interchange
FOURTH EDITION

Jack C. Richards
With Jonathan Hull and Susan Proctor

Series Editor: David Bohlke

CAMBRIDGE
UNIVERSITY PRESS

STUDENT'S BOOK **1**

CAMBRIDGE
UNIVERSITY PRESS

32 Avenue of the Americas, New York, NY 10013-2473, USA

Cambridge University Press is part of the University of Cambridge.

It furthers the University's mission by disseminating knowledge in the pursuit of education, learning and research at the highest international levels of excellence.

www.cambridge.org
Information on this title: www.cambridge.org/9781107679931

First published 2005
10th printing 2015

Printed in Mexico by Editorial Impresora Apolo, S.A. de C.V.

A catalog record for this publication is available from the British Library.

ISBN 978-1-107-64867-8 Student's Book 1 with Self-study DVD-ROM
ISBN 978-1-107-69443-9 Student's Book 1A with Self-study DVD-ROM
ISBN 978-1-107-67396-0 Student's Book 1B with Self-study DVD-ROM
ISBN 978-1-107-64872-2 Workbook 1
ISBN 978-1-107-61687-5 Workbook 1A
ISBN 978-1-107-69959-5 Workbook 1B
ISBN 978-1-107-69917-5 Teacher's Edition 1 with Assessment Audio CD/CD-ROM
ISBN 978-1-107-64725-1 Class Audio CDs 1
ISBN 978-1-107-67993-1 Full Contact 1 with Self-study DVD-ROM
ISBN 978-1-107-61136-8 Full Contact 1A with Self-study DVD-ROM
ISBN 978-1-107-63780-1 Full Contact 1B with Self-study DVD-ROM

For a full list of components, visit www. cambridge.org/interchange

Art direction, book design, layout services, and photo research: Integra
Audio production: CityVox, NYC
Video production: Nesson Media Boston, Inc.

Welcome to *Interchange Fourth Edition*, the world's most successful English series!

Interchange offers a complete set of tools for learning how to communicate in English.

Student's Book
with **NEW Self-study DVD-ROM**

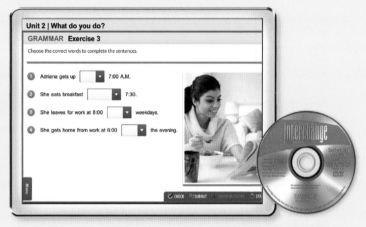

- **Complete video program** with additional **video exercises**

- Additional **vocabulary**, **grammar**, **speaking**, **listening**, and **reading** practice
- Printable **score reports** to submit to teachers

Available online

Interchange Arcade

- **Free** self-study website
- **Fun**, interactive, self-scoring activities
- Practice **vocabulary**, **grammar**, **listening**, and **reading**
- **MP3s** of the class audio program

Online Workbook

- A variety of **interactive activities** that correspond to each Student's Book lesson
- **Instant feedback** for hundreds of activities
- **Easy to use** with clear, easy-to-follow instructions
- Extra **listening practice**
- Simple tools for teachers to **monitor progress** such as scores, attendance, and time spent online

Authors' acknowledgments

A great number of people contributed to the development of *Interchange Fourth Edition*. Particular thanks are owed to the reviewers using *Interchange, Third Edition* in the following schools and institutes – their insights and suggestions have helped define the content and format of the fourth edition:

Ian Geoffrey Hanley, **The Address Education Center**, Izmir, Turkey

James McBride, **AUA Language Center**, Bangkok, Thailand

Jane Merivale, **Centennial College**, Toronto, Ontario, Canada

Elva Elena Peña Andrade, **Centro de Auto Aprendizaje de Idiomas**, Nuevo León, Mexico

José Paredes, **Centro de Educación Continua de la Escuela Politécnica Nacional** (CEC-EPN), Quito, Ecuador

Chia-jung Tsai, **Changhua University of Education**, Changhua City, Taiwan

Kevin Liang, **Chinese Culture University**, Taipei, Taiwan

Roger Alberto Neira Perez, **Colegio Santo Tomás de Aquino**, Bogotá, Colombia

Teachers at **Escuela Miguel F. Martínez**, Monterrey, Mexico

Maria Virgínia Goulart Borges de Lebron, **Great Idiomas**, São Paulo, Brazil

Gina Kim, **Hoseo University**, Chungnam, South Korea

Heeyong Kim, Seoul, South Korea

Elisa Borges, **IBEU-Rio**, Rio de Janeiro, Brazil

Jason M. Ham, **Inha University**, Incheon, South Korea

Rita de Cássia S. Silva Miranda, **Instituto Batista de Idiomas**, Belo Horizonte, Brazil

Teachers at **Instituto Politécnico Nacional**, Mexico City, Mexico

Victoria M. Roberts and Regina Marie Williams, **Interactive College of Technology**, Chamblee, Georgia, USA

Teachers at **Internacional de Idiomas**, Mexico City, Mexico

Marcelo Serafim Godinho, **Life Idiomas**, São Paulo, Brazil

J. Kevin Varden, **Meiji Gakuin University**, Yokohama, Japan

Rosa Maria Valencia Rodríguez, Mexico City, Mexico

Chung-Ju Fan, **National Kinmen Institute of Technology**, Kinmen, Taiwan

Shawn Beasom, **Nihon Daigaku**, Tokyo, Japan

Gregory Hadley, **Niigata University of International and Information Studies**, Niigata, Japan

Chris Ruddenklau, **Osaka University of Economics and Law**, Osaka, Japan

Byron Roberts, **Our Lady of Providence Girls' High School**, Xindian City, Taiwan

Simon Banha, **Phil Young's English School**, Curitiba, Brazil

Flávia Gonçalves Carneiro Braathen, **Real English Center**, Viçosa, Brazil

Márcia Cristina Barboza de Miranda, **SENAC**, Recife, Brazil

Raymond Stone, **Seneca College of Applied Arts and Technology**, Toronto, Ontario, Canada

Gen Murai, **Takushoku University**, Tokyo, Japan

Teachers at **Tecnológico de Estudios Superiores de Ecatepec**, Mexico City, Mexico

Teachers at **Universidad Autónoma Metropolitana–Azcapotzalco**, Mexico City, Mexico

Teachers at **Universidad Autónoma de Nuevo León**, Monterrey, Mexico

Mary Grace Killian Reyes, **Universidad Autónoma de Tamaulipas**, Tampico Tamaulipas, Mexico

Teachers at **Universidad Estatal del Valle de Ecatepec**, Mexico City, Mexico

Teachers at **Universidad Nacional Autónoma de Mexico – Zaragoza**, Mexico City, Mexico

Teachers at **Universidad Nacional Autónoma de Mexico – Iztacala**, Mexico City, Mexico

Luz Edith Herrera Diaz, Veracruz, Mexico

Seri Park, **YBM PLS**, Seoul, South Korea

Self-assessment charts revised by Alex Tilbury

Grammar plus written by Karen Davy

Plan of Book 1

Titles/Topics	Speaking	Grammar
UNIT 1 PAGES 2–7		
Please call me Beth. Introductions and greetings; names, countries, and nationalities	Introducing yourself; introducing someone; checking information; exchanging personal information; saying hello and good-bye	Wh-questions and statements with *be*; questions with *what, where, who,* and *how*; yes/no questions and short answers with *be*; subject pronouns; possessive adjectives
UNIT 2 PAGES 8–13		
What do you do? Jobs, workplaces, and school; daily schedules; clock time	Describing work and school; asking for and giving opinions; describing daily schedules	Simple present Wh-questions and statements; question: *when*; time expressions: *at, in, on, around, early, late, until, before,* and *after*
PROGRESS CHECK PAGES 14–15		
UNIT 3 PAGES 16–21		
How much is it? Shopping and prices; clothing and personal items; colors and materials	Talking about prices; giving opinions; discussing preferences; making comparisons; buying and selling things	Demonstratives: *this, that, these, those; one* and *ones*; questions: *how much* and *which*; comparisons with adjectives
UNIT 4 PAGES 22–27		
I really like hip-hop. Music, movies, and TV programs; entertainers; invitations and excuses; dates and times	Talking about likes and dislikes; giving opinions; making invitations and excuses	Yes/no and Wh-questions with *do*; question: *what kind*; object pronouns; modal verb *would*; verb + *to* + verb
PROGRESS CHECK PAGES 28–29		
UNIT 5 PAGES 30–35		
I come from a big family. Families; typical families	Talking about families and family members; exchanging information about the present; describing family life	Present continuous yes/no and Wh-questions, statements, and short answers; quantifiers: *all*, nearly *all, most, many, a lot of, some, not many,* and *few*; pronoun: *no one*
UNIT 6 PAGES 36–41		
How often do you exercise? Sports, fitness activities, and exercise; routines	Asking about and describing routines and exercise; talking about frequency; discussing sports and athletes; talking about abilities	Adverbs of frequency: *always, almost always, usually, often, sometimes, hardly ever, almost never,* and *never*; questions: *how often, how long, how well,* and *how good*; short answers
PROGRESS CHECK PAGES 42–43		
UNIT 7 PAGES 44–49		
We had a great time! Free-time and weekend activities	Talking about past events; giving opinions about past experiences; talking about vacations	Simple past yes/no and Wh-questions, statements, and short answers with regular and irregular verbs; past of *be*
UNIT 8 PAGES 50–55		
What's your neighborhood like? Stores and places in a city; neighborhoods; houses and apartments	Asking about and describing locations of places; asking about and describing neighborhoods; asking about quantities	*There is/there are; one, any,* and *some*; prepositions of place; quantifiers; questions: *how many* and *how much*; count and noncount nouns
PROGRESS CHECK PAGES 56–57		

1 Please call me Beth.

1 CONVERSATION *Where are you from?*

▶ Listen and practice.

David: Hello, I'm David Garza. I'm a new club member.

Beth: Hi. My name is Elizabeth Silva, but please call me Beth.

David: OK. Where are you from, Beth?

Beth: Brazil. How about you?

David: I'm from Mexico.

Beth: Oh, I love Mexico! It's really beautiful.

Beth: Oh, good. Sun-hee is here.

David: Who's Sun-hee?

Beth: She's my classmate. We're in the same math class.

David: Where's she from?

Beth: South Korea. Let's go and say hello. Sorry, what's your last name again? Garcia?

David: Actually, it's Garza.

Beth: How do you spell that?

David: G-A-R-Z-A.

2 SPEAKING *Checking information*

A ▶ Match the questions with the responses. Listen and check. Then practice with a partner. Give your own information.

1. I'm sorry. What's your name again? ....
2. What do people call you? ....
3. How do you spell your last name? ....

a. S-I-L-V-A.
b. It's Elizabeth Silva.
c. Everyone calls me Beth.

B GROUP WORK Introduce yourself with your full name. Use the expressions in part A. Make a list of names for your group.

A: Hi! I'm Yuriko Noguchi.
B: I'm sorry. What's your last name again? . . .

3 CONVERSATION *What's Seoul like?*

A Listen and practice.

Beth: Sun-hee, this is David Garza. He's a new club member from Mexico.

Sun-hee: Nice to meet you, David. I'm Sun-hee Park.

David: Hi. So, you're from South Korea?

Sun-hee: That's right. I'm from Seoul.

David: That's cool. What's Seoul like?

Sun-hee: It's really nice. It's a very exciting city.

B Listen to the rest of the conversation. What city is David from? What's it like?

4 PRONUNCIATION *Linked sounds*

 Listen and practice. Notice how final consonant sounds are often linked to the vowels that follow them.

I'm a new club member.   Sun-hee is over there.   My name is Elizabeth Silva.

5 GRAMMAR FOCUS

Statements with be; possessive adjectives

Statements with **be**	Contractions of **be**	Possessive adjectives
I**'m** from Mexico.	I**'m** = I am	my
You**'re** from Brazil.	you**'re** = you are	your
He**'s** from Japan.	he**'s** = he is	his
She**'s** a new club member.	she**'s** = she is	her
It**'s** an exciting city.	it**'s** = it is	its
We**'re** in the same class.	we**'re** = we are	our
They**'re** my classmates.	they**'re** = they are	their

A Complete these sentences. Then tell a partner about yourself.

1. ..My.. name is Mariko Kimura. .... from Japan. .... family is in Osaka. .... brother is a university student. .... name is Kenji.

2. .... name is Antonio. .... from Buenos Aires. .... a really nice city. .... sister is a student here, too. .... parents are in Argentina right now.

3. .... Katherine, but everyone calls me Katie. .... last name is Martin. .... a student at City College. .... parents are on vacation this week. .... in Los Angeles.

Wh-questions with be ▶

Where's your friend?	He's in class.
Who's Sun-hee?	She's my classmate.
What's Seoul **like**?	It's a very exciting city.
Where are you and Luisa from?	We're from Brazil.
How are your classes?	They're pretty interesting.
What are your classmates **like**?	They're really nice.

B Complete these questions. Then practice with a partner.

1. A: ...._Who's_........ that?
   B: Oh, that's Miss West.

2. A: .... she from?
   B: She's from Miami.

3. A: .... her first name?
   B: It's Celia.

4. A: .... the two students over there?
   B: Their names are Jeremy and Karen.

5. A: .... they from?
   B: They're from Vancouver, Canada.

6. A: .... they .... ?
   B: They're shy, but very friendly.

C **GROUP WORK** Write five questions about your classmates. Then ask and answer the questions.

> What's your last name?
> Where's Ming from?

6 SNAPSHOT

GREETINGS *from around the world*

- a handshake — the United States
- a kiss on the cheek
- a bow
- a hug
- a pat on the back
- a fist bump

Sources: www.familyeducation.com; www.time.com

Which greetings are typical in your country?
Can you write the name of a country for each greeting?
What are other ways to greet people?

7 CONVERSATION *How's it going?*

▶ Listen and practice.

Sun-hee: Hey, David. How's it going?
David: Fine, thanks. How are you?
Sun-hee: Pretty good. So, are your classes interesting this semester?
David: Yes, they are. I really love chemistry.
Sun-hee: Chemistry? Are you and Beth in the same class?
David: No, we aren't. My class is in the morning. Her class is in the afternoon.
Sun-hee: Listen, I'm on my way to the cafeteria now. Are you free?
David: Sure. Let's go.

8 GRAMMAR FOCUS

Yes/No questions and short answers with be ▶

Are you free?	Yes, I **am**.	No, I**'m not**.
Is David from Mexico?	Yes, he **is**.	No, he**'s not**./No, he **isn't**.
Is Beth's class in the morning?	Yes, it **is**.	No, it**'s not**./No, it **isn't**.
Are you and Beth in the same class?	Yes, we **are**.	No, we**'re not**./No, we **aren't**.
Are your classes interesting?	Yes, they **are**.	No, they**'re not**./No, they **aren't**.

A Complete these conversations. Then practice with a partner.

1. A: ....Is........ Ms. Gray from the United States?
   B: Yes, she .... from Chicago.

2. A: .... English class at 10:00?
   B: No, it .... at 11:00.

3. A: .... you and Monique from France?
   B: Yes, we .... from Paris.

4. A: .... Mr. and Mrs. Tavares American?
   B: No, they .... Brazilian.

B Answer these questions. If you answer "no," give the correct information. Then ask your partner the questions.

1. Are you from the United States? ....
2. Is your teacher from Canada? ....
3. Is your English class in the morning? ....
4. Are you and your best friend the same age? ....

C GROUP WORK Write five questions about your classmates. Then ask and answer the questions.

Are Cindy and Brian from Los Angeles?

Please call me Beth. ■ 5

9 WORD POWER Hello and good-bye

A Do you know these expressions? Which ones are "hellos" and which ones are "good-byes"? Complete the chart. Add expressions of your own.

✓ Bye.
✓ Good morning.
  Good night.
  Have a good day.
  Hey.
  Hi.

How are you?
How's it going?
See you later.
See you tomorrow.
Talk to you later.
What's up?

Hello	Good-bye
Good morning.	Bye.

B Match each expression with the best response.

1. Have a good day.
2. Hi. How are you?
3. What's up?
4. Good morning.

a. Oh, not much.
b. Thank you. You, too.
c. Good morning.
d. Pretty good, thanks.

C CLASS ACTIVITY Practice saying hello. Then practice saying good-bye.

A: Hi, Aki. How's it going?
B: Pretty good, thanks. How are you?

10 LISTENING What's your last name again?

▶ Listen to the conversations. Complete the information about each person.

	First name	Last name	Where from?
1.	Chris		
2.		Sanchez	
3.	Min-ho		

11 INTERCHANGE 1 Getting to know you

Find out about your classmates. Go to Interchange 1 on page 114.

What's in a Name?

Look at the names in the article. Do you know any people with these names? What are they like?

Your name is very important. When you think of yourself, you probably think of your name first. It is an important part of your identity.

Right now, the two most popular names for babies in the United States are "Jacob" for boys and "Emma" for girls. Why are these names popular? And why are other names unpopular?

Names can become popular because of famous actors, TV or book characters, or athletes. Popular names suggest very positive things. Unpopular names suggest negative things. Surprisingly, people generally agree on the way they feel about names. Here are some common opinions about names from a recent survey.

HELLO
my name is
_____

Boys' names

George: average, boring
Jacob: creative, friendly
Michael: good-looking, athletic
Stanley: nerdy, serious

Girls' names

Betty: old-fashioned, average
Emma: independent, adventurous
Jane: plain, ordinary
Nicole: beautiful, intelligent

So why do parents give their children unpopular names? One reason is tradition. Many people are named after a family member. Of course, opinions can change over time. A name that is unpopular now may become popular in the future. That's good news for all the Georges and Bettys out there!

A Read the article. Then check (✓) the statements that are true.

☐ 1. Your name is part of your identity.
☐ 2. People often feel the same way about a particular name.
☐ 3. Boys' names are more popular than girls' names.
☐ 4. People are often named after family members.
☐ 5. Opinions about names can change.

B According to the article, which names suggest positive things? Which suggest negative things? Complete the chart.

Positive names		Negative names	
....	....	....	....
....	....	....	....

C **PAIR WORK** What names are popular in your country? Why are they popular?

2 What do you do?

Top Six Student Part-Time Jobs in the United States

1 usher
2 tutor
3 team assistant
4 caregiver
5 server
6 fitness instructor

Source: www.snagajob.com

Which jobs are easy? Which are difficult? Why?
What's your opinion? Are these good jobs for students?
What are some other student jobs?

2 **WORD POWER**

A Complete the word map with jobs from the list.

✓ accountant
✓ cashier
  chef
✓ dancer
✓ flight attendant
  musician
  pilot
  receptionist
  server
  singer
  tour guide
  website designer

Office work
accountant

Food service
cashier

Jobs

Travel industry
flight attendant

Entertainment business
dancer

B Add two more jobs to each category. Then compare with a partner.

3 SPEAKING *Work and workplaces*

A Look at the pictures. Match the information in columns A, B, and C.

A	B	C
a salesperson	builds houses	in a restaurant
a chef	cares for patients	for a construction company
a mechanic	writes stories	in a hospital
a carpenter	cooks food	in a garage
a reporter	fixes cars	in a department store
a nurse	sells clothes	for a newspaper

B PAIR WORK Take turns describing each person's job.

A: She's a salesperson. She sells clothes. She works in a department store.
B: And he's a chef. He . . .

4 CONVERSATION *Where do you work?*

A ▶ Listen and practice.

Jason: Where do you work, Andrea?
Andrea: I work at Thomas Cook Travel.
Jason: Oh, really? What do you do there?
Andrea: I'm a guide. I take people on tours to countries in South America, like Peru.
Jason: How interesting!
Andrea: Yeah, it's a great job. I really love it. And what do you do?
Jason: Oh, I'm a student. I have a part-time job, too.
Andrea: Where do you work?
Jason: In a fast-food restaurant.
Andrea: Which restaurant?
Jason: Hamburger Heaven.

B ▶ Listen to the rest of the conversation. What does Jason do, exactly? How does he like his job?

Simple present Wh-questions and statements ▶

			I/You	He/She
What do you **do**?	I**'m** a student. I **have** a part-time job, too.		work	works
Where do you **work**?	I **work** at Hamburger Heaven.		take	takes
Where do you **go** to school?	I **go** to the University of Texas.		study	studies
			teach	teaches
What does Andrea **do**?	She's a guide. She **takes** people on tours.		do	does
Where does she **work**?	She **works** at Thomas Cook Travel.		go	goes
How does she **like** it?	She **loves** it.		have	has

A Complete these conversations. Then practice with a partner.

1. A: What ......*do*...... you ......*do*...... ?
   B: I'm a full-time student. I study the violin.
   A: And .... do you .... to school?
   B: I .... to the New York School of Music.
   A: Wow! .... do you like your classes?
   B: I .... them a lot.

2. A: What .... Tanya do?
   B: She's a teacher. She .... an art class
      at a school in Denver.
   A: And what about Ryan? Where .... he work?
   B: He .... for a big computer company in
      San Francisco.
   A: .... does he do, exactly?
   B: He's a website designer. He .... fantastic
      websites.

B **PAIR WORK** What do you know about these jobs?
Complete the chart. Then write sentences about each job.

A reporter	A flight attendant	A teacher
works for a newspaper	....	....
interviews people	....	....
writes stories	....	....

> A reporter works for a newspaper, interviews people, and writes stories.

C **PAIR WORK** Ask your partner questions like these about work
and school. Take notes to use in Exercise 6.

What do you do?	Do you go to school?	How do you like . . . ?
Where do you live?	Do you have a job?	What's your favorite . . . ?

6 WRITING A biography

A Use your notes from Exercise 5 to write a biography of your partner. Don't use your partner's name. Use *he* or *she* instead.

> My partner is a student. She lives near the university. She studies fashion design at the Fashion Institute. Her favorite class is History of Design. She has a part-time job in a clothing store. She loves her job and . . .

B **CLASS ACTIVITY** Pass your biographies around the class. Guess who each biography is about.

7 CONVERSATION *I start work at five.*

A ● Listen and practice.

Kevin: So, do you usually come to the gym in the morning?
Allie: Yeah, I do. I usually come here at 10:00.
Kevin: Really? What time do you go to work?
Allie: Oh, I work in the afternoon. I start work at five.
Kevin: Wow, that's late. When do you get home at night?
Allie: I usually get home at midnight.
Kevin: Midnight? That *is* late. What do you do, exactly?
Allie: I'm a chef. I work at the Pink Elephant.
Kevin: That's my favorite restaurant! By the way, I'm Kevin. . . .

B ● Listen to the rest of the conversation. What time does Kevin get up? start work?

8 PRONUNCIATION *Syllable stress*

A ● Listen and practice. Notice which syllable has the main stress.

● ○	● ○ ○	○ ● ○
dancer	salesperson	accountant
....	....	....
....	....	....

B ● Which stress pattern do these words have? Add them to the columns in part A. Then listen and check.

carpenter   caregiver   musician   reporter   server   tutor

9 GRAMMAR FOCUS

Time expressions ▶

				Expressing clock time
I get up	**at** 6:00	**in** the morning	**on** weekdays.	6:00
I go to bed	**around** ten	**in** the evening	**on** weeknights.	six
I leave work	**early**	**in** the afternoon	**on** weekends.	six o'clock
I get home	**late**	**at** night	**on** Fridays.	6:00 A.M. = 6:00 in the morning
I stay up	**until** midnight	**on** Saturdays.		6:00 P.M. = 6:00 in the evening
I exercise	**before** noon	**on** Sundays.		
I wake up	**after** noon	**on** Sundays.		

A Circle the correct words.

1. I get up **at** / **until** six **at** / **on** weekdays.
2. I have lunch **at** / **early** 11:30 **in** / **on** Mondays.
3. I have a little snack **in** / **around** 10:00 **in** / **at** night.
4. **In** / **On** Fridays, I leave school **early** / **before**.
5. I stay up **before** / **until** 1:00 A.M. **in** / **on** weekends.
6. I sleep **until** / **around** noon **in** / **on** Sundays.

B Rewrite the sentences in part A so that they are true for you. Then compare with a partner.

C PAIR WORK Take turns asking and answering these questions.

1. Which days do you get up early? late?
2. What's something you do before 8:00 in the morning?
3. What's something you do on Saturday evenings?
4. What do you do only on Sundays?

10 LISTENING Daily schedules

A ▶ Listen to Greg, Megan, and Lori talk about their daily schedules. Complete the chart.

	Job	Gets up at . . .	Gets home at . . .	Goes to bed at . . .
Greg	mechanic			
Megan		7:00 a.m.		
Lori				

B CLASS ACTIVITY Who do you think has the best daily schedule? Why?

11 INTERCHANGE 2 Common ground

Find out about your classmates' schedules. Go to Interchange 2 on page 115.

Why do you need a job?

Scan the profiles. Who is in high school? Who is in college? Who is a new parent?

These people need jobs. Read about their schedules, experience, and why they need a job.

Julia Brown

I study French and want to be a teacher someday. I have classes all day on Monday, Tuesday, and Thursday, and on Wednesday and Friday afternoons. I usually study on weekends. I need a job because college is really expensive! I don't have any experience, but I'm a fast learner.

Eddie Chen

I'm 16 now, and my parents don't give me an allowance anymore. I want to earn some money because I like to go out with my friends on the weekend. I go to school at 8:00 and get home around 4:30. My parents own a restaurant, so I know a little about restaurant work.

Denise Parker

My husband is an accountant and makes good money, but we don't save very much. We live in a small apartment, and we have a new baby. We want to save money to buy a house. I take care of the baby, so I need a job I can do at home. I can type well, and I have a new computer.

A Read the article. Why do these people need jobs? Check (✓) the correct boxes.

	Julia	Denise	Eddie
1. To save money	☐	☐	☐
2. To pay for college	☐	☐	☐
3. To go out on the weekend	☐	☐	☐
4. To buy a house	☐	☐	☐

B PAIR WORK Choose the best job for each person. Explain why.

Chef	**English Tutor**	**Caregiver**
French and Italian cooking *Weekends only*	*Flexible work hours* *$10 an hour*	*Work with children* *Earn great money*
Server	**Receptionist**	**Online Salesperson**
Evenings only *Experience a plus*	*Mornings and afternoons* *No experience necessary*	*Work at home* *Earn up to $20 an hour*

Units 1–2 Progress check

SELF-ASSESSMENT

How well can you do these things? Check (✔) the boxes.

I can	Very well	OK	A little
Make an introduction and use basic greeting expressions (Ex. 1)	☐	☐	☐
Show I didn't understand and ask for repetition (Ex. 1)	☐	☐	☐
Ask and answer questions about myself and other people (Ex. 2)	☐	☐	☐
Ask and answer questions about work (Ex. 3, 4)	☐	☐	☐
Ask and answer questions about habits and routines (Ex. 5)	☐	☐	☐

1 ROLE PLAY Introductions

A PAIR WORK You are talking to someone at school. Have a conversation.

A: Hi. How are you?
B: ...
A: By the way, my name is ...
B: I'm sorry. What's your name again?
A: ...
B: I'm .... Are you a student here?
A: ... And how about you?
B: ...
A: Oh, really? And where are you from?

B GROUP WORK Join another pair.
Introduce your partner.

2 SPEAKING Interview

Write questions for these answers. Then use the questions to interview a classmate.

1. What's _____? My name is Keiko Kawakami.
2. _____? I'm from Osaka, Japan.
3. _____? Yes, my classes are very interesting.
4. _____? My favorite class is English.
5. _____? No, my teacher isn't American.
6. _____? My classmates are very nice.
7. _____? My best friend is Maria.

3 SPEAKING *What a job!*

A What do you know about these jobs? List three things each person does.

receptionist

tour guide

cashier

teacher

takes messages ....

....

....

....

B GROUP WORK Compare your lists. Take turns asking about the jobs.

4 LISTENING *Work and school*

A Listen to James and Lindsey talk at a party. Complete the chart.

	James	Lindsey
What do you do?	....	....
Where do you work/study?	....	....
How do you like your job/classes?	....	....
What do you do after work/school?	....	....

B PAIR WORK Practice the questions in part A. Answer with your own information.

5 SURVEY *My perfect day*

A Imagine your perfect day. Complete the chart with your own answers.

What time do you get up?	....
What do you do after you get up?	....
Where do you go?	....
What do you do in the evening?	....
When do you go to bed?	....

B PAIR WORK Talk about your perfect day. Answer any questions.

WHAT'S NEXT?

Look at your Self-assessment again. Do you need to review anything?

3 How much is it?

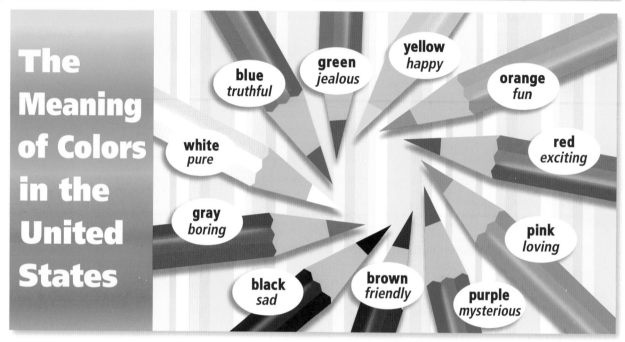

The Meaning of Colors in the United States

blue
truthful

green
jealous

yellow
happy

orange
fun

white
pure

red
exciting

gray
boring

pink
loving

black
sad

brown
friendly

purple
mysterious

Sources: Based on information from Think Quest; Hewlett-Packard, *The Meaning of Color*

Which words have a positive meaning? Which have a negative meaning?
What meanings do these colors have for you?
What does your favorite color make you think of?

2 CONVERSATION *It's really pretty.*

A ⏵ Listen and practice.

Salesclerk: Can I help you?
Customer: Yes, thank you. How much are these gloves?
Salesclerk: The gray ones? They're $18.
Customer: Oh, that's not bad. Do they come in black?
Salesclerk: No, sorry, just gray.
Customer: OK. Um, how much is that scarf?
Salesclerk: Which one? The blue and orange one?
Customer: No, the yellow one.
Salesclerk: Let's see . . . it's $24.95.
Customer: It's really pretty. I'll take it.

B ⏵ Listen to the rest of the conversation. What else does the customer look at? Does she buy it?

Demonstratives; one, ones ▶

saying prices ▶
79¢ = seventy-nine cents
$18 = eighteen dollars
$24.95 = twenty-four ninety-five

How much is	**this** scarf?	**that** scarf?	Which **one**?	**It's** $24.95.
	this one?	**that one**?	The yellow **one**.	
How much are	**these** gloves?	**those** gloves?	Which **ones**?	**They're** $18.
	these?	**those**?	The gray **ones**.	

A Complete these conversations. Then practice with a partner.

1

2

A: Excuse me. How much
   are ....*those*.... jeans?
B: Which .... ? Do you
   mean .... ?
A: No, the light blue ....
B: Oh, ... are $59.95.
A: Wow! That's expensive!

A: How much is .... backpack?
B: Which .... ?
A: The red ....
B: It's $36.99. But ....
   green .... is only $22.25.
A: That's not bad. Can I see it, please?

B **PAIR WORK** Add prices to the items. Then ask and answer questions.

A: How much are these sunglasses?
B: Which ones?
A: The pink ones.
B: They're $86.99.
A: That's expensive!

useful expressions
That's cheap.
That's reasonable.
That's OK/not bad.
That's expensive.

4 PRONUNCIATION *Sentence stress*

A ▶ Listen and practice. Notice that the important words in a sentence have more stress.

Excuse me. That's expensive. I'll take it. Do you mean these?

B **PAIR WORK** Practice the conversations in Exercise 3, part B again. Pay attention to the sentence stress.

5 ROLE PLAY *Can I help you?*

A **PAIR WORK** Put items "for sale" on your desk, such as notebooks, watches, phones, or bags.

Student A: You are a salesclerk. Answer the customer's questions.
Student B: You are a customer. Ask the price of each item. Say if you want to buy it.

A: Can I help you?
B: Yes. I like these sunglasses. How much are they?
A: Which ones?

B Change roles and try the role play again.

6 LISTENING *Look at this!*

A ▶ Listen to two friends shopping. Write the color and price for each item.

Item	Color	Price	Do they buy it?	
			Yes	**No**
1. phone	....	....	☐	☐
2. watch	....	....	☐	☐
3. sunglasses	....	....	☐	☐
4. T-shirt	....	....	☐	☐

B ▶ Listen again. Do they buy the items? Check (✓) Yes or No.

7 INTERCHANGE 3 *Flea market*

See what kinds of deals you can make as a buyer and a seller.
Go to Interchange 3 on pages 116–117.

8 WORD POWER Materials

A What are these things made of? Label each one. Use the words from the list.

cotton   gold   leather   plastic
rubber   silk   silver   wool

 1. a ....silk.... tie

 2. a .... bracelet

 3. a .... ring

 4. a .... shirt

 5. a .... jacket

 6. .... earrings

 7. .... boots

 8. .... socks

B **PAIR WORK** What other materials are the things in part A sometimes made of? Make a list.

C **CLASS ACTIVITY** Which materials can you find in your classroom?

"Pedro has a cotton shirt, and Ellen has leather shoes."

9 CONVERSATION *I prefer the blue one.*

A ▶ Listen and practice.

Brett: These wool sweaters are really nice.
      Which one do you like better?
Lisa: Let's see . . . I like the green one more.
Brett: The green one? Why?
Lisa: It looks warmer.
Brett: That's true, but I think I prefer the blue one.
      It's more stylish than the green one.
Lisa: Hmm. There's no price tag.
Brett: Excuse me. How much is this sweater?
Clerk: It's $139. Would you like to try it on?
Brett: Uh, no. That's OK. But thanks anyway.
Clerk: You're welcome.

B ▶ Listen to the rest of the conversation.
What does Brett buy? What does Lisa think of it?

Preferences; comparisons with adjectives ▶

		Spelling
Which sweater do you **prefer**?	It's **nicer than** the green one.	cheap ⟶ cheaper
I **prefer** the blue one.		nice ⟶ nicer
Which one do you **like more**?	It's **prettier than** the green one.	pretty ⟶ prettier
I **like** the blue one **more**.		big ⟶ bigger
Which one do you **like better**?	It's **more stylish than** the green one.	
I **like** the blue one **better**.		

A Complete these conversations. Then practice with a partner.

1. A: Which of these jackets do you like more?
   B: I prefer the leather one. The design is .... (nice), and it looks .... (expensive) the wool one.

2. A: These T-shirts are nice. Which one do you prefer?
   B: I like the green and white one better. The colors are .... (pretty). It's .... (attractive) the gray and black one.

3. A: Which earrings do you like better?
   B: I like the silver ones more. They're .... (big) the gold ones. And they're .... (cheap).

B **PAIR WORK** Compare the things in part A. Give your own opinions.

A: Which jacket do you like more?
B: I like the wool one better. The color is prettier.

useful expressions
The color is prettier.
The design is nicer.
The style is more attractive.
The material is better.

11 WRITING *Comparing prices*

How much do these things cost in your country? Complete the chart.
Then compare the prices in your country with the prices in the U.S.

	Price in my country	Price in the U.S.
a cup of coffee	....	$1.40
a movie ticket	....	$12.50
a paperback novel	....	$8.95
a video game	....	$50.00

Many things are more expensive in my country than in the United States. For example, a cup of coffee costs about $2.00 at home. In the U.S., it's cheaper. It's only $1.40. A movie ticket costs . . .

Tools for Better Shopping

Scan the article. Find the names of popular websites. Do you use any of them for shopping?

1 Do you like to shop online? Like millions of people, you want to find the best things for the best price. There are so many choices that it can be difficult to find the things you need and want. Here's where technology comes in! Popular websites like Facebook and Twitter aren't just for social networking anymore.

2 The websites Facebook and Twitter are popular because people can connect to friends and get their most recent news. But people also use these sites as powerful shopping tools. Members can ask about an item and then get opinions from people they trust. Twitterers can also search for news from other users and then find stores nearby that sell the item.

3 Another helpful shopping tool is the smartphone. Smartphone users can go into a store, find an item they like, and then type the item number into their smartphone. They can compare prices, read reviews, and make better decisions about their purchase. Many people find a better price online or at another store. People often want to see and touch an item before they buy. They can do just that – and pay a lower price, too.

4 But you don't have to be a Facebook or Twitter member or have a smartphone to find a bargain. Websites like Shopzilla compare prices, give reviews, and find stores near you with the best bargains. Google does all these things but also lets you buy items directly through its site. Be a smart shopper. The information you need is at your fingertips!

A Read the article. Answer these questions. Then write the number of the paragraph where you find each answer.

.... a. How are Shopzilla and Google similar? ....
.... b. What are Twitter users called? ....
.... c. How do smartphones help find bargains? ....
.... d. What are two social networking sites? ....

B According to the article, which shopping tools do these things? Check (✓) the correct boxes.

	Facebook	Twitter	Smartphone	Shopzilla	Google
1. get opinions from friends	☐	☐	☐	☐	☐
2. find product reviews	☐	☐	☐	☐	☐
3. compare prices	☐	☐	☐	☐	☐
4. find stores with items you want	☐	☐	☐	☐	☐
5. buy items directly	☐	☐	☐	☐	☐

C **PAIR WORK** Do you shop mostly in stores or online? How do you find good prices?

4 I really like hip-hop.

1 SNAPSHOT

Source: The Recording Industry Association of America, *2008 Consumer Profile*

Listen and number the musical styles from 1 to 9.
Which of these styles of music are popular in your country?
What other kinds of music are popular in your country?

2 WORD POWER

A Complete the word map with words from the list.

action
electronic
game show
heavy metal
horror
musical

reality show
reggae
salsa
science fiction
soap opera
talk show

B Add two more words to each category.
Then compare with a partner.

C GROUP WORK Number the items
in each list from 1 (you like it the most)
to 6 (you like it the least). Then compare
your ideas.

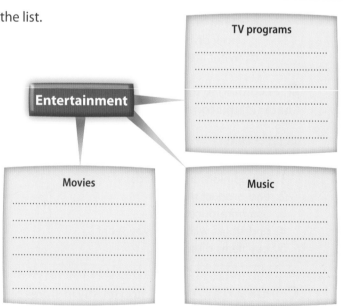

22

3 CONVERSATION *Who's your favorite singer?*

A Listen and practice.

Marissa: Do you like country music, Brian?
   Brian: No, I don't like it very much. Do you?
Marissa: Yeah, I do. I'm a big fan of Taylor Swift.
   Brian: I think I know her. Does she play the guitar?
Marissa: Yes, she does. She's a really good musician.
         So, what kind of music do you like?
   Brian: I really like hip-hop.
Marissa: Oh, yeah? Who's your favorite singer?
   Brian: Jay-Z. Do you like him?
Marissa: No, I don't. I don't like hip-hop very much.

B Listen to the rest of the conversation. Who is Brian's favorite group? Does Marissa like them?

4 GRAMMAR FOCUS

Simple present questions; short answers

		Object pronouns
Do you **like** country music?	**What kind of** music **do** you **like**?	me
Yes, I **do**. I love it.	I really like hip-hop.	you
No, I **don't**. I don't like it very much.		him
Does she **play** the piano?	**What does** she **play**?	her
Yes, she **does**. She plays very well.	She plays the guitar.	it
No, she **doesn't**. She doesn't		us
play an instrument.		them
Do they **like** Green Day?	**Who do** they **like**?	
Yes, they **do**. They like them a lot.	They like Coldplay.	
No, they **don't**. They don't like		
them at all.		

Complete these conversations. Then practice with a partner.

1. A: I like Kings of Leon a lot. .... you
      know .... ?
   B: Yes, I .... , and I love this song. Let's
      download ....
2. A: .... you like science fiction movies?
   B: Yes, I .... I like .... very much.
3. A: .... Kevin and Emma like soap operas?
   B: Kevin .... , but Emma .... She
      hates ....
4. A: What kind of music .... Noriko like?
   B: Classical music. She loves Yo-Yo Ma.
   A: Yeah, he's amazing. I like .... a lot.

Kings of Leon

I really like hip-hop. ■ 23

5 **PRONUNCIATION** *Intonation in questions*

A ▶ Listen and practice. Yes/No questions usually have rising intonation. Wh-questions usually have falling intonation.

Do you like pop music?　　　　　　　What kind of music do you like?

B **PAIR WORK** Practice these questions.

Do you like TV?	What programs do you like?
Do you like video games?	What games do you like?
Do you play a musical instrument?	What instrument do you play?

6 **SPEAKING** *Entertainment survey*

A **GROUP WORK** Write five questions about entertainment and entertainers. Then ask and answer your questions in groups.

What kinds of . . . do you like?
　(music, TV programs, video games)
Do you like . . . ?
　(reggae, game shows, action movies)
Who's your favorite . . . ?
　(singer, actor, athlete)

B **GROUP WORK** Complete this information about your group. Ask any additional questions.

Our Group Favorites

What's your favorite kind of . . . ?
music ....
movie ....
TV program ....

What's your favorite . . . ?
song ....
movie ....
video game ....

Who's your favorite . . . ?
singer ....
actor ....
athlete ....

Utada Hikaru

reality show

Cristiano Ronaldo

3-D movie

C **CLASS ACTIVITY** Read your group's list to the class. Find out the class favorites.

7 LISTENING *Who's my date?*

A ▶ Listen to four people on a TV game show. Three men want to invite Linda on a date. What kinds of things do they like? Complete the chart.

	Music	Movies	TV programs
Bill			
John			
Tony			
Linda			

B CLASS ACTIVITY Who do you think is the best date for Linda? Why?

8 CONVERSATION *An invitation*

A ▶ Listen and practice.

Dave: I have tickets to the soccer match on Friday night. Would you like to go?

Susan: Thanks. I'd love to. What time does it start?

Dave: At 8:00.

Susan: That sounds great. So, do you want to have dinner at 6:00?

Dave: Uh, I'd like to, but I have to work late.

Susan: Oh, that's OK. Let's just meet at the stadium before the match, around 7:30.

Dave: OK. Why don't we meet at the gate?

Susan: That sounds fine. See you there.

B ▶ Listen to Dave and Susan at the soccer match. Which team does each person like?

GRAMMAR FOCUS

Would; *verb* **+ to +** *verb* ▶

| **Would** you **like to go** out on Friday?
Yes, I **would**.
Yes, I**'d love to**. Thanks. | **Would** you **like to go** to a soccer match?
I**'d like to**, but I **have to work** late.
I**'d like to**, but I **need to save** money.
I**'d like to**, but I **want to visit** my parents. | **Contraction**
I**'d** = I would |

A Respond to three invitations. Then write three invitations for the given responses.

1. A: I have tickets to the baseball game on Saturday. Would you like to go?
    B: ....

2. A: Would you like to come over for dinner tomorrow night?
    B: ....

3. A: Would you like to go to a pop concert with me this weekend?
    B: ....

4. A: ....
    ....
    B: Yes, I'd love to. Thank you!

5. A: ....
    ....
    B: Well, I'd like to, but I have to study.

6. A: ....
    ....
    B: Yes, I would. They're my favorite band.

B **PAIR WORK** Ask and answer the questions in part A. Give your own responses.

C **PAIR WORK** Think of three things you would like to do. Then invite a partner to do them with you. Your partner responds and asks follow-up questions like these:

When is it?   What time does it start?   When does it end?   Where is it?

---

10 **WRITING** *A text message*

A What does this text message say?

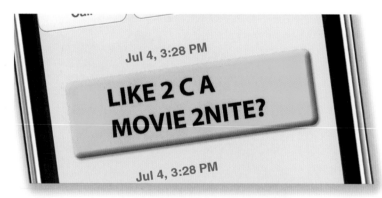

text message abbreviations			
M = am		L8	= late
U = you		W8	= wait
R = are		GR8	= great
C = see		THX	= thanks
4 = for		LUV	= love
2 = to		NITE	= night

B **GROUP WORK** Write a text message to each person in your group. Then exchange messages. Write a response to each message.

---

11 **INTERCHANGE 4** *Are you free this weekend?*

Make weekend plans with your classmates. Go to Interchange 4 on page 118.

Fergie of the Black Eyed Peas

Scan the article and look at the pictures. In what year did each event take place?

She has many hit singles and several Grammy awards with her band the Black Eyed Peas. She has fans all over the world. She's a singer, a rapper, a songwriter, a fashion designer, and an actress. Her name is Stacy Ann Ferguson, but her fans call her Fergie.

Here are some highlights of Fergie's life and career.

▶ **1975** Fergie is born on March 27 in California.

▶ **1984** Fergie starts acting, doing the voice of Sally in the *Peanuts* cartoons. She also stars in the popular TV show *Kids Incorporated,* with actress Jennifer Love Hewitt.

▶ **1991** Fergie forms the all-female band Wild Orchid.

▶ **2003** Fergie records a song with the band Black Eyed Peas. The band likes her, and she records five more songs on the album.

▶ **2004** Fergie joins the Black Eyed Peas.

▶ **2005** Fergie and the Black Eyed Peas win their first Grammy award for "Let's Get It Started."

▶ **2006** Fergie makes a solo album and has six big hits. "Big Girls Don't Cry" is her first worldwide number one single.

▶ **2008** Fergie records "That Ain't Cool" with Japanese R&B singer Kumi Koda. She becomes famous in Japan.

▶ **2009** Fergie acts and sings in the movie *Nine*.

▶ **2010** Fergie and the Black Eyed Peas perform five songs at the 2010 World Cup celebration concert in South Africa.

Fergie says she's the "luckiest girl in the world." Why? Her song "Glamorous" says it all: "All the fans, I'd like to thank. Thank you really though, 'cause I remember yesterday when I dreamed about the days when I'd rock on MTV...."

▲ performing at the World Cup

▲ on the TV show *Kids Incorporated*

▲ on stage with the Black Eyed Peas

A Read the article. Then number these sentences from 1 (first event) to 8 (last event).

.... a. She sings at the World Cup concert.
.... b. She is born in California.
.... c. She acts and sings in a movie.
.... d. Her band wins its first Grammy.

.... e. She forms her first band.
.... f. She is on TV with Jennifer Love Hewitt.
.... g. She becomes very popular in Japan.
.... h. She has her first worldwide number one song.

B **PAIR WORK** Who is your favorite musician? What do you know about his or her life?

Units 3–4 Progress check

SELF-ASSESSMENT

How well can you do these things? Check (✓) the boxes.

I can	Very well	OK	A little
Give and understand information about prices (Ex. 1)	☐	☐	☐
Say what I like and dislike (Ex. 1, 2, 3)	☐	☐	☐
Explain what I like or dislike about something (Ex. 2)	☐	☐	☐
Describe and compare objects and possessions (Ex. 2)	☐	☐	☐
Make and respond to invitations (Ex. 4)	☐	☐	☐

1 LISTENING *Weekend sale*

A ▶ Listen to a commercial for Dave's Discount Store. Circle the correct prices.

DAVE'S DISCOUNT STORE

leather pants
$19
$90

wool pants
$15
$50

silk shirt
$14
$40

laptop computer
$1,015
$1,050

cotton shirt
$18
$80

desktop computer
$813
$830

B PAIR WORK What do you think of the items in part A? Give your own opinions.

2 ROLE PLAY *Shopping trip*

Student A: Choose things from Exercise 1 for your family. Ask for Student B's opinion.

Student B: Help Student A choose presents for his or her family.

      A: I want to buy a computer for my parents. Which one do you like better?
      B: Well, I like the laptop better. It's nicer, and . . .

Change roles and try the role play again.

SURVEY *Likes and dislikes*

A Write answers to these questions.

	Me	My classmate
When do you usually watch TV?	....	....
What kinds of TV programs do you like?	....	....
Do you like game shows?	....	....
Do you listen to the radio?	....	....
Who is your favorite singer?	....	....
What do you think of heavy metal?	....	....
What is your favorite movie?	....	....
Do you like musicals?	....	....
What kinds of movies do you dislike?	....	....

B **CLASS ACTIVITY** Find someone who has the same answers. Go around the class. Write a classmate's name only once!

4 SPEAKING *What an excuse!*

A Make up three invitations to interesting activities. Write them on cards.

> *I want to see the frog races tomorrow. They're at the park at 2:00. Would you like to go?*

B Write three response cards. One is an acceptance card, and two are refusals. Think of silly or unusual excuses.

That sounds great! What time do you want to meet?	*I'd like to, but I have to wash my cat tomorrow.*	*I'd love to, but I want to take my bird to a singing contest.*

C **GROUP WORK** Shuffle the invitation cards together and the response cards together. Take three cards from each pile. Then invite people to do the things on your invitation cards. Use the response cards to accept or refuse.

WHAT'S NEXT?

Look at your Self-assessment again. Do you need to review anything?

5 I come from a big family.

WORD POWER *Family*

A Look at Sam's family tree. How are these people related to him?
Add the words to the family tree.

cousin
daughter
father
grandmother
niece
sister-in-law
uncle
wife

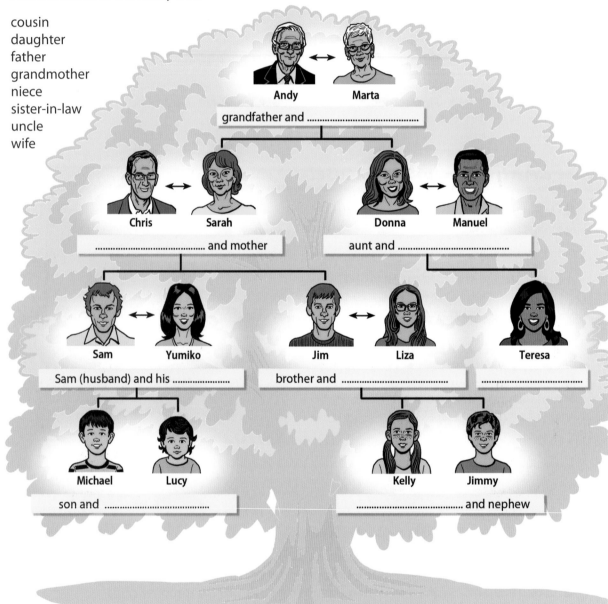

grandfather and ....

.... and mother   aunt and ....

Sam (husband) and his ....   brother and ....

son and .... and nephew

B Draw your family tree (or a friend's family tree). Then take turns talking
about your families. Ask follow-up questions to get more information.

A: There are five people in my family. I have two brothers and a sister.
B: How old is your sister?

2 LISTENING *How are they related?*

▶ Listen to four conversations about famous people. How is the second person related to the first person?

1.
Chris Martin

Gwyneth Paltrow

....

2.
Francis Ford Coppola

Nicholas Cage

....

3.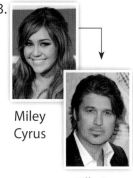
Miley Cyrus

Billy Ray Cyrus

....

4.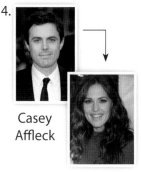
Casey Affleck

Jennifer Garner

....

3 CONVERSATION *Asking about families*

A ▶ Listen and practice.

Rita: Tell me about your brother and sister, Sue.
Sue: Well, my sister works for the government.
Rita: Oh, what does she do?
Sue: I'm not sure. She's working on a very secret project right now.
Rita: Wow! And what about your brother?
Sue: He's a wildlife photographer.
Rita: What an interesting family! Can I meet them?
Sue: Sure, but not now. My sister's away. She's not working in the United States this month.
Rita: And your brother?
Sue: He's traveling in the Amazon.

B ▶ Listen to the rest of the conversation. Where do Rita's parents live? What do they do?

4 PRONUNCIATION *Intonation in statements*

A ▶ Listen and practice. Notice that statements usually have falling intonation.

He's traveling in the Amazon.   She's working on a very secret project.

B **PAIR WORK** Practice the conversation in Exercise 3 again. Pay attention to the intonation in the statements.

5 GRAMMAR FOCUS

Present continuous ▶

Are you **living** at home now?	Yes, I **am**. No, I**'m not**.
Is your sister **working** for the government?	Yes, she **is**. No, she**'s not**./No, she **isn't**.
Are Ed and Jill **taking** classes this year?	Yes, they **are**. No, they**'re not**./No, they **aren't**.
Where **are** you **working** now?	I**'m not working**. I need a job.
What **is** your brother **doing**?	He**'s traveling** in the Amazon.
What **are** your friends **doing** these days?	They**'re studying** for their exams.

A Complete these phone conversations using the present continuous.

A: Hi, Stephanie. What .... you
.... (do)?
B: Hey, Mark. I .... (stand) in an
elevator, and it's stuck!
A: Oh, no! Are you OK?
B: Yeah. I – wait! It .... (move)
now. Thank goodness!

A: Marci, how .... you and Justin
.... (enjoy) your shopping trip?
B: We .... (have) a lot of fun.
A: .... your brother
.... (spend) a lot of money?
B: No, Mom. He .... (buy) only
one or two things. That's all!

B PAIR WORK Practice the phone conversations with a partner.

6 DISCUSSION *Is anyone . . . ?*

GROUP WORK Ask your classmates about people in their families. What are
they doing? Ask follow-up questions to get more information.

A: Is anyone in your family traveling right now?
B: Yes, my dad is. He's in South Korea.
C: What's he doing there?

topics to ask about	
traveling	going to high school or college
living abroad	moving to a new home
taking a class	studying a foreign language

7 INTERCHANGE 5 *Family facts*

Find out about your classmates' families. Go to Interchange 5 on page 119.

8 SNAPSHOT

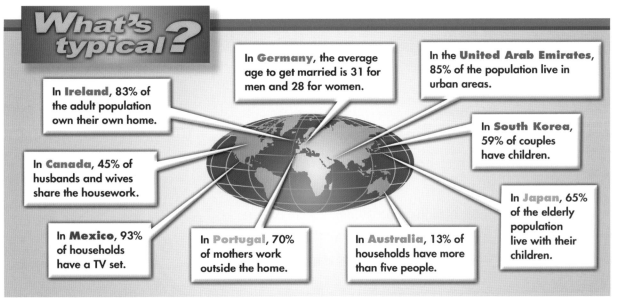

What's typical?

In **Ireland**, 83% of the adult population own their own home.

In **Germany**, the average age to get married is 31 for men and 28 for women.

In the **United Arab Emirates**, 85% of the population live in urban areas.

In **South Korea**, 59% of couples have children.

In **Canada**, 45% of husbands and wives share the housework.

In **Japan**, 65% of the elderly population live with their children.

In **Mexico**, 93% of households have a TV set.

In **Portugal**, 70% of mothers work outside the home.

In **Australia**, 13% of households have more than five people.

Source: nationmaster.com

Which facts surprise you? Why?
Which facts seem like positive things? Which seem negative?
How do you think your country compares?

9 CONVERSATION *Is that typical?*

A ⊙ Listen and practice.

Marcos: How many brothers and sisters do you have, Mei-li?
  Mei-li: Actually, I'm an only child.
Marcos: Really?
  Mei-li: Yeah, a lot of families in China have only one child these days.
Marcos: I didn't know that.
  Mei-li: What about you, Marcos?
Marcos: I come from a big family. I have three brothers and two sisters.
  Mei-li: Wow! Is that typical in Peru?
Marcos: I'm not sure. Many families are smaller these days. But big families are great because you get a lot of birthday presents!

B ⊙ Listen to the rest of the conversation. What does Mei-li like about being an only child?

I come from a big family. ▪ **33**

10 GRAMMAR FOCUS

Quantifiers ▶

100%	**All** **Nearly all** **Most**	families have only one child.
	Many **A lot of** **Some**	families are smaller these days.
	Not many **Few**	couples have more than one child.
0%	**No one**	gets married before the age of 18.

A Rewrite these sentences using quantifiers. Then compare with a partner.

1. In the U.S., 75% of high school students go to college.

....

2. Seven percent of the people in Brazil are age 65 or older.

....

3. In India, 0% of the people vote before the age of 18.

....

4. Forty percent of the people in Sweden live alone.

....

5. In Singapore, 23% of the people speak English at home.

....

B PAIR WORK Rewrite the sentences in part A so that they are true about your country.

> In . . . , many high school students go to college.

11 WRITING *An email about your family*

A Write an email to your e-pal about your family.

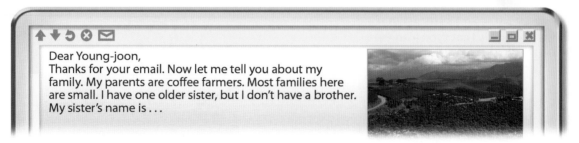

> ↑ ↓ ↺ ⊗ ✉
>
> Dear Young-joon,
> Thanks for your email. Now let me tell you about my family. My parents are coffee farmers. Most families here are small. I have one older sister, but I don't have a brother. My sister's name is . . .

B GROUP WORK Take turns reading your emails. Ask questions to get more information.

Stay-at-Home Dads

Read the title of the article. Then check (✓) the question you think the interviews will answer. ☐ *Why do men decide to stay at home with their children?* ☐ *What happens when both parents work?*

Families in the U.S. are changing. One important change is that many fathers are staying home with their children. They take care of the kids, and their wives go to work. *Modern Family* magazine asked three stay-at-home dads the question "What's it like being a stay-at-home dad?"

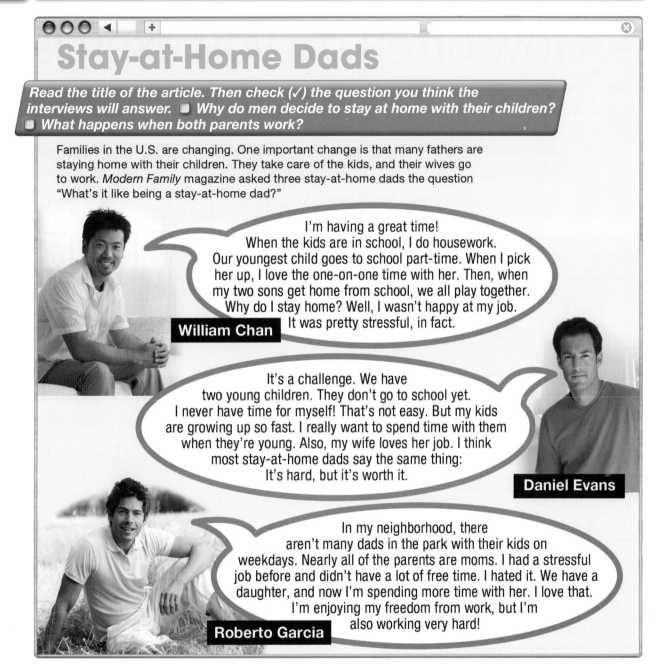

William Chan

I'm having a great time! When the kids are in school, I do housework. Our youngest child goes to school part-time. When I pick her up, I love the one-on-one time with her. Then, when my two sons get home from school, we all play together. Why do I stay home? Well, I wasn't happy at my job. It was pretty stressful, in fact.

Daniel Evans

It's a challenge. We have two young children. They don't go to school yet. I never have time for myself! That's not easy. But my kids are growing up so fast. I really want to spend time with them when they're young. Also, my wife loves her job. I think most stay-at-home dads say the same thing: It's hard, but it's worth it.

Roberto Garcia

In my neighborhood, there aren't many dads in the park with their kids on weekdays. Nearly all of the parents are moms. I had a stressful job before and didn't have a lot of free time. I hated it. We have a daughter, and now I'm spending more time with her. I love that. I'm enjoying my freedom from work, but I'm also working very hard!

A Read the interviews. Check (✓) the correct names.

Who . . . ?	William	Daniel	Roberto
1. has more than two children	☐	☐	☐
2. has an only child	☐	☐	☐
3. had a stressful career	☐	☐	☐
4. thinks it's hard to stay at home	☐	☐	☐
5. has a wife with a great job	☐	☐	☐

B **PAIR WORK** What do the dads like about staying at home? What challenges are they having? What are some other reasons dads stay at home?

6 How often do you exercise?

1 SNAPSHOT

The Top Five Sports and Fitness Activities in the United States

Sports
- [ ] basketball
- [ ] baseball
- [ ] soccer
- [ ] football
- [ ] softball

Fitness Activities
- [ ] walking
- [ ] weight training
- [ ] treadmill
- [ ] stretching
- [ ] jogging

Source: SGMA International, *Sports Participation in America*

Do people in your country enjoy any of these sports or activities?
Check (✓) the sports or fitness activities you enjoy.
Make a list of other sports or activities you do. Then compare with the class.

2 WORD POWER Sports and exercise

A Which of these activities are popular with the following age groups?
Check (✓) the activities. Then compare with a partner.

	Children	Teens	Young adults	Middle-aged people	Older people
aerobics	[ ]	[ ]	[ ]	[ ]	[ ]
bicycling	[ ]	[ ]	[ ]	[ ]	[ ]
bowling	[ ]	[ ]	[ ]	[ ]	[ ]
golf	[ ]	[ ]	[ ]	[ ]	[ ]
karate	[ ]	[ ]	[ ]	[ ]	[ ]
swimming	[ ]	[ ]	[ ]	[ ]	[ ]
tennis	[ ]	[ ]	[ ]	[ ]	[ ]
volleyball	[ ]	[ ]	[ ]	[ ]	[ ]
yoga	[ ]	[ ]	[ ]	[ ]	[ ]

B **PAIR WORK** Which activities in part A are used with *do*, *go*, or *play*?

do aerobics	go bicycling	play golf
....	....	....
....	....	....

3 CONVERSATION *I hardly ever exercise.*

A Listen and practice.

Marie: You're really fit, Paul. Do you exercise a lot?
Paul: Well, I almost always get up early, and I lift weights for an hour.
Marie: Seriously?
Paul: Sure. And then I often go swimming.
Marie: Wow! How often do you exercise like that?
Paul: About five times a week. What about you?
Marie: Oh, I hardly ever exercise. I usually just watch TV in my free time. I guess I'm a real couch potato!

B ▶ Listen to the rest of the conversation. What else does Paul do in his free time?

4 GRAMMAR FOCUS

Adverbs of frequency ▶

How often do you exercise?	Do you **ever** watch TV in the evening?	**100%** **always**
I lift weights **every day**.	Yes, I **often** watch TV after dinner.	**almost always**
I go jogging **once a week**.	I **sometimes** watch TV before bed.	**usually**
I play soccer **twice a month**.	**Sometimes** I watch TV before bed.*	**often**
I swim about **three times a year**.	I **hardly ever** watch TV.	**sometimes**
I don't exercise very **often/much**.	No, I **never** watch TV.	**hardly ever**
Usually I exercise before work.*		**almost never**
	*****Usually** and **sometimes** *can begin a sentence.* **0%**	**never**

A Put the adverbs in the correct place. Then practice with a partner.

1. A: Do you play sports? (ever)
   B: Sure. I play soccer. (twice a week)

2. A: What do you do on Saturday mornings? (usually)
   B: Nothing much. I sleep until noon. (almost always)

3. A: Do you do aerobics at the gym? (often)
   B: No, I do aerobics. (hardly ever)

4. A: Do you exercise on Sundays? (always)
   B: No, I exercise on Sundays. (never)

5. A: What do you do after class? (usually)
   B: I go out with my classmates. (about three times a week)

B **PAIR WORK** Take turns asking the questions in part A. Give your own information when answering.

PRONUNCIATION *Intonation with direct address*

A Listen and practice. Notice these statements with direct address.
There is usually falling intonation and a pause before the name.

You're really fit, Paul.   You look tired, Marie.   I feel great, Dr. Lee.

B **PAIR WORK** Write four statements using direct address.
Then practice them.

6 **SPEAKING** *Fitness poll*

A GROUP WORK Take a poll in your group. One person takes notes.
Take turns asking each person these questions.

1. Do you have a regular fitness program? How often do you exercise?

2. Do you ever go to a gym? How often do you go? What do you do there?

3. Do you play any sports? Which ones? How often do you play them?

4. Do you ever take long walks? How often? Where do you go?

5. What else do you do to keep fit?

B GROUP WORK Study the results of the poll. Who in your group
has a good fitness program?

7 **LISTENING** *In the evening*

A Listen to three people discuss what they like to do in the evening.
Complete the chart.

	Activity	How often?
Justin	....	....
Carrie	....	....
Marcos	....	....

B Listen again. Who is most similar to you – Justin, Carrie, or Marcos?

8 DISCUSSION *Sports and athletes*

GROUP WORK Take turns asking and answering these questions.

Who's your favorite male athlete? Why?
Who's your favorite female athlete? Why?
Who are three famous athletes in your country?
What's your favorite sports team? Why?
Do you ever watch sports on TV? Which ones?
Do you ever watch sports live? Which ones?
What are two sports you don't like?
What sport or activity do you want to try?

9 WRITING *About favorite activities*

A Write about your favorite activities. Include one activity that is false.

> I love to exercise! I usually work out every day. I get up early in the morning and go jogging for about 30 minutes. Then I often go to the gym and do yoga. Sometimes I play tennis in the afternoon. I play . . .

B **GROUP WORK** Take turns reading your descriptions. Can you guess the false information?

"You don't play tennis in the afternoon. Right?"

10 CONVERSATION *I'm a real fitness freak.*

A ▶ Listen and practice.

Ruth: You're in great shape, Keith.
Keith: Thanks. I guess I'm a real fitness freak.
Ruth: How often do you work out?
Keith: Well, I do aerobics twice a week. And I play tennis every week.
Ruth: Tennis? That sounds like a lot of fun.
Keith: Oh, do you want to play sometime?
Ruth: Uh, . . . how well do you play?
Keith: Pretty well, I guess.
Ruth: Well, all right. But I'm not very good.
Keith: No problem. I'll give you a few tips.

B ▶ Listen to Keith and Ruth after their tennis match. Who's the winner?

11 GRAMMAR FOCUS

A Complete these questions. Then practice with a partner.

1. A: .... at volleyball?
   B: I guess I'm pretty good. I often play on weekends.

2. A: .... spend online?
   B: About an hour after dinner. I like to chat with my friends.

3. A: .... play chess?
   B: Once or twice a month. It's a good way to relax.

4. A: .... swim?
   B: Not very well. I need to take swimming lessons.

B GROUP WORK Take turns asking the questions in part A.
Give your own information when answering.

12 LISTENING *I'm terrible at sports.*

▶ Listen to Dan, Jean, Sally, and Phil discuss sports and exercise.
Who is a couch potato? a fitness freak? a sports nut? a gym rat?

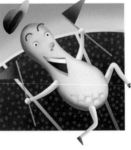

a couch potato	**a fitness freak**	**a sports nut**	**a gym rat**
1.	2.	3.	4. ....

13 INTERCHANGE 6 *Do you dance?*

Find out what your classmates can do. Go to Interchange 6 on page 120.

Health and Fitness Quiz

How healthy and fit do you think you are? Skim the questions below. Then guess your health and fitness score from 0 (very unhealthy) to 50 (very healthy).

Your Food and Nutrition

1. How many meals do you eat each day? — Points
- Four or five small meals — 5
- Three meals — 3
- One or two big meals — 0

2. How often do you eat at regular times during the day?
- Almost always — 5
- Usually — 3
- Hardly ever — 0

3. How many servings of fruits or vegetables do you eat each day?
- Five or more — 5
- One to four — 3
- None — 0

4. How much junk food do you eat?
- Very little — 5
- About average — 3
- A lot — 0

5. Do you take vitamins?
- Yes, every day — 5
- Sometimes — 3
- No — 0

Your Fitness

6. How often do you exercise or play a sport? — Points
- Three or more days a week — 5
- One or two days a week — 3
- Never — 0

7. Which best describes your exercise program? — Points
- Both weight training and aerobic exercise — 5
- Either weight training or aerobic exercise — 3
- None — 0

8. How important is your fitness program to you?
- Very important — 5
- Fairly important — 3
- Not very important — 0

Your Health

9. How often do you get a physical exam? — Points
- Once a year — 5
- Every two or three years — 3
- Rarely — 0

10. How often do you sleep well?
- Always — 5
- Usually or sometimes — 3
- Hardly ever or never — 0

Rate yourself

TOTAL POINTS
- **42 to 50:** Excellent job! Keep up the good work!
- **28 to 41:** Good! Your health and fitness are above average.
- **15 to 27:** Your health and fitness are a little below average.
- **14 or below:** You can improve your health and fitness.

A Take the quiz and add up your score. Is your score similar to your original guess? Do you agree with your quiz score? Why or why not?

B GROUP WORK Compare your scores. Who is the healthiest and fittest? What can you do to improve your health and fitness?

Units 5–6 Progress check

How well can you do these things? Check (✓) the boxes.

I can	Very well	OK	A little
Ask about and describe present activities (Ex. 1, 2, 3)	☐	☐	☐
Describe family life (Ex. 3)	☐	☐	☐
Ask for and give personal information (Ex. 3)	☐	☐	☐
Give information about quantities (Ex. 3)	☐	☐	☐
Ask and answer questions about free time (Ex. 4)	☐	☐	☐
Ask and answer questions about routines and abilities (Ex. 4)	☐	☐	☐

1 LISTENING What are they doing?

A ▶ Listen to people do different things. What are they doing? Complete the chart.

B PAIR WORK Compare your answers.

A: In number one, someone is watching TV.
B: I don't think so. I think someone is . . .

What are they doing?
1. ....
2. ....
3. ....
4. ....

2 GAME Memory test

GROUP WORK Choose a person in the room, but don't say who! Other students ask yes/no questions to guess the person.

A: I'm thinking of someone in the classroom.
B: Is it a woman?
A: Yes, it is.
C: Is she sitting in the front of the room?
A: No, she isn't.
D: Is she sitting in the back?
A: Yes, she is.
E: Is she wearing jeans?
A: No, she isn't.
B: Is it . . . ?

The student with the correct guess has the next turn.

3 SURVEY Family life

A GROUP WORK Add two more yes/no questions about family life to the chart. Then ask and answer the questions in groups. Write down the number of "yes" and "no" answers. (Remember to include yourself.)

	Number of "yes" answers	Number of "no" answers
1. Are you living with your family?	....	....
2. Do your parents both work?	....	....
3. Do you eat dinner with your family?	....	....
4. Are you working these days?	....	....
5. Are you married?	....	....
6. Do you have any children?	....	....
7.	....	....
8.	....	....

B GROUP WORK Write up the results of the survey. Then tell the class.

> 1. In our group, most people are living with their family.
> 2. Few of our parents both work.

4 DISCUSSION Routines and abilities

GROUP WORK Choose three questions. Then ask your questions in groups. When someone answers "yes," think of other questions to ask.

Do you ever . . . ?
- [ ] sing karaoke
- [ ] listen to English songs
- [ ] chat online
- [ ] do weight training
- [ ] play golf
- [ ] play video games
- [ ] cook for friends
- [ ] go swimming
- [ ] watch old movies

A: **Do you ever** sing karaoke?
B: Yes, I often do.
C: **What** song do you like to sing?
B: "I Love Rock 'n' Roll."
A: **When** do you sing karaoke?
B: In the evenings.
C: **How often** do you go?
B: Every weekend!
D: **How well** do you sing?
B: Not very well. But I have a lot of fun!

WHAT'S NEXT?

Look at your Self-assessment again. Do you need to review anything?

7 We had a great time!

1 SNAPSHOT

The Top Eight Leisure-Time Activities in the United States

☐ read   ☐ watch TV   ☐ spend time with family   ☐ play sports

☐ go to the gym   ☐ use the computer   ☐ go fishing   ☐ go to the movies

Source: The Harris Poll

Check (✓) the activities you do in your free time.
List three other activities you do in your free time.
What are your favorite leisure-time activities?

2 CONVERSATION *Did you do anything special?*

A ▶ Listen and practice.

Rick: So, what did you do last weekend, Meg?

Meg: Oh, I had a great time. I went to a karaoke bar and sang with some friends on Saturday.

Rick: How fun! Did you go to Lucky's?

Meg: No, we didn't. We went to that new place downtown. How about you? Did you go anywhere?

Rick: No, I didn't go anywhere all weekend. I just stayed home and studied for today's Spanish test.

Meg: Our test is today? I forgot about that!

Rick: Don't worry. You always get an A.

B ▶ Listen to the rest of the conversation.
What does Meg do on Sunday afternoons?

GRAMMAR FOCUS

Simple past ▶

Did you **work** on Saturday?
   Yes, I **did**. I **worked** all day.
   No, I **didn't**. I **didn't work** at all.

Did you **go** anywhere last weekend?
   Yes, I **did**. I **went** to the movies.
   No, I **didn't**. I **didn't go** anywhere.

What **did** Rick **do** on Saturday?
He **stayed** home and **studied** for a test.

How **did** Meg **spend** her weekend?
She **went** to a karaoke bar and **sang**
   with some friends.

A Complete these conversations. Then practice with a partner.

1. A: .... you .... (stay) home on Saturday?
   B: No, I .... (call) my friend. We .... (drive)
      to a café for lunch.
2. A: How .... you .... (spend) your last birthday?
   B: I .... (have) a party. Everyone .... (enjoy) it,
      but the neighbors .... (not, like) the noise.
3. A: What .... you .... (do) last night?
   B: I .... (see) a 3-D movie at the Cineplex.
      I .... (love) it!
4. A: .... you .... (do) anything special over the weekend?
   B: Yes, I .... I .... (go) shopping. Unfortunately,
      I .... (spend) all my money. Now I'm broke!
5. A: .... you .... (go) out on Friday night?
   B: No, I .... I .... (invite) friends over,
      and I .... (cook) dinner for them.

| regular verbs |
| work ⟶ work**ed** |
| invite ⟶ invite**d** |
| study ⟶ stud**ied** |
| stop ⟶ stop**ped** |

| irregular verbs |
| do ⟶ **did** |
| drive ⟶ **drove** |
| have ⟶ **had** |
| go ⟶ **went** |
| sing ⟶ **sang** |
| see ⟶ **saw** |
| spend ⟶ **spent** |

B **PAIR WORK** Take turns asking the questions in part A.
Give your own information when answering.

A: Did you stay home on Saturday?
B: No, I didn't. I went out with some friends.

4 PRONUNCIATION *Reduction of* did you

A ▶ Listen and practice. Notice how **did you** is reduced in the
following questions.

[dɪdʒə]   [wədɪdʒə]   [haʊdɪdʒə]
Did you have a good time?   **What did you** do last night?   **How did you** like the movie?

B **PAIR WORK** Practice the questions in Exercise 3, part A again.
Pay attention to the pronunciation of **did you**.

5 WORD POWER Chores and activities

A Find two other words or phrases from the list that usually go with each verb.

a lot of fun	dancing	a good time	shopping	a vacation
the bed	the dishes	the laundry	a trip	a video

do	my homework	....	....
go	online	....	....
have	a party	....	....
make	a phone call	....	....
take	a day off	....	....

B Circle the things you did last weekend. Then compare with a partner.

A: I went shopping with my friends. We had a good time.
B: I didn't have a very good time. I did the laundry and . . .

6 DISCUSSION Any questions?

GROUP WORK Take turns. One student makes a statement about the weekend. Other students ask questions. Each student answers at least three questions.

A: I went dancing on Saturday night.
B: **Where** did you go?
A: To the Rock-it Club.
C: **Who** did you go with?
A: I went with my friends.
D: **What time** did you go?
A: We went around 10:00.

7 LISTENING What did you do last night?

A Listen to John and Laura describe what they did last night. Check (✓) the correct information about each person.

Who . . . ?	John	Laura
went to a party	☐	☐
had a good meal	☐	☐
watched a video	☐	☐
met an old friend	☐	☐
got home late	☐	☐

B Listen again. Who had a good time? Who didn't have a good time? Why or why not?

8

INTERCHANGE 7 *Thinking back*

Play a board game. Go to Interchange 7 on page 121.

9 CONVERSATION *How was your vacation?*

A ▶ Listen and practice.

Celia: Hi, Don. How was your vacation?
 Don: It was excellent! I went to Hawaii with
       my cousin. We had a great time.
Celia: Lucky you. How long were you there?
 Don: About a week.
Celia: Fantastic! Was the weather OK?
 Don: Not really. It was cloudy a lot. But we went
       surfing every day. The waves were amazing.
Celia: So, what was the best thing about the trip?
 Don: Well, something incredible happened. . . .

B ▶ Listen to the rest of the conversation.
What happened?

10 *GRAMMAR FOCUS*

Past of be ▶

		Contractions
Were you in Hawaii?	Yes, I **was**.	was**n't** = was not
Was the weather OK?	No, it **wasn't**.	were**n't** = were not
Were you and your cousin on vacation?	Yes, we **were**.	
Were your parents there?	No, they **weren't**.	
How long **were** you away?	I **was** away for a week.	
How **was** your vacation?	It **was** excellent!	

Complete these conversations. Then practice with a partner.

1. A: .... you in Los Angeles last weekend?
   B: No, I .... I .... in San Francisco.
   A: How .... it?
   B: It .... great! But it .... foggy and
      cool as usual.

2. A: How long .... your parents in Europe?
   B: They .... there for two weeks.
   A: .... they in London the whole time?
   B: No, they .... They also went to Paris.

3. A: .... you away last week?
   B: Yes, I .... in Istanbul.
   A: Really? How long .... you there?
   B: For almost a week. I .... there on business.

Golden Gate Bridge

We had a great time! ▪ **47**

11 DISCUSSION On vacation

A GROUP WORK Ask your classmates about their last vacations.
Ask these questions or your own ideas.

Where did you spend your last vacation?
How long was your vacation?
Who were you with?

What did you do?
How was the weather?
What would you like to do on your next vacation?

B CLASS ACTIVITY Who had an interesting vacation? Tell the class who and why.

12 WRITING An online post

A Read this online post.

Search [ ] Go

Kathy

Chichen Itza

Greetings from Cancun! I'm having a great time. Yesterday I took a tour to the Mayan ruins of Chichen Itza. They were amazing! This morning I went to the beach and then went shopping in the city. I bought some beautiful Mexican silver jewelry. Last night I tried the famous local lime soup. This was a great vacation!

B Write an online post to a partner about your last vacation. Then exchange messages. Do you have any questions about the vacation?

13 LISTENING Welcome back.

A ▶ Listen to Jason and Barbara talk about their vacations.
Write where they went and what they did there.

	Where they went	What they did	Did they enjoy it?	
			Yes	No
Jason	....	....	☐	☐
Barbara	....	....	☐	☐

B ▶ Listen again. Did they enjoy their vacations? Check (✓) Yes or No.

Look at the pictures. What do you think each person did on his or her vacation?

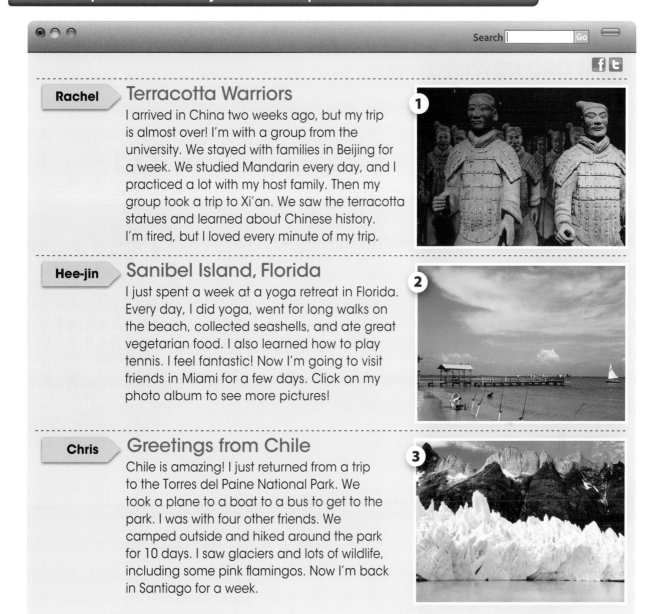

Search [   ] Go

Rachel ▶ Terracotta Warriors

I arrived in China two weeks ago, but my trip is almost over! I'm with a group from the university. We stayed with families in Beijing for a week. We studied Mandarin every day, and I practiced a lot with my host family. Then my group took a trip to Xi'an. We saw the terracotta statues and learned about Chinese history. I'm tired, but I loved every minute of my trip.

Hee-jin ▶ Sanibel Island, Florida

I just spent a week at a yoga retreat in Florida. Every day, I did yoga, went for long walks on the beach, collected seashells, and ate great vegetarian food. I also learned how to play tennis. I feel fantastic! Now I'm going to visit friends in Miami for a few days. Click on my photo album to see more pictures!

Chris ▶ Greetings from Chile

Chile is amazing! I just returned from a trip to the Torres del Paine National Park. We took a plane to a boat to a bus to get to the park. I was with four other friends. We camped outside and hiked around the park for 10 days. I saw glaciers and lots of wildlife, including some pink flamingos. Now I'm back in Santiago for a week.

A Read the online posts. Then write the number of the post where each sentence could go.

.... It was a long trip, but I was so happy after we got there!
.... I really recommend this place – it's very relaxing.
.... I had a great trip, but now I need a vacation!

B PAIR WORK Answer these questions.

1. Which person had a fitness vacation?
2. Who learned a lot on vacation?
3. Who had a vacation that was full of adventure?
4. Which vacation sounds the most interesting to you? Why?

8 What's your neighborhood like?

1 WORD POWER Places

A Match the words and the definitions. Then ask and answer the questions with a partner.

What's a...?   *It's a place where you...*

1. barbershop ....   a. wash and dry clothes
2. grocery store ....   b. buy food
3. laundromat ....   c. buy cards and paper
4. library ....   d. get a haircut
5. stationery store ....   e. see a movie or play
6. theater ....   f. make reservations for a trip
7. travel agency ....   g. borrow books

B **PAIR WORK** Write definitions for these places.

clothing store   drugstore   Internet café   music store   post office

> It's a place where you find new fashions. (clothing store)

C **GROUP WORK** Read your definitions. Can others guess the places?

2 CONVERSATION *I'm your new neighbor.*

▶ Listen and practice.

Jack: Excuse me. I'm your new neighbor, Jack. I just moved in.

Mrs. Day: Oh. Yes?

Jack: I'm looking for a grocery store. Are there any around here?

Mrs. Day: Yes, there are some on Pine Street.

Jack: Oh, good. And is there a laundromat near here?

Mrs. Day: Well, I think there's one across from the shopping center.

Jack: Thank you.

Mrs. Day: By the way, there's a barbershop in the shopping center, too.

Jack: A barbershop?

There is, there are; one, any, some ▶

Is there a laundromat near here? Yes, **there is**. There's **one** across from the shopping center. No, **there isn't**, but there's **one** next to the library. **Are there any** grocery stores around here? Yes, **there are**. There are **some** nice stores on Pine Street. No, **there aren't**, but there are **some** on Third Avenue. No, **there aren't any** around here.	**Prepositions** on next to near/close to across from/opposite in front of in back of/behind between on the corner of

A Look at the map below. Write questions about these places.

a bank	an electronics store	grocery stores	hotels	a post office
a department store	gas stations	a gym	a pay phone	restaurants

> Is there a bank around here?
>
> Are there any gas stations on Main Street?

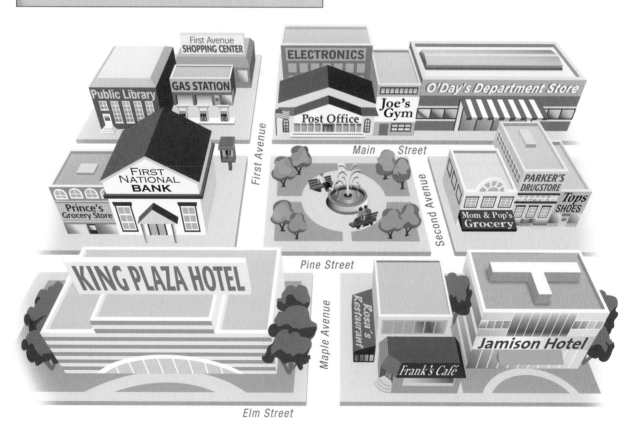

B **PAIR WORK** Ask and answer the questions you wrote in part A.

A: Is there a pay phone around here?
B: Yes, there is. There's one across from the gas station.

4 PRONUNCIATION *Reduction of* there is/there are

A Listen and practice. Notice how **there is** and **there are** are reduced in conversation, except for short answers.

Is there a laundromat near here?
    Yes, **there is**. **There's** one across from the shopping center.

Are there any grocery stores around here?
    Yes, **there are**. **There are** some on Pine Street.

B Practice the questions and answers in Exercise 3, part B again.

5 SPEAKING *My neighborhood*

GROUP WORK Take turns asking and answering questions about places like these in your neighborhood.

a bookstore	an Internet café
coffee shops	a karaoke bar
dance clubs	a library
drugstores	movie theaters
an electronics store	a park
a gym	restaurants

A: Is there a good bookstore in your
    neighborhood?
B: Yes, there's an excellent one across
    from the park.
C: Are there any coffee shops?
B: Sorry, I don't know.
D: Are there any cool dance clubs?
B: I'm not sure, but I think there's one . . .

useful expressions
Sorry, I don't know.
I'm not sure, but I think . . .
Of course. There's one . . .

6 LISTENING *What are you looking for?*

A Listen to hotel guests ask about places to visit. Complete the chart.

Place	Location	Interesting?	
		Yes	**No**
Hard Rock Cafe	....	☐	☐
Science Museum	....	☐	☐
Aquarium	....	☐	☐

B **PAIR WORK** Which place sounds the most interesting to you? Why?

7 SNAPSHOT

Common Complaints About Neighbors

Noise

☐ "My neighbor's dog barks all night."

☐ "My neighbor always listens to loud music."

Cleanliness

☐ "My neighbor puts his garbage in the hall."

☐ "There are always shoes outside my door."

Pets

☐ "My neighbor's cats go everywhere."

☐ "My neighbor has six dogs. It's like a zoo!"

Privacy

☐ "My neighbor's kids visit every day. It's too much!"

☐ "My neighbor always asks me for things."

Source: Based on information from njcooperator.com

Check (✓) the complaints you have about your neighbors.
What other complaints do you have about neighbors?
What do you do when you have complaints?

8 CONVERSATION *It's pretty safe.*

Listen and practice.

Nick: How do you like your new apartment?

Pam: I love it. It's downtown, so it's very convenient.

Nick: Downtown? Is there much noise?

Pam: No, there isn't any. I live on the fifth floor.

Nick: How many restaurants are there near your place?

Pam: A lot. In fact, there's an excellent Korean place just around the corner.

Nick: What about parking?

Pam: Well, there aren't many parking garages. But I usually find a place on the street.

Nick: Is there much crime?

Pam: No, it's pretty safe. Hold on. That's my car alarm! I'll call you back later.

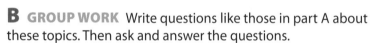

Quantifiers; how many *and* how much ⊙

Count nouns	**Noncount nouns**
Are there **many restaurants**?	Is there **much crime**?
Yes, there are **a lot**.	Yes, there's **a lot**.
Yes, there are **a few**.	Yes, there's **a little**.
No, there are**n't many**.	No, there is**n't much**.
No, there are**n't any**.	No, there is**n't any**.
No, there are **none**.	No, there's **none**.
How many restaurants are there?	**How much** crime is there?
There are ten or twelve.	There's a lot of street crime.

A Write answers to these questions about your neighborhood. Then practice with a partner.

1. Is there much parking? ....
2. Are there many apartment buildings? ....
3. How much traffic is there? ....
4. How many dance clubs are there? ....
5. Is there much noise? ....
6. Are there many pay phones? ....
7. Is there much pollution? ....
8. How many swimming pools are there? ....

B GROUP WORK Write questions like those in part A about these topics. Then ask and answer the questions.

cafés   crime   parks   pollution   public transportation   schools   traffic lights

 INTERCHANGE 8 *Where am I?*

Play a guessing game. Go to Interchange 8 on page 122.

 WRITING *A "roommate wanted" ad*

A Read these ads asking for roommates.

B Now write a "roommate wanted" ad. Use your real name at the end, but you can use a false phone number or email address.

C CLASS ACTIVITY Put your ads on the wall. Read the ads and choose one. Then find the person who wrote it. Ask questions to get more information.

Roommates 🏠 Wanted

Roommate needed to share large 3-bedroom apt. in nice neighborhood. Great park across the street. Only $440 a month! Parking available. Call Sheri or Jen at 352-555-8381.

Quiet student looking for roommate to share 2-bedroom house near university. Near public transportation. Pets OK. $550 a month plus utilities. Email Greg at g.adams@cup.com.

The World in One Neighborhood

1 The sidewalks are crowded with people chatting in Cantonese. An Indian man sells spices from his corner shop. Brazilian music plays loudly from a café. Is it China? India? Brazil? No, it's Kensington Market, a neighborhood in Toronto, Canada. Kensington Market was once an Eastern European and Italian neighborhood, but the area changed along with its residents. First came the Portuguese, then East Asians, then people from Iran, Vietnam, Sudan, Brazil, the Caribbean, and the Middle East.

2 Today, the neighborhood is truly multicultural – you can hear more than 100 languages on its streets. New residents bring many new traditions. "What's really cool about Kensington is that as soon as you're in it, you feel as though you're not in Toronto anymore," says one resident. "I think what makes Kensington Market unique is that it's always changing," says another.

3 It isn't surprising that the area in and around Kensington Market is becoming a popular place to live. The rents are reasonable, the neighborhood is exciting, and it has good public transportation. There are apartments of every size and for every budget. It has inexpensive stores, fun cafés, fresh fruit and vegetable markets, and restaurants with almost every type of cuisine. As one resident says, "This place is the heart of Toronto."

A Read the article. Then write the number of each paragraph next to its main idea.

.... The residents and their traditions make Kensington Market a multicultural neighborhood.
.... People from all over the world live in Kensington Market.
.... The neighborhood has many good characteristics.

B Check (✓) the things you can find in Kensington Market.

☐ inexpensive stores ☐ beautiful beaches ☐ many different cultures
☐ big apartments ☐ great markets ☐ interesting old buildings
☐ good schools ☐ good restaurants ☐ good public transportation

C PAIR WORK Do you know of a neighborhood that is similar to Kensington Market? Describe it.

Units 7–8 Progress check

SELF-ASSESSMENT

How well can you do these things? Check (✓) the boxes.

I can	Very well	OK	A little
Understand descriptions of past events (Ex. 1)	☐	☐	☐
Describe events in the past (Ex. 1)	☐	☐	☐
Ask and answer questions about past activities (Ex. 2)	☐	☐	☐
Give and understand simple directions (Ex. 3)	☐	☐	☐
Talk about my neighborhood (Ex. 4)	☐	☐	☐

1 LISTENING *Frankie's weekend*

A A thief robbed a house on Saturday. A detective is questioning Frankie. The pictures show what Frankie really did on Saturday. Listen to their conversation. Are Frankie's answers true (**T**) or false (**F**)?

1:00 P.M. T F   **3:00** P.M. T F   **5:00** P.M. T F   **6:00** P.M. T F   **8:00** P.M. T F   **10:30** P.M. T F

B **PAIR WORK** What did Frankie really do? Use the pictures to retell the story.

2 DISCUSSION *What do you remember?*

A Do you remember what you did yesterday? Check (✓) the things you did. Then add two other things you did.

☐ got up early   ☐ went shopping   ☐ did the dishes   ☐ went to bed late
☐ went to class   ☐ ate at a restaurant ☐ watched TV   ☐ ....
☐ made phone calls ☐ did the laundry   ☐ exercised   ☐ ....

B **GROUP WORK** Ask questions about each thing in part A.

A: Did you get up early yesterday?
B: No, I didn't. I got up at 10:00. I was very tired.

3 SPEAKING The neighborhood

A Create a neighborhood. Add five places to "My map."
Choose from this list.

a bank   cafés   a dance club   a drugstore   gas stations   a gym   a theater

My map

My partner's map

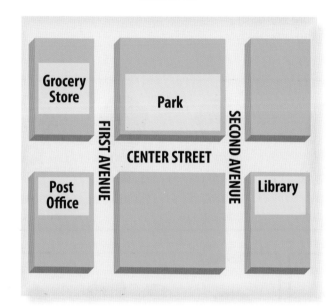

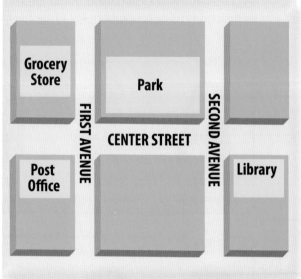

B **PAIR WORK** Ask questions about your partner's map. (But don't look!)
Draw the places on "My partner's map." Then compare your maps.

A: Are there any cafés in the neighborhood?
B: Yes, there's one on the corner of Center Street and First Avenue.

4 ROLE PLAY What's it like?

Student A: Imagine you are a visitor in Student B's neighborhood.
           Ask questions about it.
Student B: Imagine a visitor wants to find out about your
           neighborhood. Answer the visitor's questions.

     A: How much crime is there?
     B: There isn't much. It's a very safe neighborhood.
     A: Is there much noise?
     B: Well, yes, there's a lot. . . .

Change roles and try the role play again.

topics to ask about
crime
noise
parks
places to shop
pollution
public transportation
schools
traffic

WHAT'S NEXT?

Look at your Self-assessment again. Do you need to review anything?

What does she look like?

 WORD POWER *Appearance*

A Look at these expressions. What are three more words or expressions to describe people? Write them in the box below.

Hair

| long brown hair | short blond hair | straight black hair | curly red hair | bald | a mustache and beard |

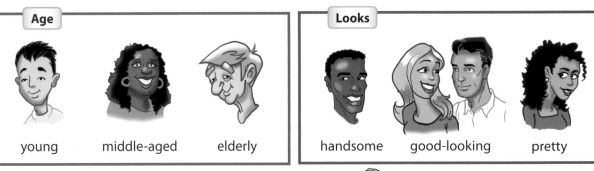

Age

young   middle-aged   elderly

Looks

handsome   good-looking   pretty

Other words or expressions
....
....
....

Height

short   fairly short   medium height   pretty tall   very tall

B **PAIR WORK** Choose at least four expressions to describe yourself and your partner. Then compare. Do you agree?

A: You have curly black hair. You're young and good-looking.
B: I don't agree. My hair isn't very curly.

Me	My partner
....	....
....	....
....	....
....	....

2 CONVERSATION *She's very tall.*

A ▶ Listen and practice.

Emily: I hear you have a new girlfriend, Randy.
Randy: Yes. Her name's Ashley, and she's
        gorgeous!
Emily: Really? What does she look like?
Randy: Well, she's very tall.
Emily: How tall?
Randy: About 6 feet 2, I suppose.
Emily: Wow, that *is* tall. What color is her hair?
Randy: She has beautiful red hair.
Emily: And how old is she?
Randy: I don't know. She won't tell me.

B ▶ Listen to the rest of the conversation.
What else do you learn about Ashley?

3 GRAMMAR FOCUS

Describing people ▶

General appearance	Age	Height	Hair
What does she look like?	How old is she?	How tall is she?	How long is her hair?
She's tall, with red hair.	She's about 32.	She's 1 meter 88.	It's medium length.
She's gorgeous.	She's in her thirties.	She's 6 feet 2.	
Does he wear glasses?	How old is he?	How tall is he?	What color is his hair?
Yes, and he has a beard.	He's in his twenties.	He's pretty short.	It's dark/light brown.
			He has brown hair.

A Write questions to match these statements. Then compare with a partner.

1. .... ?   My brother is 26.
2. .... ?   I'm 173 cm (5 feet 8).
3. .... ?   My mother has brown hair.
4. .... ?   No, she wears contact lenses.
5. .... ?   He's tall and very good-looking.
6. .... ?   My sister's hair is medium length.
7. .... ?   I have dark brown eyes.

B **PAIR WORK** Choose a person in your class. Don't tell your partner who
it is. Your partner will ask questions to guess the person's name.

A: Is it a man or a woman?
B: It's a man.
A: How tall is he?
B: . . .

4 LISTENING *Who is it?*

A ▶ Listen to descriptions of six people. Number them from 1 to 6.

B ▶ Listen again. How old is each person?

5 INTERCHANGE 9 *Find the differences*

Compare two pictures of a party. Student A go to Interchange 9A on page 123. Student B go to Interchange 9B on page 124.

6 WRITING *An email describing people*

A Imagine your e-pal is coming to visit you for the first time. You and a classmate are meeting him or her at the airport. Write an email describing yourself and your classmate. (Don't give the classmate's name.)

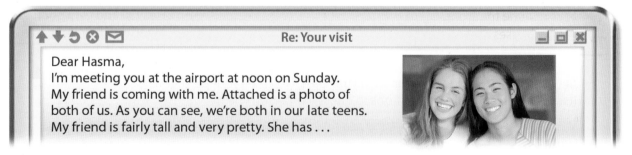

Re: Your visit

Dear Hasma,
I'm meeting you at the airport at noon on Sunday.
My friend is coming with me. Attached is a photo of
both of us. As you can see, we're both in our late teens.
My friend is fairly tall and very pretty. She has . . .

B GROUP WORK Read your email to the group. Can they guess the classmate you are describing?

7 SNAPSHOT

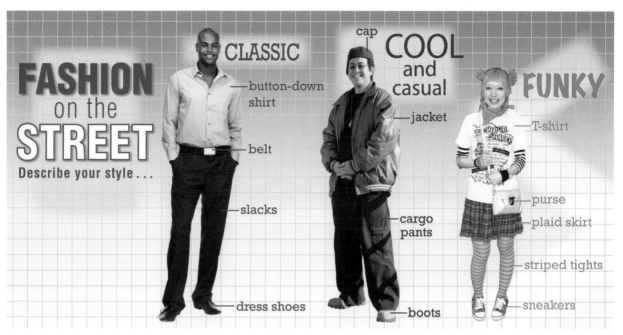

FASHION on the STREET
Describe your style...

CLASSIC
- button-down shirt
- belt
- slacks
- dress shoes

COOL and casual
- cap
- jacket
- cargo pants
- boots

FUNKY
- T-shirt
- purse
- plaid skirt
- striped tights
- sneakers

Source: Based on an idea from *Time Out New York*

Which clothing items do you often wear? Circle the items.
What are three more things you like to wear?
What's your style? Is it classic? cool and casual? funky? something else?

8 CONVERSATION *Which one is she?*

A ▶ Listen and practice.

Liz: Hi, Raoul! Good to see you! Where's Maggie?

Raoul: Oh, she couldn't make it. She went to a concert with Alex.

Liz: Oh! Well, why don't you go and talk to Julia? She doesn't know anyone here.

Raoul: Julia? Which one is she? Is she the woman wearing glasses over there?

Liz: No, she's the tall one in jeans. She's standing near the window.

Raoul: Oh, I'd like to meet her.

B ▶ Listen to the rest of the conversation. Label Joe, Michiko, Rosa, and John in the picture.

9 GRAMMAR FOCUS

Modifiers with participles and prepositions ▶

		Participles
Who's Raoul?	He's **the man**	**wearing** a green shirt.
Which one is Raoul?	He's **the one**	**talking** to Liz.
		Prepositions
Who's Liz?	She's **the woman**	**with** short black hair.
Which one is Julia?	She's **the tall one**	**in** jeans.
Who are the Smiths?	They're **the people**	**next to** the window.
Which ones are the Smiths?	They're **the ones**	**on** the couch.

A Rewrite these statements using modifiers with participles or prepositions.

1. Clark is the tall guy. He's wearing a button-down shirt and cargo pants.
   Clark is the tall guy wearing a button-down shirt and cargo pants.

2. Adam and Louise are the good-looking couple. They're talking to Tom.
   ....

3. Lynne is the young girl. She's in a striped T-shirt and blue jeans.
   ....

4. Jessica is the attractive woman. She's sitting to the left of Antonio.
   ....

5. A.J. is the serious-looking boy. He's playing a video game.
   ....

B PAIR WORK Complete these questions using your classmates' names and information. Then take turns asking and answering the questions.

1. Who's the man sitting next to .... ?
2. Who's the woman wearing .... ?
3. Who is .... ?
4. Which one is .... ?
5. Who are the people .... ?
6. Who are the ones .... ?

10 PRONUNCIATION *Contrastive stress in responses*

A ▶ Listen and practice. Notice how the stress changes to emphasize a contrast.

A: Is Anthony the one wearing the red shirt?

B: No, he's the one wearing the black shirt.

A: Is Judy the woman on the couch?

B: No, Diana is the woman on the couch.

B ▶ Mark the stress changes in these conversations. Listen and check. Then practice the conversations.

A: Is Britney the one sitting next to Katy?

B: No, she's the one standing next to Katy.

A: Is Donald the one on the couch?

B: No, he's the one behind the couch.

DEAR KEN AND PIXIE

Your style questions answered!

Look at the pictures. What is each an example of? Match the descriptions with the pictures. a. mixing old and new   b. mixing baggy and slim   c. mixing colors and patterns

All of your questions this week are about mixing and matching styles, patterns, and colors.

Dear Ken and Pixie,
I'm reading a lot about how to mix prints in the latest fashion magazines. But when I wear different prints together, I look silly. What's the trick?
– Mixed-up

Dear Mixed-up,
It's not difficult to wear different prints together. Find the similarity in each item of clothing you want to wear. Mix two or three items with the same background color, like white or another neutral color. Mix a large print with a small one. Mix similar patterns, like stripes with plaid. But if you don't feel comfortable in it, don't wear it!

Dear Ken and Pixie,
In college, I wore vintage clothes, but now I'm 30 and need a modern look. How can I wear vintage styles without looking outdated?
– Oldie but Goodie

Dear Oldie but Goodie,
Vintage clothing is always in! But mix it with something new for a modern look. Wear a vintage shirt with pants. Pair an old belt with a new bag. Wear vintage shoes with new jeans. But sometimes you need to alter the clothes. For example, take a baggy vintage skirt and make it slim, or cut the shoulder pads out of a vintage jacket.

Dear Ken and Pixie,
I'm seeing both baggy pants and skinny pants on the designer runways. Also, short pants and long pants. What's in style?
– Confused Carrie

Dear Confused Carrie,
It's all in style! For pants, anything goes this year. The trick is to wear something on top that is the opposite of the style of the pants. So, if you're wearing baggy pants, try a slim shirt. If slim pants are your thing, wear a baggy sweater. Short pants? Try funky shoes. Wear long pants with your shirt tucked in and a belt.

A Read the webpage. Find the words in *italics* in the text. Then match each word with its meaning.

.... 1. *neutral*	a. not in style
.... 2. *vintage*	b. change
.... 3. *outdated*	c. slim
.... 4. *alter*	d. from the past but still in style
.... 5. *baggy*	e. without strong color
.... 6. *skinny*	f. loose fitting

B **PAIR WORK** Answer these questions.

1. Do you mix and match patterns and colors? What does your favorite outfit look like?
2. Do you have any vintage clothing? What time period is it from?
3. Do you wear clothes because they are fashionable or because they look good on you, or both?

10 Have you ever ridden a camel?

1 SNAPSHOT

Entertainment Guide

Fun things to do in **NEW ORLEANS**

go to a jazz club
take a riverboat tour
ride in a streetcar
visit a historic home
go to a food festival

Source: www.neworleansonline.com

Which activities have you done?
Check (✓) the activities you would like to try.

2 CONVERSATION *A visit to New Orleans*

A ⊙ Listen and practice.

Jan: It's great to see you, Todd. Have you been in New Orleans long?

Todd: No, not really. Just a few days.

Jan: I can't wait to show you the city. Have you been to a jazz club yet?

Todd: Yeah, I've already been to one.

Jan: Oh. Well, how about a riverboat tour?

Todd: Uh, I've already done that, too.

Jan: Have you ridden in a streetcar? They're a lot of fun.

Todd: Actually, that's how I got here today.

Jan: Well, is there anything you want to do?

Todd: You know, I really just want to take it easy. My feet are killing me!

B ⊙ Listen to the rest of the conversation. What do they plan to do tomorrow?

Present perfect; already, yet ▶

**The present perfect is formed with
the verb have + the past participle.**

Have you **been** to a jazz club?

   Yes, I**'ve been** to several.   No, I **haven't been** to one.

Has he **called** home lately?

   Yes, he**'s called** twice this week.   No, he **hasn't called** in months.

Have they **eaten** dinner yet?

   Yes, they**'ve** already **eaten**.   No, they **haven't eaten** yet.

Contractions		
I**'ve**	=	I have
you**'ve**	=	you have
he**'s**	=	he has
she**'s**	=	she has
it**'s**	=	it has
we**'ve**	=	we have
they**'ve**	=	they have
has**n't**	=	has not
have**n't**	=	have not

A How many times have you done these things in the past week?
Write your answers. Then compare with a partner.

1. clean the house
2. make your bed
3. cook dinner
4. do laundry
5. wash the dishes
6. go grocery shopping

regular past participles
call → call**ed**
hike → hike**d**
jog → jog**ged**
try → tr**ied**

> I've cleaned the house once this week.
> OR
> I haven't cleaned the house this week.

irregular past participles
be → **been**
do → **done**
eat → **eaten**
go → **gone**
have → **had**
make → **made**
ride → **ridden**
see → **seen**

B Complete these conversations using the present perfect.
Then practice with a partner.

1. A: ....Have.... you ....done.... much exercise this week? (do)
   B: Yes, I .... already .... to aerobics class four times. (be)

2. A: .... you .... any sports this month? (play)
   B: No, I .... the time. (have)

3. A: How many movies .... you .... to this month? (be)
   B: Actually, I .... any yet. (see)

4. A: .... you .... to any interesting parties recently? (be)
   B: No, I .... to any parties for quite a while. (go)

5. A: .... you .... any friends today? (call)
   B: Yes, I .... already .... three calls. (make)

6. A: How many times .... you .... out to eat this week? (go)
   B: I .... at fast-food restaurants a couple of times. (eat)

C **PAIR WORK** Take turns asking the questions in part B.
Give your own information when answering.

4 CONVERSATION *Actually, I have.*

A ▶ Listen and practice.

Peter: I'm sorry I'm late. Have you been here long?

Mandy: No, only for a few minutes.

Peter: Have you chosen a restaurant yet?

Mandy: I can't decide. Have you ever eaten Moroccan food?

Peter: No, I haven't. Is it good?

Mandy: It's delicious. I've had it several times.

Peter: Or how about Thai food? Have you ever had green curry?

Mandy: Actually, I have. I lived in Thailand as a teenager. I ate it a lot there.

Peter: I didn't know that. How long did you live there?

Mandy: I lived there for two years.

B ▶ Listen to the rest of the conversation. Where do they decide to have dinner?

5 GRAMMAR FOCUS

Present perfect vs. simple past ▶

Use the present perfect for an indefinite time in the past.
Use the simple past for a specific event in the past.

Have you ever **eaten** Moroccan food?	Yes, I **have**. I **ate** it once in Paris.
	No, I **haven't**. I**'ve** never **eaten** it.
Have you ever **had** green curry?	Yes, I **have**. I **tried** it several years ago.
	No, I **haven't**. I**'ve** never **had** it.

A Complete these conversations. Use the present perfect and simple past of the verbs given and short answers. Then practice with a partner.

1. A: .... you ever .... in a karaoke bar? (sing)
   B: Yes, I .... I .... in one on my birthday.

2. A: .... you ever .... something valuable? (lose)
   B: No, I .... But my brother .... his camera on a trip once.

3. A: .... you ever .... a traffic ticket? (get)
   B: Yes, I .... Once I .... a ticket and had to pay $50.

4. A: .... you ever .... a live concert? (see)
   B: Yes, I .... I .... the Black Eyed Peas at the stadium last year.

5. A: .... you ever .... late for an important appointment? (be)
   B: No, I .... But my sister .... 30 minutes late for her wedding!

B **PAIR WORK** Take turns asking the questions in part A. Give your own information when answering.

For *and* since

How long **did** you **live** in Thailand?	I **lived** there **for** two years. It was wonderful.
How long **have** you **lived** in Miami?	I**'ve lived** here **for** six months. I love it here. I**'ve lived** here **since** last year. I'm really happy here.

C Complete these sentences with *for* or *since*.
Then compare with a partner.

1. Pam was in Central America .... a month last year.
2. I've been a college student .... almost four years.
3. Hiroshi has been at work .... 6:00 A.M.
4. I haven't gone to a party .... a long time.
5. Josh lived in Venezuela .... two years as a kid.
6. My parents have been on vacation .... Monday.
7. Natalie was engaged to Danny .... six months.
8. Pat and Valeria have been best friends .... high school.

expressions with *for*

two weeks
a few months
several years
a long time

expressions with *since*

6:45
last weekend
1997
elementary school

D **PAIR WORK** Ask and answer these questions.

How long have you had your current hairstyle?   How long have you known your best friend?
How long have you studied at this school?   How long have you been awake today?

6 PRONUNCIATION *Linked sounds*

A Listen and practice. Notice how final /t/ and /d/ sounds in
verbs are linked to the vowels that follow them.

A: Have you cooked lunch yet?   A: Have you ever tried Cuban food?
　　　　　　　　　/t/　　　　　　　　　　　　　/d/
B: Yes, I've already cooked it.   B: Yes, I tried it once in Miami.

B **PAIR WORK** Ask and answer these questions. Use *it* in your
responses. Pay attention to the linked sounds.

Have you ever cut your hair?
Have you ever tasted blue cheese?
Have you ever tried Korean food?
Have you ever lost your ID?
Have you looked at Unit 11 yet?

7 LISTENING *I'm impressed!*

 Listen to Clarice and Karl talk about interesting things they've
done recently. Complete the chart.

	Where they went	Why they liked it
Clarice	....	....
Karl	....	....

Have you ever ridden a camel? ▪ **67**

8 WORD POWER Activities

A Find two phrases to go with each verb. Write them in the chart.

| a camel | a costume | iced coffee | a motorcycle | your phone | a truck |
| chicken's feet | herbal tea | your keys | octopus | a sports car | a uniform |

eat	....	....	....
drink	....	....	....
drive	....	....	....
lose	....	....	....
ride	....	....	....
wear	....	....	....

B Add another phrase for each verb in part A.

9 SPEAKING Have you ever...?

A GROUP WORK Ask your classmates questions about the activities in Exercise 8 or your own ideas.

A: Have you ever ridden a camel?
B: Yes, I have.
C: Really? Where were you?

B CLASS ACTIVITY Tell the class one interesting thing you learned about a classmate.

10 WRITING An email to an old friend

A Write an email to someone you haven't seen for a long time. Include three things you've done since you last saw that person.

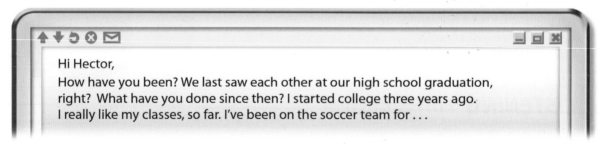

Hi Hector,
How have you been? We last saw each other at our high school graduation, right? What have you done since then? I started college three years ago. I really like my classes, so far. I've been on the soccer team for ...

B PAIR WORK Exchange emails with a partner. Write a response to it.

11 INTERCHANGE 10 Lifestyle survey

What kind of lifestyle do you have? Go to Interchange 10 on page 125.

TAKING THE RISK

///////////////////

Look at the pictures and skim the interviews.
Then write the name of the sport below each picture.

Sports World magazine recently spoke with Josh Parker, Lisa Kim, and Alex Costas about risky sports.

SW: Wingsuit flying is a dangerous sport, Josh. What do you enjoy about it? And have you ever had an accident?

Josh: No, I've never been hurt. But, yes, it is dangerous, even for experienced flyers. I've been doing it for five years, but I still get a little nervous before I jump out of the plane. That's the most dangerous thing. Once, I jumped too fast, and I started to spin. That was scary! But it's amazing to be able to fly like a bird.

SW: Lisa, you've been kiteboarding for years now. What are some of the dangers?

Lisa: Oh, there are many dangers. When you're in the ocean, the conditions can be unpredictable. The wind can lift you up too fast and then drop you against something hard, like sand, or even water. You can also hit another surfer. But I like the challenge, and I like overcoming danger. That's why I do it.

SW: Alex, have you ever experienced any dangers while ice climbing?

Alex: Yes, absolutely. When you're high up on a mountain, the conditions are hard on the body. The air is thin, and it's very cold. I've seen some really dangerous storms. But the great thing about it is how you feel when you're done. Your body feels good, and you have a beautiful view of the snowy mountaintops.

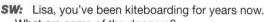

▶ _____

▶ _____

//////////////////

▶ _____

A Read the interviews. Then complete the chart.

	Sport	What they enjoy	The danger(s)
1. Josh	....	....	....
2. Lisa	....	....	....
3. Alex	....	....	....

B **PAIR WORK** Would you like to try any of these sports? Why or why not?

Units 9–10 Progress check

SELF-ASSESSMENT

How well can you do these things? Check (✓) the boxes.

I can	Very well	OK	A little
Ask about and describe people's appearance (Ex. 1)	☐	☐	☐
Identify people by describing what they're doing, what they're wearing, and where they are (Ex. 2)	☐	☐	☐
Find out whether or not things have been done (Ex. 3)	☐	☐	☐
Understand descriptions of experiences (Ex. 4)	☐	☐	☐
Ask and answer questions about experiences (Ex. 4)	☐	☐	☐
Find out how long people have done things (Ex. 5)	☐	☐	☐

1 ROLE PLAY *Missing person*

Student A: One of your classmates is lost. You are talking to a police officer. Answer the officer's questions and describe your classmate.

Student B: You are a police officer. Someone is describing a lost classmate. Ask questions to complete the form. Can you identify the classmate?

Change roles and try the role play again.

MISSING PERSON REPORT

NAME _____   # 78439122475

HEIGHT: _____   WEIGHT: _____   AGE: _____

EYE COLOR		HAIR COLOR	
☐ BLUE	☐ BROWN	☐ BLOND	☐ BROWN
☐ GREEN	☐ HAZEL	☐ RED	☐ BLACK
		☐ GRAY	☐ BALD

CLOTHING: _____
_____

GLASSES, ETC: _____

2 SPEAKING *Which one is . . . ?*

A Look at this picture. How many sentences can you write to identify the people?

> Amy and T.J. are the people in sunglasses.
> They're the ones looking at the picture.

B PAIR WORK Close your books. Who do you remember? Take turns asking about the people.

A: Which one is Bill?
B: I think Bill is the guy sitting . . .

Kate   Louisa   Bill

Amy and T.J.

3 SPEAKING *Reminders*

A Imagine you are preparing for these situations. Make a list of four things you need to do for each situation.

Your first day of school is in a week.
You are moving to a new apartment.
You are going to the beach.

> "To do" list: first day of school
> 1. buy notebooks

B **PAIR WORK** Exchange lists. Take turns asking about what has been done. When answering, decide what you have or haven't done.

A: Have you bought notebooks yet?
B: Yes, I've already gotten them.

4 LISTENING *What have you done?*

A ▶ Jamie is on a cruise. Listen to her talk about things she has done. Check (✓) the correct things.

- ☐ won a contest
- ☐ flown in a plane
- ☐ stayed in an expensive hotel
- ☐ met a famous person
- ☐ gone windsurfing
- ☐ lost her wallet
- ☐ been seasick
- ☐ kept a diary

B **GROUP WORK** Have you ever done the things in part A? Take turns asking about each thing.

5 SURVEY *How long . . . ?*

A Write answers to these questions using *for* and *since*.

How long have you . . . ?	My answers	Classmate's name
owned this book	....	....
studied English	....	....
known your best friend	....	....
lived in this town or city	....	....
been a student	....	....

B **CLASS ACTIVITY** Go around the class. Find someone who has the same answers. Write a classmate's names only once.

WHAT'S NEXT?

Look at your Self-assessment again. Do you need to review anything?

11 It's a very exciting place!

1 WORD POWER Adjectives

A **PAIR WORK** Match each word in column A with its opposite in column B. Then add two more pairs of adjectives to the list.

A
1. beautiful ....
2. cheap ....
3. clean ....
4. interesting ....
5. quiet ....
6. relaxing ....
7. safe ....
8. spacious ....
9. ....
10. ....

B
a. boring
b. crowded
c. dangerous
d. expensive
e. noisy
f. polluted
g. stressful
h. ugly
i. ....
j. ....

beautiful

ugly

B **PAIR WORK** Choose two places you know. Describe them to your partner using the words in part A.

2 CONVERSATION It's a fairly big city.

A ⏵ Listen and practice.

Eric: So, where are you from, Carmen?
Carmen: I'm from San Juan, Puerto Rico.
Eric: Wow, I've heard that's a really nice city.
Carmen: Yeah, it is. The weather is great, and there are some fantastic beaches nearby.
Eric: Is it expensive there?
Carmen: No, it's not very expensive. Prices are pretty reasonable.
Eric: How big is the city?
Carmen: It's a fairly big city. It's not *too* big, though.
Eric: It sounds perfect to me. Maybe I should plan a trip there sometime.

B ⏵ Listen to the rest of the conversation. What does Carmen say about entertainment in San Juan?

San Juan

Adverbs before adjectives ▶

San Juan is **really** nice.
It's **fairly** big.
It's not **very** expensive.

It's a **really** nice city.
It's a **fairly** big city.
It's not a **very** expensive place.

It's **too** noisy, and it's **too** crowded for me.

adverbs
extremely
very
really
pretty
fairly
somewhat
too

A Match the questions with the answers. Then practice the conversations with a partner.

1. What's Seoul like?
   Is it an interesting place? ....

2. Do you like your hometown?
   Why or why not? ....

3. What's Sydney like?
   I've never been there. ....

4. Have you ever been to
   São Paulo? ....

5. What's the weather like
   in Chicago? ....

a. Oh, really? It's beautiful and very clean. It has a great harbor and beautiful beaches.

b. Yes, I have. It's an extremely large and crowded place, but I love it. It has excellent restaurants.

c. It's really nice in the summer, but it's too cold for me in the winter.

d. Not really. It's too small, and it's really boring. That's why I moved away.

e. Yes. It has amazing shopping, and the people are pretty friendly.

Conjunctions ▶

It's a big city, **and** the weather is nice.
It's a big city, **but** it's not too big.

It's a big city. It's not too big, **though**.
It's a big city. It's not too big, **however**.

B Choose the correct conjunctions and rewrite the sentences.

1. Taipei is very nice. Everyone is extremely friendly. (and / but)
   ....

2. The streets are crowded. It's easy to get around. (and / though)
   ....

3. The weather is nice. Summers get pretty hot. (and / however)
   ....

4. Shopping is great. You have to bargain in the markets. (and / but)
   ....

5. It's an amazing city. I love to go there. (and / however)
   ....

C **GROUP WORK** Describe three cities or towns in your country. State two positive features and one negative feature for each.

A: Lima is very exciting and there are a lot of things to do, but it's too cold.
B: The weather in Shanghai is ...

It's a very exciting place! ▪ 73

4 LISTENING My hometown

Listen to Joyce and Nicholas talk about their hometowns.
What do they say? Check (✓) the correct boxes.

	Big?		Interesting?		Expensive?		Beautiful?	
	Yes	No	Yes	No	Yes	No	Yes	No
1. Joyce	☐	☐	☐	☐	☐	☐	☐	☐
2. Nicholas	☐	☐	☐	☐	☐	☐	☐	☐

5 WRITING An interesting place

A Write about an interesting town or city for tourists to visit in your country.

> Otavalo is a very interesting town in Ecuador. It's to the north of Quito. It has a fantastic market, and a lot of tourists go there to buy local handicrafts. The scenery around Otavalo is very pretty and . . .

B **PAIR WORK** Exchange papers and read each other's articles. Which place sounds more interesting?

6 SNAPSHOT

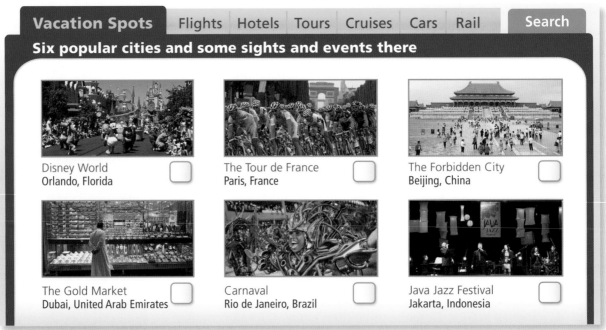

| Vacation Spots | Flights | Hotels | Tours | Cruises | Cars | Rail | Search |

Six popular cities and some sights and events there

Disney World
Orlando, Florida ☐

The Tour de France
Paris, France ☐

The Forbidden City
Beijing, China ☐

The Gold Market
Dubai, United Arab Emirates ☐

Carnaval
Rio de Janeiro, Brazil ☐

Java Jazz Festival
Jakarta, Indonesia ☐

Source: www.fodors.com

Which places would you like to visit? Why?
Put the places you would like to visit in order from most interesting to least interesting.
What three other places in the world would you like to visit? Why?

CONVERSATION *What should I see there?*

A ⊙ Listen and practice.

Thomas: Can you tell me a little about Mexico City?

Elena: Sure. What would you like to know?

Thomas: Well, I'm going to be there next month, but for only two days. What should I see?

Elena: Oh, you should definitely visit the Palace of Fine Arts. It's really beautiful.

Thomas: OK. Anything else?

Elena: You shouldn't miss the Museum of Modern Art. It has some amazing paintings.

Thomas: Great! And is there anything I can do for free?

Elena: Sure. You can walk in the parks, go to outdoor markets, or just watch people. It's a fascinating city!

B ⊙ Listen to the rest of the conversation.
Where is Thomas from? What should you do there?

8 **GRAMMAR FOCUS**

Modal verbs can *and* should ⊙

What **can** I do in Mexico City?   What **should** I see there?
   You **can** go to outdoor markets.   You **should** visit the Palace of Fine Arts.
   You **can't** visit some museums on Mondays.   You **shouldn't** miss the Museum of Modern Art.

A Complete these conversations using *can, can't, should,* or *shouldn't.*
Then practice with a partner.

1. A: I .... decide where to go on my vacation.
   B: You .... go to India. It's my favorite place to visit.
2. A: I'm planning to go to Bogotá next year. When do you think I .... go?
   B: You .... go anytime. The weather is nice almost all year.
3. A: .... I rent a car when I arrive in Cairo? What do you recommend?
   B: No, you .... definitely use the subway. It's fast and efficient.
4. A: Where .... I get some nice jewelry in Bangkok?
   B: You .... miss the weekend market. It's the best place for bargains.
5. A: What .... I see from the Eiffel Tower?
   B: You .... see all of Paris, but in bad weather, you .... see anything.

B Write answers to these questions about your country.
Then compare with a partner.

What time of year should you go there?   What can you do for free?
What are three things you can do there?   What shouldn't a visitor miss?

It's a very exciting place! ▪ 75

9 PRONUNCIATION Can't *and* shouldn't

A ▶ Listen and practice these statements. Notice how the *t* in **can't** and **shouldn't** is not strongly pronounced.

You can get a taxi easily.
You can**'t** get a taxi easily.
You should visit in the summer.
You shouldn**'t** visit in the summer.

B ▶ Listen to four sentences.
Circle the modal verb you hear.

1. can / can't   2. should / shouldn't   3. can / can't   4. should / shouldn't

10 LISTENING *Three capital cities*

A ▶ Listen to speakers talk about Japan, Argentina, and Egypt. Complete the chart.

	Capital city	What visitors should see or do
1. Japan	....	....
2. Argentina	....	....
3. Egypt	....	....

B ▶ Listen again. One thing about each country is incorrect. What is it?

11 SPEAKING *Interesting places*

GROUP WORK Has anyone visited an interesting place in your country? Find out more about it. Start like this and ask questions like the ones below.

A: I visited Istanbul once.
B: Really? What's the best time of year to visit?
A: It's nice all year. I went in March.
C: What's the weather like then?

What's the best time of year to visit?
What's the weather like then?
What should tourists see and do there?
What special foods can you eat?
What's the shopping like?
What things should people buy?
What else can visitors do there?

Istanbul, Turkey

12 INTERCHANGE 11 *City guide*

Make a guide to fun places in your city. Go to Interchange 11 on page 126.

Fez is so interesting! I've been to the medina (the old city) every day. It has walls all the way around it, and more than 9,000 streets! It's always crowded and noisy. My favorite places to visit are the small shops where people make local crafts. Fez is famous for its leather products. I visited a place where they dye the leather in dozens of beautiful colors.

I came at the perfect time, because the World Sacred Music festival is happening right now!

Kathy

I've discovered that Cartagena has two different personalities. One is a lively city with fancy restaurants and crowded old plazas. And the other is a quiet and relaxing place with sandy beaches.

If you come here, you should stay in the historic district – a walled area with great shopping, nightclubs, and restaurants. It has some wonderful old Spanish buildings.

Last night, I learned some salsa steps at a great dance club.

Today, I went on a canoe tour of La Ciénaga mangrove forest.

Mike

Hanoi is the capital of Vietnam and its second-largest city. It's a fun city, but six days is not enough time for a visit. I'm staying near the Old Quarter of the city. It's a great place to meet people. Last night I went to a water puppet show. Tomorrow I'm going to Ha Long Bay.

I took a cooking class at the Vietnam Culinary School. I bought some fruits and vegetables at a local market and then prepared some local dishes. My food was really delicious! I'll cook you something when I get home.

Belinda

A Read the emails. Check (✓) the cities where you can do these things. Then complete the chart with examples from the emails.

Activity	Fez	Cartagena	Hanoi	Specific examples
1. go shopping	☐	☐	☐	....
2. see old buildings	☐	☐	☐	....
3. go dancing	☐	☐	☐	....
4. attend a festival	☐	☐	☐	....
5. take a boat trip	☐	☐	☐	....

B **PAIR WORK** Which city is the most interesting to you? Why?

12 It really works!

1 SNAPSHOT

Common Health Complaints

- a headache
- a backache
- sore muscles
- a stomachache
- a cold
- a cough
- the flu
- insomnia

Source: National Center for Health Statistics

Check (✓) the health problems you have had recently.
What do you do for the health problems you checked?
How many times have you been sick in the past year?

2 CONVERSATION *Health problems*

A ▶ Listen and practice.

Joan: Hi, Craig! How are you?
Craig: Not so good. I have a terrible cold.
Joan: Really? That's too bad! You should be at home in bed. It's really important to get a lot of rest.
Craig: Yeah, you're right.
Joan: And have you taken anything for it?
Craig: No, I haven't.
Joan: Well, it's sometimes helpful to eat garlic soup. Just chop up a whole head of garlic and cook it in chicken stock. Try it! It really works!
Craig: Yuck! That sounds awful!

B ▶ Listen to advice from two more of Craig's co-workers. What do they suggest?

3 GRAMMAR FOCUS

Adjective + infinitive; noun + infinitive ▶

What should you do for a cold?	It's **important**	**to get** a lot of rest.
	It's sometimes **helpful**	**to eat** garlic soup.
	It's a **good idea**	**to take** some vitamin C.

A Look at these health problems. Choose several pieces of good advice for each problem.

Problems
1. a sore throat ....
2. a cough ....
3. a backache ....
4. a fever ....
5. a toothache ....
6. a bad headache ....
7. a burn ....
8. the flu ....

Advice
a. take some vitamin C
b. put some ointment on it
c. drink lots of liquids
d. go to bed and rest
e. put a heating pad on it
f. put it under cold water
g. take some aspirin
h. see a dentist
i. see a doctor
j. get some medicine

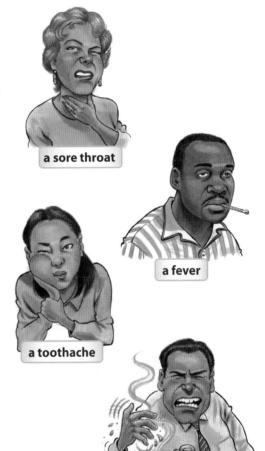

a sore throat

a fever

a toothache

a burn

B **GROUP WORK** Talk about the problems in part A and give advice. What other advice do you have?

A: What should you do for a sore throat?
B: It's a good idea to get some medicine from the drugstore.
C: And it's important to drink lots of liquids and . . .

C Write advice for these problems. (You will use this advice in Exercise 4.)

a cold   sore eyes   a sunburn   sore muscles

For a cold, it's a good idea to . . .

4 PRONUNCIATION *Reduction of* to

A ▶ Listen and practice. In conversation, **to** is often reduced to /tə/.

A: What should you do for a fever?
B: It's important **to** take some aspirin. And it's a good idea **to** see a doctor.

B **PAIR WORK** Look back at Exercise 3, part C. Ask for and give advice about each health problem. Pay attention to the pronunciation of **to**.

Play a board game. Go to Interchange 12 on page 127.

6 **DISCUSSION** *Difficult situations*

A GROUP WORK Imagine these situations are true for you. Get three suggestions for each one.

I get really hungry before I go to bed.
I sometimes feel really stressed.
I need to study, but I can't concentrate.
I feel sick before every exam.
I forget about half the new words I learn.
I get nervous when I speak English to foreigners.

A: I get really hungry before I go to bed. What should I do?
B: It's a bad idea to eat late at night.
C: It's sometimes helpful to drink herbal tea.

B CLASS ACTIVITY Have any of the above situations happened to you recently? Share what you did with the class.

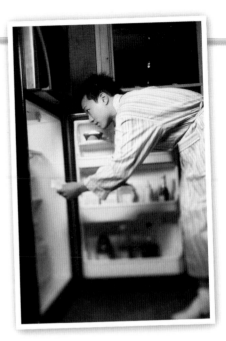

7 **WORD POWER** *Containers*

A Use the words in the list to complete these expressions. Then compare with a partner.

bag	jar
bottle	pack
box	stick
can	tube

1. a .... of toothpaste
2. a .... of aspirin
3. a .... of bandages
4. a .... of shaving cream
5. a .... of tissues
6. a .... of face cream
7. a .... of cough drops
8. a .... of deodorant

B PAIR WORK What is one more thing you can buy in each of the containers above?

"You can buy a bag of breath mints."

C PAIR WORK What are the five most useful items in your medicine cabinet?

8 CONVERSATION *What do you suggest?*

A ▶ Listen and practice.

Pharmacist: Hi. May I help you?

Mrs. Webb: Yes, please. Could I have something for a cough? I think I'm getting a cold.

Pharmacist: Sure. Why don't you try these cough drops? They work very well.

Mrs. Webb: OK, I'll take one box. And what do you suggest for dry skin?

Pharmacist: Well, you could get a jar of this new lotion. It's very good.

Mrs. Webb: OK. And one more thing. My husband has no energy these days. Can you suggest anything?

Pharmacist: He should try some of these multivitamins. They're excellent.

Mrs. Webb: Great! May I have three large bottles, please?

B ▶ Listen to the pharmacist talk to the next customer. What does the customer want?

9 GRAMMAR FOCUS

> ### Modal verbs can, could, may *for requests; suggestions* ▶
>
> | | |
> |---|---|
> | **Can/May** I help you? | What do you suggest/have for dry skin? |
> | **Can** I have a box of cough drops? | You could try this lotion. |
> | **Could** I have something for a cough? | You should get some skin cream. |
> | **May** I have a bottle of aspirin? | Why don't you try this new ointment? |

Circle the correct words. Then compare and practice with a partner.

1. A: **Can / Could** I help you?
   B: Yes. **May / Do** I have something for itchy eyes?
   A: Sure. You **could / may** try a bottle of eyedrops.

2. A: What do you **suggest / try** for sore muscles?
   B: Why don't you **suggest / try** this ointment? It's excellent.
   A: OK. I'll take it.

3. A: Could I **suggest / have** a box of bandages, please?
   B: Here you are.
   A: And what do you **suggest / try** for insomnia?
   B: You **should / may** try this herbal tea. It's very relaxing.
   A: OK. Thanks.

10 LISTENING *Try this!*

A ▶ Listen to four people talk to a pharmacist. Check (✓) each person's problem.

1. ☐ The man's feet are sore.
   ☐ The man's feet are itchy.
2. ☐ The woman can't eat.
   ☐ The woman has an upset stomach.
3. ☐ The man has difficulty sleeping.
   ☐ The man is sleeping too much.
4. ☐ The woman burned her hand.
   ☐ The woman has a bad sunburn.

B ▶ Listen again. What does the pharmacist suggest for each person?

11 ROLE PLAY *Can I help you?*

Student A: You are a customer in a drugstore. You need:

> something for low energy
> something for the flu
> something for a backache
> something for dry skin
> something for an upset stomach
> something for sore feet

Ask for some suggestions.

Student B: You are a pharmacist in a drugstore. A customer needs some things. Make some suggestions.

Change roles and try the role play again.

12 WRITING *A letter to an advice columnist*

A Read these letters to an online advice columnist.

Dear Fix-it Fred

Dear Fix-it Fred

I have a problem and need your advice. My parents don't like how I dress. I think I have an interesting style, but my parents say I just look strange. Weren't they ever teenagers? Can you please help?

Funky Frida

Dear Fix-it Fred

Several months ago, I started college. I study a lot and have a part-time job, so I don't have much of a social life. I haven't made many friends, but I really want to. What do you suggest?

Too Busy

B Now imagine you want some advice about a problem. Write a short letter to an advice columnist. Think of an interesting way to sign it.

C GROUP WORK Exchange letters. Read and write down some advice at the bottom of each letter. Then share the most interesting letter and advice with the class.

WORLD NEWS

HOME | LOG IN | SETTINGS

HOME | CURRENT ISSUE | ARCHIVES | WEB EXTRAS | RADIO | CONTACT US | SUBSCRIBE

Rain Forest Remedies?

Look at the title, pictures, and captions. What do you think the article is about?

Carol writes a column on health.
Recently she took a trip to Tortuguero National Park in Costa Rica.

1 Rodrigo Bonilla turns off the motor of the boat. We get off the boat and follow him along the path into the rain forest. Above us, a monkey with a baby hangs from a tree.

2 On this hot January day, Rodrigo is not looking for wild animals, but for medicinal plants – plants that can cure or treat illnesses. Medicinal plants grow in rain forests around the world.

A broom tree

3 Rodrigo is Costa Rican. He learned about jungle medicine from his grandmother. He shows us many different plants, such as the broom tree. He tells us that parts of the broom tree can help stop bleeding.

4 People have always used natural products as medicine. In fact, about 50 percent of Western medicines, such as aspirin, come from natural sources. And some animals eat certain kinds of plants when they are sick.

5 This is why medical researchers are so interested in plants. Many companies are now working with local governments and searching the rain forests for medicinal plants.

6 So far, the search has not produced any new medicines. But it's a good idea to keep looking. That's why we are now here in the Costa Rican rain forest.

MORE >>

A Read the article. Then check (✓) the best description of the article.

☐ 1. The article starts with a description and then gives facts.
☐ 2. The article gives the writer's opinion.
☐ 3. The article starts with facts and then gives advice.

B Answer these questions. Then write the number of the paragraph where you find each answer.

.... Where did Rodrigo learn about jungle medicine?
.... Who is interested in studying medicinal plants?
.... What is Rodrigo looking for in the rain forest?
.... How many new medicines have come from Rodrigo's search?
.... How many Western medicines come from natural sources?

C GROUP WORK Can you think of other reasons why rain forests are important?

Units 11–12 Progress check

SELF-ASSESSMENT

How well can you do these things? Check (✓) the boxes.

I can	Very well	OK	A little
Understand descriptions of towns and cities (Ex. 1)	☐	☐	☐
Get useful information about towns and cities (Ex. 1, 2)	☐	☐	☐
Describe towns and cities (Ex. 2)	☐	☐	☐
Ask for and make suggestions on practical questions (Ex. 2, 3, 4)	☐	☐	☐
Ask for and give advice about problems (Ex. 3, 4)	☐	☐	☐

1 LISTENING *I'm from Honolulu.*

A ▶ Listen to Jenny talk about Honolulu. What does she say about these things? Complete the chart.

1. size of city ....
2. weather ....
3. prices of things ....
4. most famous place ....

B Write sentences comparing Honolulu with your hometown. Then discuss with a partner.

> Honolulu isn't too big, but Seoul is really big.

2 ROLE PLAY *My hometown*

Student A: Imagine you are planning to visit Student B's hometown. Ask questions using the ones in the box or your own questions.

Student B: Answer Student A's questions about your hometown.

A: What's your hometown like?
B: It's quiet but fairly interesting. . . .

possible questions

What's your hometown like?
How big is it?
What's the weather like?
Is it expensive?
What should you see there?
What can you do there?

Change roles and try the role play again.

DISCUSSION *Medicines and remedies*

A GROUP WORK Write advice and remedies for these problems. Then discuss your ideas in groups.

| a stomachache | an insect bite | a nosebleed | the hiccups |

> For a stomachache, it's a good idea to . . .

A: What can you do for a stomachache?
B: I think it's a good idea to buy a bottle of antacid.
C: Yes. And it's helpful to drink herbal tea.

B GROUP WORK What health problems do you visit a doctor for? go to a drugstore for? use a home remedy for? Ask for advice and remedies.

SPEAKING *Advice column*

A GROUP WORK Look at these problems from an advice column. Suggest advice for each problem. Then choose the best advice.

I'm visiting the United States. I'm staying with a family while I'm here. What small gifts can I get for them?

My co-worker always talks loudly to her friends – during work hours. I can't concentrate! What can I do?

Our school wants to buy some new gym equipment. Can you suggest some good ways to raise money?

A: Why doesn't she give them some flowers? They're always nice.
B: That's a good idea. Or she could bring chocolates.
C: I think she should . . .

B CLASS ACTIVITY Share your group's advice for each problem with the class.

WHAT'S NEXT?

Look at your Self-assessment again. Do you need to review anything?

13 May I take your order?

1 SNAPSHOT

FOOD FIRSTS

NOODLES
first made in China around 1000 B.C.E.

COFFEE
first farmed in the Middle East in 850

CHOCOLATE
brought to Spain from Mexico in 1520

FRENCH FRIES
first made in Belgium around 1680

SUSHI
modern-style sushi first made in Japan in the 1700s

THE SANDWICH
named for the English Earl of Sandwich in 1760

PIZZA
first pizzeria in New York City opened in 1895

THE HAMBURGER
invented in Connecticut, USA, in 1900

Sources: *New York Public Library Book of Chronologies;* www.digitalsushi.net; www.belgianfries.com

What are these foods made of?
Put the foods in order from your favorite to your least favorite.
What are three other foods you enjoy?

2 CONVERSATION *Getting something to eat*

A ⊙ Listen and practice.

Jeff: Say, do you want to get something to eat?
Bob: Sure. I'm tired of studying.
Jeff: So am I. So, what do you think of Indian food?
Bob: I love it, but I'm not really in the mood for it today.
Jeff: Yeah. I'm not either, I guess. It's a bit spicy.
Bob: Do you like Japanese food?
Jeff: Yeah, I like it a lot.
Bob: So do I. And I know a great restaurant near here –
it's called Iroha.
Jeff: Oh, I've always wanted to go there.

B ⊙ Listen to the rest of the conversation. What time do they decide to have dinner? Where do they decide to meet?

So, too, neither, either ▶

I like Japanese food a lot.
So do I./I do, **too**.
Really? I don't like it very much.

I'm crazy about Italian food.
So am I./I am, **too**.
Oh, I'm not.

I can eat really spicy food.
So can I./I can, **too**.
Really? I can't.

I don't like salty food.
Neither do I./I don't **either**.
Oh, I like it a lot.

I'm not in the mood for Indian food.
Neither am I./I'm not **either**.
Really? I am.

I can't stand fast food.
Neither can I./I can't **either**.
Oh, I love it!

healthy

salty

spicy

bland

greasy

rich

delicious

A Write responses to show agreement with these statements.
Then compare with a partner.

1. I'm not crazy about French food. ....
2. I can eat any kind of food. ....
3. I think Mexican food is delicious. ....
4. I can't stand greasy food. ....
5. I don't like salty food. ....
6. I'm in the mood for something spicy. ....
7. I'm tired of fast food. ....
8. I don't enjoy rich food very much. ....
9. I always eat healthy food. ....
10. I can't eat bland food. ....

B **PAIR WORK** Take turns responding to the statements in part A again.
Give your own opinion when responding.

C Write statements about these things. (You will use the statements in Exercise 4.)

1. two kinds of food you like
2. two kinds of food you can't stand
3. two kinds of food you are in the mood for

4 PRONUNCIATION *Stress in responses*

A ▶ Listen and practice. Notice how the last word of each response is stressed.

●	●	●	●
I do, too.	So do I.	I don't either.	Neither do I.
I am, too.	So am I.	I'm not either.	Neither am I.
I can, too.	So can I.	I can't either.	Neither can I.

B PAIR WORK Read and respond to the statements you wrote in Exercise 3, part C. Pay attention to the stress in your responses.

5 WORD POWER *Food categories*

A Complete the chart. Then add one more word to each category.

bread	fish	mangoes	peas	shrimp
chicken	grapes	octopus	potatoes	strawberries
corn	lamb	pasta	rice	turkey

Meat	Seafood	Fruit	Vegetables	Grains
....	....	....	....	....
....	....	....	....	....
....	....	....	....	....
....	....	....	....	....

B GROUP WORK What's your favorite food in each category? Are there any you haven't tried?

6 CONVERSATION *Ordering a meal*

A ▶ Listen and practice.

Server: May I take your order?
Customer: Yes. I'd like the spicy fish and rice.
Server: All right. And would you like a salad?
Customer: Yes, I'll have a mixed green salad.
Server: OK. What kind of dressing would you like? We have blue cheese and vinaigrette.
Customer: Blue cheese, please.
Server: And would you like anything to drink?
Customer: Yes, I'd like a large iced tea, please.

B ▶ Listen to the server talk to the next customer. What does she order?

TODAY'S SPECIALS
CHEESEBURGER AND FRIES
TURKEY SANDWICH WITH CHIPS
CHEESE PASTA AND SALAD

7 GRAMMAR FOCUS

Modal verbs *would* and *will* *for requests*

What **would** you **like**?	I**'d like** the fish and rice. I**'ll have** a small salad.	**Contractions** I**'ll** = I will
What kind of dressing **would** you **like**?	I**'d like** blue cheese, please. I**'ll have** vinaigrette.	I**'d** = I would
What **would** you **like** to drink?	I**'d like** an iced tea. I**'ll have** coffee.	
Would you **like** anything else?	Yes, please. I**'d like** some water. No, thank you. That**'ll be** all.	

Complete this conversation. Then practice with a partner.

Server: What .... you like to order?
Customer: I .... have the spicy chicken.
Server: .... you like rice or potatoes?
Customer: I .... like rice, please.
Server: OK. And .... you like anything to drink?
Customer: I .... just have a glass of water.
Server: Would you .... anything else?
Customer: No, that .... be all for now, thanks.

Later

Server: Would you .... dessert?
Customer: Yes, I .... like ice cream.
Server: What flavor .... you like?
Customer: Hmm. I .... have strawberry, please.

8 ROLE PLAY *In a coffee shop*

Student A: You are a customer in a coffee shop. Order what you want for lunch.
Student B: You are the server. Take your customer's order.

Today's Lunch Specials
Spicy beef and potatoes   Vegetable curry and rice
Lamb with french fries   Chicken salad sandwich
Shrimp pizza and salad   Sushi plate with miso soup
DRINKS
Coffee   Tea   Soda   Milk   Fresh juice
DESSERTS
Ice cream   Chocolate cake   Apple pie   Fresh fruit

Change roles and try the role play again.

9 LISTENING Let's order.

A ▶ Listen to Rex and Hannah order in a restaurant.
What did each of them order? Fill in their check.

Phil's DINER No. 399825

....

....

....

....

....

....

Thank You! **TOTAL** _____

B ▶ Listen to the rest of the conversation. Circle the two items that the server forgot to bring.

10 INTERCHANGE 13 Plan a menu

Create a menu of dishes to offer at your very own restaurant. Go to Interchange 13 on page 128.

11 WRITING A restaurant review

A Have you eaten out recently? Write a restaurant review.
Answer these questions and add ideas of your own.

What's the name of the restaurant?
When did you go there?
What did you have?
What did/didn't you like about it?
Would you recommend it? Why or why not?

| Overview | Review | Menu | Photos | | Search |

Luigi's ★★★★☆

Last week, I had lunch at Luigi's, a new Italian restaurant in my neighborhood.
I had a green salad and a cheese pizza. For dessert, I had chocolate cake.
The pizza was excellent, but the salad wasn't very good. The lettuce wasn't
very fresh. The cake was rich and delicious. I would recommend this restaurant
because the pizza is great and not very expensive.

B GROUP WORK Take turns reading your reviews.
Which restaurant would you like to try?

To Tip or Not to Tip?

Scan the article. How much should you tip someone in the United States who: carries your suitcase at a hotel? parks your car? serves you in a fast-food restaurant?

The word *tip* comes from an old English slang word that means "to give." It's both a noun and a verb. People in the U.S. usually tip people in places like restaurants, airports, hotels, and hair salons. People who work in these places often get paid low wages. A tip shows that the customer is pleased with the service.

Sometimes it's hard to know how much to tip. The size of the tip usually depends on the service. People such as parking valets or bellhops usually get smaller tips. The tip for people such as taxi drivers and servers is usually larger. Here are a few guidelines for tipping in the United States:

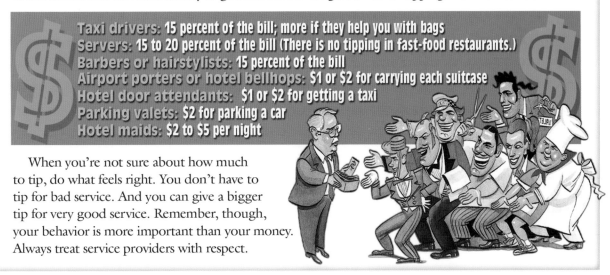

Taxi drivers: 15 percent of the bill; more if they help you with bags
Servers: 15 to 20 percent of the bill (There is no tipping in fast-food restaurants.)
Barbers or hairstylists: 15 percent of the bill
Airport porters or hotel bellhops: $1 or $2 for carrying each suitcase
Hotel door attendants: $1 or $2 for getting a taxi
Parking valets: $2 for parking a car
Hotel maids: $2 to $5 per night

When you're not sure about how much to tip, do what feels right. You don't have to tip for bad service. And you can give a bigger tip for very good service. Remember, though, your behavior is more important than your money. Always treat service providers with respect.

A Read the article. Find the words in italics in the article.
Then check (✓) the meaning of each word.

1. *wages*
   ☐ regular pay for a job
   ☐ tips received for a job

2. *pleased*
   ☐ happy or satisfied
   ☐ annoyed or bothered

3. *depend on*
   ☐ be the same as
   ☐ change according to

4. *behavior*
   ☐ a way of acting
   ☐ a way of feeling

5. *treat*
   ☐ ignore
   ☐ act toward

6. *respect*
   ☐ courtesy
   ☐ rudeness

B Check (✓) the statements that describe appropriate tipping behavior.
For the other items, what is acceptable?

☐ 1. Your haircut costs $40. You love it. You tip the stylist $3.
☐ 2. A porter at the airport helps you with three suitcases. You tip him $6.
☐ 3. Your fast-food meal costs $8. You don't leave a tip.
☐ 4. You stay in a hotel for a week. You leave a $10 tip for the hotel maid.
☐ 5. Your taxi ride costs $14. The driver carries your bag. You tip him $3.

C GROUP WORK Is tipping customary in your country? Do you like the idea of tipping? Why or why not?

The biggest and the best!

1 WORD POWER *Geography*

A Label the picture with words from the list. Then compare with a partner.

a. beach
b. desert
c. forest
d. hill
e. island
f. lake
g. mountain
h. ocean
i. river
j. valley
k. volcano
l. waterfall

B **PAIR WORK** What other geography words can you think of? Do you see any of them in the picture above?

C **GROUP WORK** Try to think of famous examples for each item in part A.

A: A famous beach is Waikiki in Hawaii.
B: And the Sahara is a famous . . .

2 CONVERSATION *Which is larger?*

A ▶ Listen and practice.

Mike: Here's an interesting geography quiz.
Wendy: Oh, I love geography. Ask me the questions.
Mike: Sure, first question. Which country is larger, China or Canada?
Wendy: I know. Canada is larger than China.
Mike: OK, next. What's the longest river in the Americas?
Wendy: Hmm, I think it's the Mississippi.
Mike: Here's a hard one. Which country is more crowded, Monaco or Singapore?
Wendy: I'm not sure. I think Monaco is more crowded.
Mike: OK, one more. Which South American capital city is the highest: La Paz, Quito, or Bogotá?
Wendy: Oh, that's easy. Bogotá is the highest.

B ▶ Listen to the rest of the conversation. How many questions did Wendy get right?

3 GRAMMAR FOCUS

Comparisons with adjectives ▶

Which country is **larger**, Canada or China?
  Canada is **larger than** China.

Which city has **the largest** population:
Tokyo, Mexico City, or São Paulo?
  Tokyo has **the largest** population of the three.

What is **the most beautiful** mountain in the world?
  I think Mount Fuji is **the most beautiful**.

Adjective	Comparative	Superlative
long	longer	the longest
dry	drier	the driest
big	bigger	the biggest
famous	more famous	the most famous
beautiful	more beautiful	the most beautiful
good	better	the best
bad	worse	the worst

A Complete questions 1 to 4 with comparatives and questions 5 to 8 with superlatives. Then ask and answer the questions.

1. Which country is .... , Monaco or Vatican City?   (small)
2. Which waterfall is .... , Niagara Falls or Victoria Falls?   (high)
3. Which city is .... , Hong Kong or Cairo?   (crowded)
4. Which lake is .... , the Caspian Sea or Lake Superior?   (large)
5. Which is .... : Mount Aconcagua, Mount Everest, or Mount Fuji?   (high)
6. What is .... river in the world, the Mekong, the Nile, or the Amazon?   (long)
7. Which city is .... : London, Tokyo, or Moscow?   (expensive)
8. What is .... ocean in the world, the Pacific, the Atlantic, or the Arctic?   (deep)

B CLASS ACTIVITY Write four questions like those in part A about your country or other countries. Then ask your questions around the class.

4 PRONUNCIATION *Questions of choice*

A ⊙ Listen and practice. Notice how the intonation in questions of choice drops, then rises, and then drops.

Which city is more crowded, Hong Kong or Cairo?

Which city is the most expensive: London, Tokyo, or Moscow?

B **PAIR WORK** Take turns asking these questions. Pay attention to your intonation. Can you guess the answers?

Which desert is bigger, the Gobi or the Sahara?
Which city is higher, Denver or New Orleans?
Which ocean is the smallest: the Arctic, the Indian, or the Atlantic?
Which mountains are the highest: the Alps, the Rockies, or the Himalayas?

5 SPEAKING *Our recommendations*

GROUP WORK Imagine these people are planning to visit your country. What would they enjoy doing? Agree on a recommendation for each person.

Molly

"I really like quiet places where I can relax, hike, and enjoy the views. I can't stand big crowds."

Rod

"I love to eat in nice restaurants, go dancing, and stay out late at night. I don't like small towns."

Teresa

"My favorite activity is shopping. I love to buy gifts to take home. I don't like modern shopping malls."

A: Molly should go to . . . because it has the best views in the country, and it's very quiet.
B: Or what about . . . ? I think the views there are more beautiful.
C: She also likes to hike, so . . .

6 LISTENING *Game show*

⊙ Listen to three people on a TV game show. Check (✓) the correct answers.

1. ☐ the Statue of Liberty
   ☐ the Eiffel Tower
   ☐ the Panama Canal

2. ☐ Niagara Falls
   ☐ Angel Falls
   ☐ Victoria Falls

3. ☐ gold
   ☐ butter
   ☐ feathers

4. ☐ the U.S.
   ☐ China
   ☐ Canada

5. ☐ India
   ☐ Russia
   ☐ China

6. ☐ Australia
   ☐ Argentina
   ☐ Brazil

7 **INTERCHANGE 14** *How much do you know?*

You probably know more than you think! Take a quiz.
Go to Interchange 14 on page 129.

8 **SNAPSHOT**

The World We Live In

- **France is the most popular country to visit. It has about 78 million visitors a year.**

- **The most-watched World Cup was in the United States in 1994. It had an average attendance of 70,000 fans a day.**

- **The largest clock is in Mecca, Saudi Arabia. Each of its four faces is 43 meters (141 feet).**

- **The busiest airport in the world is Hartsfield-Jackson International Airport, in Atlanta, Georgia, United States. It has more than 88 million passengers a year.**

- ***Avatar* is the most popular movie ever. It has made more than $2.4 billion.**

- **The longest nonstop flight is from New York to Singapore. It's 18.5 hours long.**

- **Antarctica is the largest desert on earth at 14 million square kilometers (5.4 million square miles). It's also the coldest, windiest continent.**

- **The highest price for a book at an auction is $11.5 million for *Birds of America* by John Audubon.**

- **The strongest animal is the rhinoceros beetle. It can lift 850 times its own weight.**

Source: *The Top 10 of Everything;* www.extremescience.com

Which facts do you find surprising?
What's the tallest building in your country? the most popular city to visit?
  the busiest airport?

9 **CONVERSATION** *Distances and measurements*

A ⊙ Listen and practice.

Scott: I'm going to Australia next year. Aren't you from Australia, Beth?
 Beth: Actually, I'm from New Zealand.
Scott: Oh, I didn't know that. So what's it like there?
 Beth: Oh, it's beautiful. There are lots of farms, and it's very mountainous.
Scott: Really? How high are the mountains?
 Beth: Well, the highest one is Mount Cook. It's about 3,800 meters high.
Scott: Wow! So how far is New Zealand from Australia?
 Beth: Well, I live in Auckland, and Auckland is about 2,000 kilometers from Sydney.
Scott: Maybe I should visit you next year, too!

Mount Cook

B ⊙ Listen to the rest of the conversation.
What else is New Zealand famous for?

Questions with how ▶

How far is New Zealand from Australia?	It's about 2,000 kilometers.	(1,200 miles)
How big is Singapore?	It's 710 square kilometers.	(274 square miles)
How high is Mount Cook?	It's 3,740 meters **high**.	(12,250 feet)
How deep is the Grand Canyon?	It's about 1,900 meters **deep**.	(6,250 feet)
How long is the Mississippi River?	It's about 5,970 kilometers **long**.	(3,710 miles)
How hot is Auckland in the summer?	It gets up to about 23° Celsius.	(74° Fahrenheit)
How cold is it in the winter?	It goes down to about 10° Celsius.	(50° Fahrenheit)

A Write the questions to these answers. Then practice with a partner.

1. A: .... ?
    B: Niagara Falls is 52 meters (170 feet) high.

2. A: .... ?
    B: California is about 403,970 square kilometers (155,973 square miles).

3. A: .... ?
    B: The Nile is 6,670 kilometers (4,145 miles) long.

4. A: .... ?
    B: Osaka is about 400 kilometers (250 miles) from Tokyo.

5. A: .... ?
    B: Mexico City gets up to about 28° Celsius (82° Fahrenheit) in the spring.

B GROUP WORK Think of five questions with *how* about places in your country or other countries you know. Ask and answer your questions.

11 *WRITING* An article

A Write an article to promote a place in your country. Describe a place in the list.

a beach
a desert
an island
a lake
a mountain
a river
a volcano
a waterfall

Web   Location   Photos   News   Ask

Jeju Island, South Korea

JEJU ISLAND

One of the most interesting places to go in South Korea is Jeju Island. Many people go there for its warm climate and beautiful beaches.
I think one of the best places to visit there is Halla Mountain, or Halla-san. It's an old volcano and you can climb it in a day, but you should go early.

Tweet   Like

B PAIR WORK Read your partner's article. Ask questions to get more information.

Things You Can Do to Help the Environment

Look at the pictures. Which show environmental problems? Which show solutions?

CARS

Cars are getting bigger. SUVs—large, truck-like vehicles—are now the most popular cars in the United States. Bigger vehicles burn more gas and increase air pollution. So try to walk, bicycle, or use public transportation. If you drive a car, keep it tuned up. This saves gas and reduces pollution.

ENERGY

The biggest use of home energy is for heating and cooling. So turn up your air conditioner and turn down the heat, especially at night. Replace regular lightbulbs with bulbs that use less energy. And remember to turn lights off.

PRODUCTS

Each American throws away about 1.8 kilograms (4 pounds) of garbage every day. Most of it goes into landfills. Reduce waste before you buy by asking yourself: Do I need this? Is it something I can only use once? Buy products that you can use over and over again. And try to buy products made from recycled materials.

WATER

Showers use a lot of water. In one week, a typical American family uses as much water as a person drinks in three years! Buy a special "low-flow" showerhead or take shorter showers. This can cut water use in half. Also, fix any leaky faucets.

A Read the article. Where do you think it is from? Check (✓) the correct answer.

☐ a textbook ☐ an encyclopedia ☐ a magazine ☐ an advertisement

B Read these statements. Then write the advice from the article that each person should follow.

1. Stephanie always takes long showers in the morning. ....
2. In the winter, Ralph keeps the heat turned up all day. ....
3. Matt buys a newspaper every day, but never reads it. ....
4. Stuart drives to work, but his office is near his home. ....
5. Sheila leaves the lights on at home all the time. ....

C GROUP WORK What other ways do you know about to help the environment?

Units 13–14 Progress check

SELF-ASSESSMENT

How well can you do these things? Check (✓) the boxes.

I can	Very well	OK	A little
Say what I like and dislike (Ex. 1)	☐	☐	☐
Agree and disagree with other people (Ex. 1)	☐	☐	☐
Understand a variety of questions in a restaurant (Ex. 2)	☐	☐	☐
Order a meal in a restaurant (Ex. 3)	☐	☐	☐
Describe and compare things, people, and places (Ex. 4, 5)	☐	☐	☐
Ask questions about distances and measurements (Ex. 5)	☐	☐	☐

1 SURVEY Food facts

A Answer these questions. Write your responses under the column "My answers."

	My answers	Classmate's name
What food are you crazy about?	....	....
What food can't you stand?	....	....
Do you like vegetarian food?	....	....
Can you eat very rich food?	....	....
What restaurant do you like a lot?	....	....
How often do you go out to eat?	....	....

B CLASS ACTIVITY Go around the class. Find someone who has the same opinions or habits.

A: I'm crazy about Korean food.
B: I am, too./So am I. OR Oh, I'm not. I'm crazy about . . .

2 LISTENING In a restaurant

 Listen to six requests in a restaurant. Check (✓) the best response.

1. ☐ Yes. This way, please.
   ☐ Yes, please.

2. ☐ No, I don't.
   ☐ Yes, I'll have tea, please.

3. ☐ I'd like a steak, please.
   ☐ Yes, I would.

4. ☐ I'll have a cup of coffee.
   ☐ Italian, please.

5. ☐ Carrots, please.
   ☐ Yes, I will.

6. ☐ Yes, I'd like some water.
   ☐ No, I don't think so.

3 ROLE PLAY *What would you like?*

Student A: Imagine you are a server and
Student B is a customer. Take his or her order
and write it on the check.

Student B: Imagine you are a hungry customer and can
order anything you like. Student A
is a server. Order a meal.

Change roles and try the role play again.

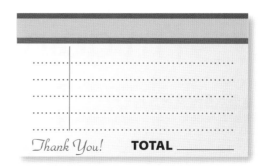

Thank You! **TOTAL** _____

4 SPEAKING *City quiz*

A **PAIR WORK** Write down six facts about your city using comparatives or
superlatives. Then write six Wh-questions based on your facts.

> 1. The busiest street is Market Drive.
> What's the busiest street in our city?

B **GROUP WORK** Join another pair. Take
turns asking the other pair your questions.
How many can they answer correctly?

5 GAME *What's the question?*

A Think of three statements that can be answered with
how questions or Wh-questions with comparatives and
superlatives. Write each statement on a separate card.

B **CLASS ACTIVITY** Divide into Teams A and B. Shuffle the
cards together. One student from Team A picks a card and
reads it to a student from Team B. That student tries to
make a question for it.

A: The Pacific Ocean is bigger than the Atlantic Ocean.
B: Which ocean is bigger, the Pacific or the Atlantic?

Keep score. The team with the most correct questions wins.

> *It's about four kilometers*
> *from my house to the school.*

> *The Pacific Ocean is bigger*
> *than the Atlantic Ocean.*

> *Ana has the longest hair in*
> *our class.*

WHAT'S NEXT?

Look at your Self-assessment again. Do you need to review anything?

15 I'm going to a soccer match.

1 SNAPSHOT

Making Excuses

Some common excuses for not accepting an invitation

I can't. I have to wash my hair.

- ☐ I'm busy that night.
- ☐ I can't find a babysitter.
- ☐ I'm not feeling well.
- ☐ I have to work then.
- ☐ I have class that night.
- ☐ My parents are visiting from out of town.
- ☐ I need to stay home with my new puppy.
- ☐ My favorite TV show is on that night.
- ☐ I have to get up early the next morning.

Sources: www.excuses.co.uk; interviews with people aged 18–45

Have you ever used any of these excuses? Have you ever heard any of them?
Which are good excuses and which are bad excuses? Check (✓) the good ones.
What other excuses can you make for not accepting an invitation?

2 CONVERSATION *Making plans*

A ▶ Listen and practice.

Lynn: Say, Miguel, what are you doing tonight? Do you want to go bowling?

Miguel: I'd love to, but I can't. I'm going to a soccer match with my brother.

Lynn: Oh, well, maybe some other time.

Miguel: Are you doing anything tomorrow? We could go then.

Lynn: Tomorrow sounds fine. I'm going to work until five.

Miguel: So let's go around six.

Lynn: OK. Afterward, maybe we can get some dinner.

Miguel: Sounds great.

B ▶ Listen to the rest of the conversation.
When are they going to have dinner? Who are they going to meet after dinner?

GRAMMAR FOCUS

Future with present continuous and be going to ⊙

With present continuous	With be going to + verb	Time expressions
What **are** you **doing** tonight?	What **is** she **going to do** tomorrow?	tonight
I**'m going** to a soccer match.	She**'s going to work** until five.	tomorrow
Are you **doing** anything tomorrow?	**Are** they **going to go** bowling?	on Friday
No, I'm not.	Yes, they are.	this weekend
		next week

A Complete the invitations in column A with the present continuous used as future. Complete the responses in column B with *be going to*.

A

1. What .... you .... (do) tonight? Would you like to go out?

2. .... you .... (do) anything on Friday night? Do you want to see a movie?

3. We .... (have) friends over for a barbecue on Sunday. Would you and your parents like to come?

4. .... you .... (stay) in town next weekend? Do you want to go for a hike?

B

a. I .... (be) here on Saturday, but not Sunday. Let's try and go on Saturday.

b. Well, my father .... (visit) my brother at college. But my mother and I .... (be) home. We'd love to come!

c. Sorry, I can't. I .... (work) overtime tonight. How about tomorrow night?

d. Can we go to a late show? I .... (stay) at the office till 7:00.

B Match the invitations in column A with the responses in column B. Then practice with a partner.

4 WORD POWER Leisure activities

A Complete the chart with words and phrases from the list. Then add one more example to each category.

barbecue	bicycle race	picnic	singing contest
baseball game	birthday party	play	tennis match
beach party	dance performance	rock concert	volleyball tournament

Spectator sports	Friendly gatherings	Live performances
....	....	....
....	....	....
....	....	....
....	....	....
....	....	....

B **PAIR WORK** Are you going to do any of the activities in part A? When are you doing them? Talk with a partner.

5 ROLE PLAY *Accept or refuse?*

Student A: Choose an activity from Exercise 4 and invite a partner to go with you. Be ready to say where and when the activity is.

> A: Say, are you doing anything on . . . ?
> Would you like to . . . ?

Student B: Your partner invites you out. Either accept the invitation and ask for more information, or say you can't go and give an excuse.

Accept	*Refuse*
B: OK. That sounds fun. Where is it?	B: Oh, I'm sorry, I can't. I'm . . .

Change roles and try the role play again.

6 INTERCHANGE 15 *Weekend plans*

Find out what your classmates are going to do this weekend.
Go to Interchange 15 on page 130.

7 CONVERSATION *Can I take a message?*

A ▶ Listen and practice.

Secretary: Good morning, Parker Industries.
  Mr. Kale: Hello. May I speak to Ms. Graham, please?
Secretary: I'm sorry. She's not in. Can I take a message?
  Mr. Kale: Yes, please. This is Mr. Kale.
Secretary: Is that G-A-L-E?
  Mr. Kale: No, it's K-A-L-E.
Secretary: All right.
  Mr. Kale: Please tell her our meeting is on Friday at 2:30.
Secretary: Friday at 2:30.
  Mr. Kale: And could you ask her to call me this afternoon? My number is (646) 555-4031.
Secretary: (646) 555-4031. Yes, Mr. Kale. I'll give Ms. Graham the message.
  Mr. Kale: Thank you. Good-bye.
Secretary: Good-bye.

B ▶ Listen to three other calls. Write down the callers' names.

8 GRAMMAR FOCUS

Messages with *tell* and *ask* ▶

Statement	Messages with a statement
The meeting is on Friday.	**Please tell her (that)** the meeting is on Friday.
	Could you tell her (that) the meeting is on Friday?
	Would you tell her (that) the meeting is on Friday?
Request	Messages with a request
Call me this afternoon.	**Please ask him to** call me this afternoon.
	Could you ask him to call me this afternoon?
	Would you ask him to call me this afternoon?

Unscramble these messages. Then compare with a partner.

1. tell / that / is / please / Ryan / the barbecue / on Saturday

....

2. call me / at 12:00 / you / Patrick / could /ask / to

....?

3. is / that / Amy / tonight / could / you / the dance performance / tell

....?

4. tell / is / Celia / in the park / would / you / that / the picnic

....?

5. meet me / to / you / would / Noriko / ask / at the stadium

....?

6. ask / to the rock concert / please / bring / Jason / to / the tickets

....

9 WRITING *Unusual favors*

A **PAIR WORK** Think of unusual messages for three people in your class.
Write a note to your partner asking him or her to pass on the messages.

Dear Rachel,
Could you tell Brian to wear two different color
socks tomorrow?

Please tell Jeff that our class tomorrow is at midnight.

Would you ask Sun-hee to bring me a hamburger
and french fries for breakfast tomorrow?

Thanks!
David

B **GROUP WORK** Compare your messages.
Which is the most unusual?

10 PRONUNCIATION *Reduction of* could you *and* would you

A ▶ Listen and practice. Notice how **could you** and **would you** are reduced in conversation.

[cʊdʒə]
Could you tell her the meeting is on Friday?

[wʊdʒə]
Would you ask him to call me this afternoon?

B PAIR WORK Practice these questions with reduced forms.

Could you tell them I'll be late?
Would you ask her to be on time?

Could you ask her to return my dictionary?
Would you tell him there's a picnic tomorrow?

11 LISTENING *Taking a message*

▶ Listen to telephone calls to Mr. Lin and Ms. Carson. Write down the messages.

1

To: Mr. _____

Date: _____ Time: _____

WHILE YOU WERE OUT

From: _____

of: City _____

Phone: _____ ext: _____

Message:

Call Mrs. _____

_____

Taken by: _____

2

To: Wendy _____

Date: _____ Time: _____

WHILE YOU WERE OUT

From: _____

of: _____ National _____

Phone: _____ ext: _____

Message:

_____

_____

Taken by: _____

12 ROLE PLAY *Who's calling?*

Student A: Call your friend Andrew to tell him this:

There's a party at Ray's house on Saturday night.
Ray's address is 414 Maple St., Apt. 202. Pick me up at 8:00 P.M.

Student B: Someone calls for your brother Andrew. He isn't in.
Take a message for him.

Change roles and try another role play.

Student A: You are a receptionist at Systex Industries. Someone calls for your boss, Ms. Park.
She isn't in. Take a message for her.

Student B: Call Ms. Park at Systex Industries to tell her this:

You can't make your lunch meeting at 12:00. You want to meet at 12:30 at the same place
instead. Call her to arrange the new time.

useful expressions
May I speak to . . . ?
Sorry, but . . . isn't here.
Can I leave a message?
Can I take a message?
I'll give . . . the message.

Cell Phone Etiquette

Scan the article. Is it OK to use a cell phone in a movie theater? in a restaurant? on the street?

What do these things have in common: a stranger's personal problems, details about a business meeting, the food in someone's refrigerator, someone's medical issues, and a private argument? These are all things you hear about when the people around you don't practice good cell phone etiquette!

Most people find cell phones a necessity in their day-to-day lives. But we've all sat next to someone talking too loudly, listening to loud music, or playing a loud beeping game on a cell phone. But a recent report shows that while most people are annoyed by cell phone rudeness, most admit to doing it, too. What can you do to practice better etiquette? Here are a few rules:

> **Off means off!** Respect the rules of restaurants and other public places. If a sign says "No cell phones," don't use your phone – for anything.

> **Keep private conversations private!** Speak softly and for a short time. Observe the 3-meter (10-feet) rule – stay away from other people.

> **Lights off, phone off!** Never take calls or send text messages in a theater, at the movies, or at a performance. Turn your phone or your ringer off.

> **Pay attention!** Talking or texting while driving is dangerous. Listening to music with headphones while driving is dangerous. Crossing the street while playing a game or checking your email is dangerous. You get the picture.

Cell phones have become mini-computers that people depend on 24 hours a day. But don't let yours become a nuisance – or a danger – to others! Next time you're getting ready to use yours, stop and consider the people around you.

FRUIT STAND

Caution: Open manhole

A Read the article. Then complete the summary with information from the article.

Many people don't practice good cell phone .... They talk too .... , listen to .... music, or check their email while .... the street. To be a better cell phone user, follow a few simple rules. For example: Turn .... your phone in public places that don't allow cell phones; speak .... on phone calls; and don't talk, text, play games, or listen to music while .... or crossing the street.

B Check (✓) the statements the writer would probably agree with.

- ☐ 1. You should never use a cell phone in public.
- ☐ 2. Cell phone users are very rude people.
- ☐ 3. Turn off your cell phone if someone asks you to.
- ☐ 4. You can talk loudly if you're more than 3 meters away from someone.
- ☐ 5. It's OK to send text messages while driving a car.
- ☐ 6. You can use a cell phone at a dance performance if you speak quietly.
- ☐ 7. Don't play games on your phone in restaurants.
- ☐ 8. Don't check your email while crossing the street.

C **PAIR WORK** Do you agree with the writer's opinions? Why or why not?

16 A change for the better!

1 SNAPSHOT

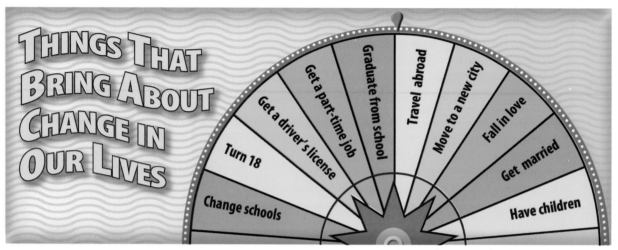

THINGS THAT BRING ABOUT CHANGE IN OUR LIVES

Turn 18
Get a driver's license
Get a part-time job
Graduate from school
Travel abroad
Move to a new city
Fall in love
Get married
Have children
Change schools

Source: Based on interviews with people between the ages of 16 and 50

Which of these events are the most important changes?
Have any of these things happened to you recently?
What other things bring about change in our lives?

2 CONVERSATION *Catching up*

A ▶ Listen and practice.

Diane: Hi, Kerry. I haven't seen you in ages. How have you been?
Kerry: Pretty good, thanks.
Diane: Are you still in school?
Kerry: No, not anymore. I graduated last year. And I got a job at Midstate Bank.
Diane: That's great news. You know, you look different. Have you changed your hair?
Kerry: Yeah, it's shorter. And I wear contacts now.
Diane: Well, you look fantastic!
Kerry: Thanks, so do you. And there's one more thing. Look! I got engaged.
Diane: Congratulations!

B ▶ Listen to the rest of the conversation. How has Diane changed?

3 GRAMMAR FOCUS

Describing changes

With the present tense
I'**m not** in school anymore.
I **wear** contacts now.

With the past tense
I **got** engaged.
I **moved** to a new place.

With the present perfect
I'**ve changed** jobs.
I'**ve fallen** in love.

With the comparative
My hair is **shorter** now.
My job is **less stressful**.

A How have you changed in the last five years?
Check (✓) the statements that are true for you.
If a statement isn't true, give the correct information.

1. I've changed my hairstyle.
2. I dress differently now.
3. I've made some new friends.
4. I got a pet.
5. I've joined a club.
6. I moved into my own apartment.
7. I'm more outgoing than before.
8. I'm not in high school anymore.
9. My life is easier now.
10. I got married.

B PAIR WORK Compare your responses in
part A. Have you changed in similar ways?

C GROUP WORK Write five sentences describing
other changes in your life. Then compare in groups.
Who in the group has changed the most?

4 LISTENING *Memory lane*

Linda and Scott are looking through a photo album.
Listen to their conversation. How have they changed?
Write down three changes.

Changes
....
....
....

5 WORD POWER

A Complete the word map with phrases from the list. Then add two more examples to each category.

dye my hair
get a bank loan
get a credit card
grow a beard
improve my English vocabulary
learn a new sport
learn how to dance
open a savings account
pierce my ears
start a new hobby
wear contact lenses
win the lottery

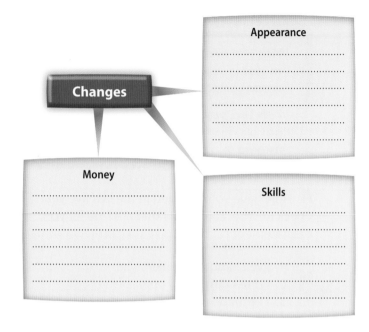

Changes

Appearance
....
....
....
....
....

Money
....
....
....
....
....

Skills
....
....
....
....
....

B **PAIR WORK** Have you changed in any of these areas? Tell your partner about a change in each category.

A: I opened a savings account last year. I've already saved $500.
B: I got my first credit card last month. Can I borrow … ?

6 CONVERSATION *Planning your future*

A ▶ Listen and practice.

Alex: So, what are you going to do after graduation, Susan?
Susan: Well, I've saved some money, and I think I'd really like to travel.
Alex: Lucky you. That sounds exciting!
Susan: Yeah. Then I plan to get a job and my own apartment.
Alex: Oh, you're not going to live at home?
Susan: No, I don't want to live with my parents – not after I start to work.
Alex: I know what you mean.
Susan: What about you, Alex? Any plans yet?
Alex: I'm going to get a job *and* live at home. I'm broke, and I want to pay off my student loan!

B ▶ Listen to the rest of the conversation. What kind of job does Alex want? Where would Susan like to travel?

7 GRAMMAR FOCUS

Verb + infinitive ⊙

What **are** you **going to do** after graduation?
I**'m** (not) **going to get** a job right away.
I (don't) **plan to get** my own apartment.
I (don't) **want to live** with my parents.

I **hope to get** a new car.
I**'d like to travel** this summer.
I**'d love to move** to a new city.

A Complete these statements so that they are true for you. Use information from the grammar box. Then add two more statements of your own.

1. I .... travel abroad.
2. I .... live with my parents.
3. I .... get married.
4. I .... have a lot of children.
5. I .... make a lot of money!
6. I .... become very successful.
7. ....
8. ....

B **PAIR WORK** Compare your responses with a partner. How are you the same? How are you different?

C **GROUP WORK** What are your plans for the future? Take turns asking and answering these questions.

What are you going to do after this English course is over?
Do you plan to study here again next year?
What other languages would you like to learn?
What countries would you like to visit? Why?
Do you want to get a (new) job in a few years?
What kind of future do you hope to have?

8 PRONUNCIATION *Vowel sounds* /oʊ/ *and* /ʌ/

A ⊙ Many words spelled with *o* are pronounced /oʊ/ or /ʌ/. Listen to the difference and practice.

/oʊ/ =	don't	smoke	go	loan	own	hope
/ʌ/ =	month	love	some	does	young	touch

B ⊙ Listen to these words. Check (✓) the correct pronunciation.

	both	cold	come	home	honey	money	mother	over
/oʊ/	☐	☐	☐	☐	☐	☐	☐	☐
/ʌ/	☐	☐	☐	☐	☐	☐	☐	☐

9 INTERCHANGE 16 *My possible future*

Imagine you could do anything, go anywhere, and meet anybody.
Go to Interchange 16 on page 131.

10 SPEAKING *A class party*

A GROUP WORK Make plans for a class party.
Talk about these things and take notes.

| Date | Transportation | Place | Food and drink |
| Time | Entertainment | Activities | Cost (if any) |

A: When are we going to have our party?
B: I'd like to have it on Saturday.
C: That sounds fine. Let's plan to have it in the afternoon.
D: Can we start the party at noon?

B GROUP WORK Decide what each person is going
to bring to the party.

A: I can bring the drinks.
B: And I can bring some snacks.
C: Hey, why don't you bring
your guitar?

11 WRITING *Party plans*

A GROUP WORK Work with your same group from Exercise 10.
As a group, write about your plans for the class party.

Baseball Fun in the Sun!
1. Date and Time: We'd like to have our end-of-the-class party
    next Saturday, on June 18th, from 12:00 – 4:00 p.m.
2. Place: We plan to meet at City Park near the baseball field.
    If it rains, meet on Sunday at the same time and place.
3. Activities: We're going to play a class baseball game. The
    game can start after lunch. Other activities are . . .

B CLASS ACTIVITY Present your plans to the class. Each person in
your group should present a different part. Then choose the best plan.

Goal Setting

Setting Personal Goals

Look at the list in the article. Which of these areas of your life would you like to change or improve?

Ask any top athlete or successful businessperson and they will tell you the importance of setting goals. Goal setting can motivate you and give your life direction. It seems easy, right? Just write down a list of things you want to achieve and then do them. Well, it's not that easy!

Effective goal setting happens on several levels. First, you create a big picture of what you want to do with your life. At this point, you decide what large-scale goals you want to achieve. Second, you divide these into smaller and smaller tasks. Third, you put the smaller tasks into a rough time line. Finally, once you have your plan, you start working to achieve it.

How do you know what your large-scale goals are? These questions can help you get started.

- **Career**
  What level do you want to reach in your career?

- **Family**
  What kind of relationship do you want with the people in your family?

- **Community Service**
  How do you want to give back to your community?

- **Financial**
  How much money do you want to earn? How much do you want to save?

- **Creative**
  Do you want to achieve any artistic goals?

- **Physical**
  How will you stay in good physical shape throughout your life?

- **Education**
  What do you want to learn? How will you learn it?

- **Recreation**
  How do you want to enjoy yourself?

PROCESS

Write down your goals and think about them carefully. Are they realistic?

How important are they?

Rank them in order from most important to least important.

Then follow the process above to make your long-term plan. Remember, your goals can change with time.

Look at them regularly and adjust them if necessary. And be sure your goals are things you hope to achieve, not things others want.

A Read the article. Who do you think the article was written for? Check (✓) the correct answer.

People who . . .

☐ have very clear goals ☐ are looking for direction ☐ don't care about their future

B Answer these questions.

1. What kinds of people set personal goals? ....
2. Why do people set personal goals? ....
3. Why should you divide your goals into steps? ....
4. Why is it important to adjust your goals? ....

C **PAIR WORK** What is one of your personal goals? What steps will you take to achieve it?

Units 15–16 Progress check

SELF-ASSESSMENT

How well can you do these things? Check (✓) the boxes.

I can	Very well	OK	A little
Discuss future plans and arrangements (Ex. 1)	☐	☐	☐
Make and respond to invitations (Ex. 2)	☐	☐	☐
Understand and pass on telephone messages (Ex. 3)	☐	☐	☐
Ask and answer questions about changes in my life (Ex. 4)	☐	☐	☐
Describe personal goals (Ex. 5)	☐	☐	☐
Discuss and decide how to accomplish goals (Ex. 5)	☐	☐	☐

1 DISCUSSION *The weekend*

A GROUP WORK Find out what your classmates are doing this weekend.
Ask for two details about each person's plans.

Name	Plans	Details
....	....	....
....	....	....
....	....	....

A: What are you going to do this weekend?
B: I'm seeing a rock concert on Saturday.
C: Which band are you going to see?

B GROUP WORK Whose weekend plans sound the best? Why?

2 ROLE PLAY *Inviting a friend*

Student A: Invite Student B to one of the events from
Exercise 1. Say where and when it is.
Student B: Student A invites you out. Accept and ask for
more information, or refuse and give an excuse.

Change roles and try the role play again.

3 LISTENING *Telephone messages*

▶ Listen to the telephone conversations. Write down the messages.

1

Message for: _____
Caller: _____
Message: _____

_____

_____

_____

2

Message for: _____
Caller: _____
Message: _____

_____

_____

_____

4 SURVEY *Changes*

A CLASS ACTIVITY Go around the class and find this information.
Write a classmate's name only once! Ask follow-up questions.

Find someone who	Name
1. got his or her hair cut last week	....
2. doesn't wear glasses anymore	....
3. has changed schools recently	....
4. goes out more often these days	....
5. got married last year	....
6. has started a new hobby	....
7. is happier these days	....
8. has gotten a part-time job recently	....

last week

this week

B CLASS ACTIVITY Compare your information.
Who in the class has changed the most?

5 SPEAKING *Setting goals*

Check (✓) the goals you have and add two more. Then choose one goal.
Plan how to accomplish it with a partner.

- ☐ own my own computer
- ☐ move to a new city
- ☐ have more free time
- ☐ have more friends
- ☐ get into a good school
- ☐ travel a lot more
- ☐ live a long time
- ☐ ....
- ☐ ....

A: I'd like to travel a lot more.
B: How are you going to do that?

WHAT'S NEXT?

Look at your Self-assessment again. Do you need to review anything?

Interchange activities

A **CLASS ACTIVITY** Go around the class and interview three classmates. Complete the chart.

> Excuse me, Lady Gaga. Is Gaga your first name or your last name?

	Classmate 1	Classmate 2	Classmate 3
What's your first name?	....	....	....
What's your last name?	....	....	....
What city are you from?	....	....	....
When's your birthday?	....	....	....
What's your favorite color?	....	....	....
What are your hobbies?	....	....	....

B **GROUP WORK** Compare your information. Then discuss these questions.

Who...?

has an interesting first name   has the next birthday
has a common last name   likes black or white
is not from a big city   has an interesting hobby

A CLASS ACTIVITY Answer these questions about yourself. Then interview two classmates. Write their names and the times they do each thing.

What time do you . . . ?	Me	Name	Name
get up during the week			
get up on weekends			
have breakfast			
leave for school or work			
get home during the week			
have dinner			
go to bed during the week			
go to bed on weekends			

B PAIR WORK Whose schedule is similar to yours? Tell your partner.

A: Keiko and I have similar schedules. We both get up at 6:00 and have breakfast at 7:00.
B: I leave for work at 7:30, but Jeff leaves for school at . . .

useful expressions
We both . . . at . . . We . . . at different times. My schedule is different from my two classmates' schedules.

Student A

A You want to sell these things. Write your "asking price" for each item.

Student B

A You want to sell these things. Write your "asking price" for each item.

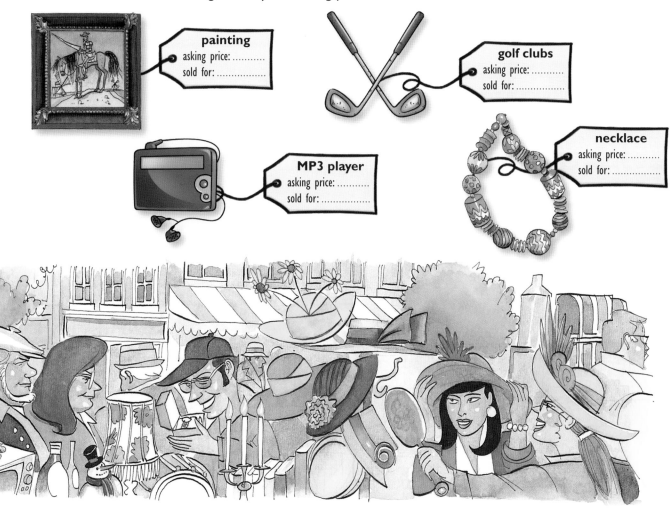

painting
asking price: ....
sold for: ....

golf clubs
asking price: ....
sold for: ....

MP3 player
asking price: ....
sold for: ....

necklace
asking price: ....
sold for: ....

Students A and B

B **PAIR WORK** Now choose three things you want to buy. Get the best price for each one. Then write what each item "sold for" on the price tag.

A: How much is the lamp?
B: It's only $30.
A: Wow! That's expensive!
B: Well, how about $25?
A: No. That's still too much. I'll give you $20 for it.
B: Sold! It's yours.

C **GROUP WORK** Compare your earnings in groups. Who made the most money at the flea market?

A Write two things you need to do this weekend. Include the times.

Saturday	Sunday
....	....
....	....

B Read the events page from your city's website. Choose three things you'd like to do.

On The Town

HOME
Log In
Register
Contact Us

Search the Calendar
What do you want to do?
GO

RESTAURANTS · LATE NIGHT · MUSIC · THEATER · MUSEUMS · OUTDOORS · KIDS · MOVIES · CALENDAR

TOP PICKS   **What's on this weekend**

Saturday, May 21

Community Art Fair
See the work of local artists at the Community Art Fair! More than 200 artists, plus food, drinks, and music. Fun for the whole family!
11:00–5:00

Play Tennis!
Free tennis lessons for all ages. Central Park Tennis Courts. Bring a partner!
2:00–4:00

Bike Now's Ride Around the City
Once a year, this group organizes a bike ride around the city. Free food and drinks for cyclists from local restaurants.
Ride starts at 4:30.

Movies at Green Park
This Saturday's movie: *Avatar.* Bring your dinner, sit on the grass, and enjoy a movie under the stars.
Movie starts at 8:30.   MORE

Sunday, May 22

Concerts on the River
Come hear your favorite music next to the White River. A different kind of music from a different country every week.
Concert starts at 1:00.

Chess in the Park
Bring a partner or find a partner at the city's biggest chess-a-thon. All levels and ages welcome. City Park, next to Park Café.
2:00–7:00

Free Tango Lessons
Learn to dance the tango! Live music and dancing. All levels. Beginners welcome. Center Street Activity Center.
5:30–7:00

City Baseball League
Green Park Team vs. the Lions. Come cheer for your favorite team! Come early to win prizes for the biggest fans!
Game at 7:30   MORE

C GROUP WORK Take turns inviting your classmates to the events. Say yes to one invitation and no to two invitations. Give a polite excuse.

A: Would you like to play tennis on Saturday? We can play from 2:00 to 4:00.
B: I'd like to, but I can't. I have to clean my room on Saturday afternoon.
A: Well, are you free in the morning?

A CLASS ACTIVITY Go around the class and find this information.
Write a classmate's name only once. Ask follow-up questions of your own.

Find someone	Name
1. who is an only child **"Do you have any brothers or sisters?"**	....
2. who has two brothers **"How many brothers do you have?"**	....
3. who has two sisters **"How many sisters do you have?"**	....
4. whose brother or sister is living abroad **"Are any of your brothers or sisters living abroad?"**	....
5. who lives with his or her grandparents **"Do you live with your grandparents?"**	....
6. who has a grandparent still working **"Is your grandmother or grandfather still working?"**	....
7. who has a family member with an unusual job **"Does anyone in your family have an unusual job?"**	....
8. whose mother or father is studying English **"Is either of your parents studying English?"**	....

B GROUP WORK Compare your information.

A CLASS ACTIVITY Does anyone in your class do these things?
How often and how well? Go around the class and find one person
for each activity.

	Name	How often?	How well?
dance	....	....	....
play an instrument	....	....	....
sing	....	....	....
act	....	....	....
tell jokes	....	....	....
do gymnastics	....	....	....
do magic tricks	....	....	....

A: Do you dance?
B: Yes, I do.
A: How often do you go dancing?
B: Every weekend.
A: Really? And how well do you dance?

B GROUP WORK Imagine there's a talent show this weekend.
Who do you want to enter? Choose three people from your class.
Explain your choices.

A: Let's enter Adam in the talent show.
B: Why Adam?
A: Because he dances very well.
C: Yes, he does. And Yvette is very good at playing the guitar.
   Let's enter her, too!

GROUP WORK Play the board game. Follow these instructions.

1. Use small pieces of paper with your initials on them as markers.
2. Take turns by tossing a coin: If the coin lands face up, move two spaces. If the coin lands face down, move one space.
3. When you land on a space, answer the question. Answer any follow-up questions.
4. If you land on "Free question," another player asks you any question.

A: I'll go first. Last night, I met my best friend.
B: Oh, yeah? Where did you go?
A: We went to the movies.

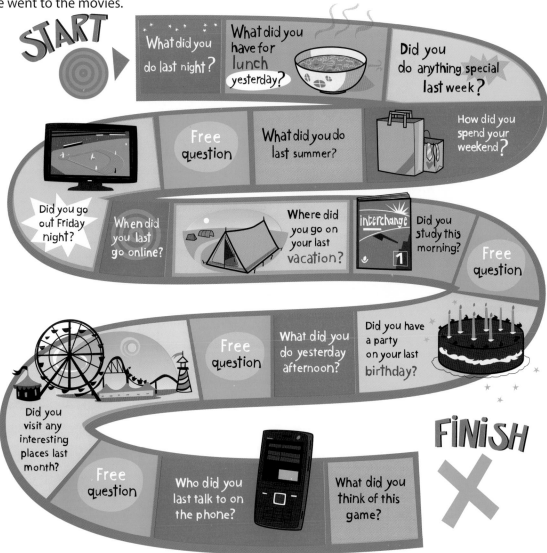

CLASS ACTIVITY Play a guessing game. Follow these instructions.

1. Get into two teams, A and B. One student from each team goes to the front of the class.
2. These two students choose a location and give four clues, using *There is/are* plus a quantifier.
3. The first student to guess the location correctly joins his or her team-mate at the front.
4. The new student chooses a different location and gives clues. His or her team answers.
5. The first team with all of its members in the front wins.

a coffee shop	a hospital	a dance club	a restaurant
a bank	a park	a post office	a hotel
a grocery store	an airport	an outdoor market	a movie theater
a library	a mall	an Internet café	a gym

A: There isn't any food in this place. There's a lot of coffee. There are a few computers. There are many emails. Where am I?

B: In an Internet café!

A: Correct! Now you come to the front.

interchange 9A FIND THE DIFFERENCES

Student A

A PAIR WORK How many differences can you find between your picture here and your partner's picture? Ask questions like these to find the differences.

How many people are standing / sitting / wearing . . . / holding a drink? Who?
What color is . . . 's T-shirt / sweater / hair?
Does . . . wear glasses / have a beard / have long hair?
What does . . . look like?

B CLASS ACTIVITY How many differences are there in the pictures?

"In picture 1, Dave's T-shirt is . . . . In picture 2, it's . . ."

Student B

A PAIR WORK How many differences can you find between your picture here and your partner's picture? Ask questions like these to find the differences.

How many people are standing / sitting / wearing . . . / holding a drink? Who?
What color is . . . 's T-shirt / sweater / hair?
Does . . . wear glasses / have a beard / have long hair?
What does . . . look like?

B CLASS ACTIVITY How many differences are there in the pictures?

"In picture 1, Dave's T-shirt is . . . . In picture 2, it's . . ."

A PAIR WORK What kind of lifestyle does your partner have? Interview him or her. Write the number of points using this scale.

never = 1 point   4–7 times = 3 points
1–3 times = 2 points   8 or more times = 4 points

SURVEY

How many times have you . . . ? ▶	Points ▶
1. eaten a meal at your desk in the last two weeks	_____
2. run to get somewhere on time in the last month	_____
3. stayed inside all weekend to work or study in the last six months	_____
4. checked your email in the last 12 hours	_____
5. worked late or studied past midnight in the last month	_____
6. had trouble sleeping in the last three weeks	_____
7. lost something important in the last year	_____
8. missed a party in the last six months	_____
9. worked or studied during a holiday or vacation in the last year	_____
10. skipped or forgotten to eat a meal in the last month	_____

B GROUP WORK Add up your partner's points. Tell the group what your partner's lifestyle is like and why.

10–19 = You are a well-balanced person who knows how to relax, breathe deeply, and stop and smell the roses. Keep it up!
20–29 = You're doing OK, but you need to be careful. Continue to take time to do the things that are important to you.
30–40 = You are overdoing it! Your life is too busy and fast-paced. You need to slow down and relax more.

"Pedro is overdoing it. His lifestyle is too busy and fast-paced. He never goes to parties, and he often studies past midnight. And he sometimes forgets to eat. He also . . ."

C CLASS ACTIVITY Do you think your partner needs to change his or her lifestyle? In what way?

"I think Pedro needs to slow down a little. He needs to try to eat regular meals and . . ."

A Where can you get information about a city? buy souvenirs? see historical sights? Complete the city guide with information about a city of your choice.

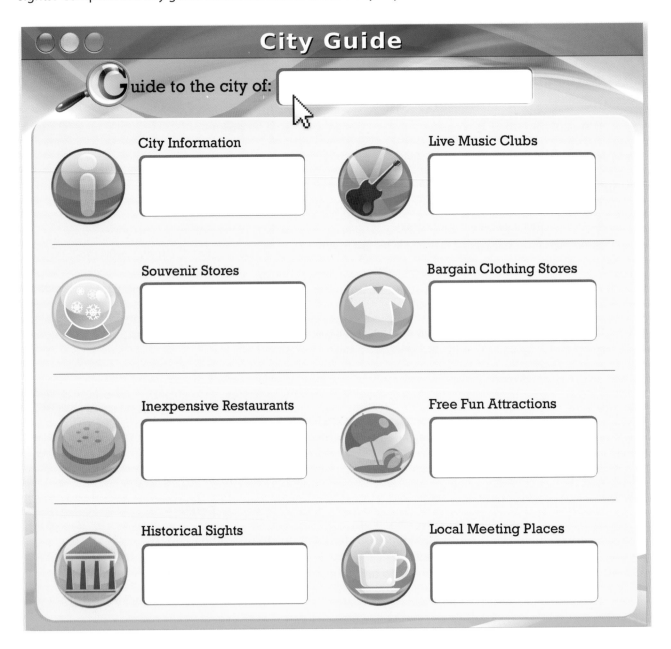

City Guide

Guide to the city of:

City Information

Live Music Clubs

Souvenir Stores

Bargain Clothing Stores

Inexpensive Restaurants

Free Fun Attractions

Historical Sights

Local Meeting Places

B GROUP WORK Compare your city guide in groups. Ask these questions and questions of your own. Add any additional or interesting information to your guide.

Where can you get information about your city?
Where's a good place to buy souvenirs?
Where's an inexpensive place to eat?
What historical sights should you visit?
Where's the best place to hear live music?
Where's a cheap place to shop for clothes?
What fun things can you do for free?
Where's a popular place to meet?

A GROUP WORK Play the board game. Follow these instructions.

1. Use small pieces of paper with your initials on them as markers.
2. Take turns by tossing a coin:
   If the coin lands face up, move two spaces.
   If the coin lands face down, move one space.
3. When you land on a space, ask two others in your group for advice.

A: I have a terrible headache. Akira, what's your advice?
B: Well, it's important to get a lot of rest.
A: Thanks. What about you, Jason? What do you think?
C: You should take two aspirin. That always works for me.

useful expressions
You should . . .
You could . . .
It's a good idea to . . .
It's important to . . .
I think it's useful to . . .

B CLASS ACTIVITY Who gave the best advice in your group? Tell the class.

interchange 13 *PLAN A MENU*

A **GROUP WORK** Imagine you are opening a new restaurant. Create a menu of dishes you'd like to offer. Then write the prices.

Today's Special

SOUPS

MAIN DISHES

SALADS

KIDS' MENU

BEVERAGES

DESSERTS

B **GROUP WORK** Choose a name for your restaurant. Write it at the top of the menu.

C **CLASS ACTIVITY** Compare your menus. Which group has . . . ?

the most interesting menu
the most typical menu
the healthiest menu
the cheapest prices
the best name for a restaurant

A **PAIR WORK** Take turns asking and answering these questions.
Check (✓) the answer you think is correct for each question.

World Knowledge Quiz

1.	Which animal lives the longest?	☐ a whale	☐ an elephant	☐ a tortoise
2.	Which one is the tallest?	☐ an elephant	☐ a giraffe	☐ a camel
3.	Which of these is the heaviest?	☐ the brain	☐ the heart	☐ the liver
4.	Which planet is the smallest?	☐ Mercury	☐ Venus	☐ Earth
5.	Which planet is the largest?	☐ Jupiter	☐ Saturn	☐ Neptune
6.	Which metal is the heaviest?	☐ gold	☐ silver	☐ aluminum
7.	Which country is the driest?	☐ Egypt	☐ Peru	☐ Chile
8.	Which is closest to the equator?	☐ Malaysia	☐ Colombia	☐ India
9.	Which place is the wettest?	☐ Kauai, Hawaii	☐ Bogor, Indonesia	☐ Manaus, Brazil
10.	Which ocean is the deepest?	☐ the Pacific	☐ the Arctic	☐ the Indian

Correct answers **1.** a tortoise **2.** a giraffe **3.** the liver **4.** Mercury **5.** Jupiter **6.** gold **7.** Egypt **8.** Colombia **9.** Kauai, Hawaii **10.** the Pacific

How many did you get correct?

10 Perfect! Brilliant! You should be a teacher.   **2–5** Just OK. How often do you go to the library?
6–9 Very good! Do you watch lots of TV game shows?   **0–1** Oh, dear. You should never be on a quiz show

B **PAIR WORK** Create your own quiz. Write 3 to 5 questions.
Then ask the questions to another pair.

A **CLASS ACTIVITY** What are your classmates' plans for the weekend?
Go around the class and find people who are going to do these things.
For each question, ask for further information.

Find someone who is going to . . .	Name	Notes
go out of town	....	....
meet friends	....	....
stay out late	....	....
visit relatives	....	....
go to a party	....	....
see a live performance	....	....
play video games	....	....
study for a test	....	....
exercise	....	....
buy something for someone	....	....

A: Omar, are you going to go out of town this weekend?
B: Yes, I am.
A: What are you going to do?
B: My friend Tom and I are going to go camping in the mountains.

B **PAIR WORK** Compare your information with a partner.
Who is going to do something fun? physical? serious?

A Complete this chart with information about yourself.

My possible future	
What are two things you plan to do next year?	....
	....
What are two things you aren't going to do next year?	....
	....
What is something you hope to buy in the next year?	....
What would you like to change about yourself?	....
Where would you like to visit someday?	....
What city would you like to live in someday?	....
What kind of job would you like to have?	....
What career goals do you hope to achieve?	....
What famous person would you like to meet?	....

B **GROUP WORK** Compare your information in groups.
Be prepared to explain the future you have planned.

A: What are two things you plan to do next year?
B: Well, I'm going to take a cooking class, and I'm also going to
go to Italy.
C: Oh, really? What part of Italy are you going to visit?
B: I'm not sure yet! What about you? What are two things you plan
to do next year?

Grammar plus

Unit 1

1 Statements with *be*; possessive adjectives (page 3)

▶ Don't confuse contractions of *be* with possessive adjectives: **You're** a student. **Your** class is English 1. (NOT: ~~You're class is English 1.~~) **He's** my classmate. **His** name is Roberto. (NOT: ~~He's name is Roberto.~~)

Circle the correct words.

1. This **is** / **are** Delia Rios. **She's** / **Her** a new student from Peru.
2. My name **am** / **is** Sergio. **I'm** / **He's** from Brazil.
3. My brother and I **is** / **are** students here. **Our** / **We're** names are Dave and Jeff.
4. **He's** / **His** Yoshi. **He's** / **His** 19 years old.
5. **They're** / **Their** in my English class. **It's** / **Its** a big class.

2 Wh-questions with *be* (page 4)

▶ Use *What* to ask about things: **What's** in your bag? Use *Where* to ask about places: **Where's** your friend from? Use *Who* to ask about people: **Who's** your teacher? Use *What . . . like?* to ask for a description: **What's** your friend **like**?

Match the questions with the answers.

1. Who's that? ....f....
2. Where's your teacher? ....
3. What are your friends like? ....
4. Where's she from? ....
5. Who are they? ....
6. What's his name? ....

a. They're really nice.
b. She's from Japan.
c. They're my brother and sister.
d. His name is Carlos.
e. He's in class.
f. That's our new classmate.

3 Yes/No questions and short answers with *be* (page 5)

▶ Use short answers to answer yes/no questions. Don't use contractions with short answers with *Yes*: **Are you** from Mexico? Yes, **I am**. (NOT: ~~Yes, I'm.~~)

Complete the conversations.

1. A: _Are they_ in your class?
   B: No, ... They're in English 2.
2. A: Hi! .... in this class?
   B: Yes, ... I'm a new student here.
3. A: .... from the United States?
   B: No, ... We're from Montreal, Canada.
4. A: Hi, Sonia. .... free?
   B: No, ... I'm on my way to class.
5. A: That's the new student. .... from Puerto Rico?
   B: No, ... He's from Costa Rica.
6. A: .... from Thailand?
   B: Yes, ... She's from Bangkok.

Unit 2

1 Simple present Wh-questions and statements (page 10)

Statements

▶ Verbs with he/she/it end in –s: He/She **walks** to school. BUT I/You/We/They **walk** to school.

▶ *Have, go,* and *do* are irregular with he/she/it: She **has** a class at 1:00. He **goes** to school at night. She **does** her homework before school.

Wh-questions

▶ Use *does* in questions with he/she/it and *do* with all the others: Where *does* he/she/it live? Where *do* I/you/we/they live?

▶ Don't add –s to the verb: Where does she **live**? (NOT: Where does she lives?)

Complete the conversations with the correct form of the verbs in parentheses.

1. A: I ....*have*.......... (have) good news! Dani .... (have) a new job.
   B: How .... she .... (like) it?
   A: She .... (love) it. The hours are great.
   B: What time .... she .... (start)?
   A: She .... (start) at nine and .... (finish) at five.
2. A: What .... you .... (do)?
   B: I'm a teacher.
   A: What .... you .... (teach)?
   B: I .... (teach) Spanish and English.
   A: Really? My sister .... (teach) English, too.

2 Time expressions (page 12)

▶ Use *in* with *the morning/afternoon/evening.* Us *at* with *night*: He goes to school **in** the afternoon and works **at** night. BUT: **on** *Friday night.*

▶ Use *at* with clock times: She gets up **at** 7:00.

▶ Use *on* with days: He gets up early **on** weekdays. She has class **on** Mondays.

Complete the conversation with time expressions from the box. You can use some words more than once.

> at   early   in   on   until

A: How's your new job?
B: I love it, but the hours are difficult. I start work .... 7:30 A.M., and I work .... 3:30.
A: That's interesting! I work the same hours, but I work .... night. I start .... 7:30 .... the evening and finish .... 3:30 .... the morning.
B: Wow! What time do you get up?
A: Well, I get home .... 4:30 and go to bed .... 5:30. And I sleep .... 2:00. But I only work .... weekends, so it's OK. What about you?
B: Oh, I work .... Monday, Wednesday, and Friday. And I get up .... – around 6:00 A.M.

Unit 3

1 Demonstratives; *one, ones* (page 17)

> ▶ With singular nouns, use *this* for a thing that is nearby and *that* for a thing that is not nearby: How much is **this** cap here? How much is **that** cap over there?
>
> ▶ With plural nouns, use *these* for things that are nearby and *those* for things that are not nearby: How much are **these** earrings here? How much are **those** earrings over there?
>
> ▶ Use *one* to replace a singular noun: I like the red <u>hat</u>. → I like the red **one**. Use *ones* to replace plural nouns: I like the green <u>bags</u>. → I like the green **ones**.

Circle the correct words.

1. A: Excuse me. How much are **this / these** shoes?
   B: **It's / They're** $279.
   A: And how much is **this / that** bag over there?
   B: **It's / They're** only $129.
   A: And are the two gray **one / ones** $129, too?
   B: No. **That / Those** are only $119.
   A: Oh! **This / That** store is really expensive.

2. A: Can I help you?
   B: Yes, please. I really like **these / those** jeans over there. How much **is it / are they**?
   A: Which **one / ones**? Do you mean **this / these**?
   B: No, the black **one / ones**.
   A: Let me look. Oh, **it's / they're** $35.99.
   B: That's not bad. And how much is **this / that** sweater here?
   A: **It's / They're** only $9.99.

2 Preferences; comparisons with adjectives (page 20)

> ▶ With adjectives of one or two syllables, add –*er* to form the comparative: cheap → cheaper; nice → nicer; pretty → prettier; big → bigger.
>
> ▶ With adjectives of three or more syllables, use *more* + adjective to form the comparative: expensive → more expensive.

A Write the comparatives of these adjectives.

1.	attractive	more attractive	5. interesting	....
2.	boring	....	6. reasonable	....
3.	exciting	....	7. sad	....
4.	friendly	....	8. warm	....

B Answer the questions. Use the words in parentheses in your answer. Then write another sentence with the second word.

1. Which pants do you prefer, the cotton ones or the wool ones? (wool / attractive)
   I prefer the wool ones. They're more attractive than the cotton ones

2. Which ring do you like better, the gold one or the silver one? (silver / interesting)
   ....

3. Which one do you prefer, the silk jacket or the wool jacket? (silk / pretty)
   ....

4. Which ones do you like more, the black shoes or the purple ones? (purple / exciting)
   ....

Unit 4

1 Simple present questions; short answers (page 23)

▶ Use *do* + base form for yes/no questions and short answers with I/you/we/they: **Do** I/you/we/they **like** rock? Yes, I/you/we/they **do**. No, I/you/we/they **don't**.

▶ Use *does* in yes/no questions and short answers with he/she/it: **Does** he/she **like** rock? Yes, he/she **does**. No, he/she **doesn't**.

▶ Use *don't* and *doesn't* + base form for negative statements: I **don't like** horror movies. He **doesn't like** action movies.

▶ Remember: Don't add *–s* to the base form: Does she **like** rock? (NOT: ~~Does she likes rock?~~)

▶ Subject pronouns (*I, you, he, she, it, we, they*) usually come before a verb. Object pronouns (*me, you, him, her, it, us, them*) usually come after a verb: He likes **her**, but she doesn't like **him**.

A Complete the questions and short answers.

1. A: _Do you play_ (play) a musical instrument?
   B: Yes, _I do_ . I play the guitar.
2. A: .... (like) Taylor Swift?
   B: No, ... Joe doesn't like country music.
3. A: .... (like) talk shows?
   B: Yes, ... Lisa is a big fan of them.
4. A: .... (watch) the news on TV?
   B: Yes, ... Kevin and I watch the news every night.
5. A: .... (like) hip-hop?
   B: No, ... But I love R&B.
6. A: .... (listen to) jazz?
   B: No, ... But my parents listen to a lot of classical music.

B Complete the sentences with object pronouns.

1. We don't listen to hip-hop because we really don't like _it_ .
2. We love your voice. Please sing for ....
3. These sunglasses are great. Do you like .... ?
4. Who is that man? Do you know .... ?
5. Beth looks great in green. It's a really good color for ....

2 *Would*; verb + *to* + verb (page 26)

▶ Don't use a contraction in affirmative short answers with *would*: **Would** you **like to go to** the game? Yes, I **would**. (NOT: ~~Yes, I'd.~~)

Unscramble the questions and answers to complete the conversation.

A: tonight   to see   would you like   with me   a movie
.... ?

B: I would.   yes,   what   to see   would you like
.... ?

A: the new Halle Berry movie   to see   I'd like
....

B: OK. That's a great idea!

Unit 5

1 Present continuous (page 32)

> ▶ Use the present continuous to talk about actions that are happening now: What **are** you **doing (these days)**? I'**m studying** English.
>
> ▶ The present continuous is present of *be* + *-ing*. For verbs ending in *e*, drop the *e* and add *-ing*: have → having, live → living.
>
> ▶ For verbs ending in vowel + consonant, double the consonant and add *-ing*: sit → sitting.

Write questions with the words in parentheses and the present continuous. Then complete the responses with short answers or the verbs in the box.

live	study	take	✓ teach	work

1. A: (what / your sister / do / these days) <u>What's your sister doing these days?</u>
   B: <u>She's teaching</u> English.
   A: Really? (she / live / abroad) ....
   B: Yes, ... She .... in South Korea
2. A: (how / you / spend / your summer) ....
   B: I .... part-time. I .... two classes also.
   A: (what / you / take) ....
   B: My friend and I .... photography and Japanese. We like our classes a lot.

2 Quantifiers (page 34)

> ▶ Use *a lot of, all, few, nearly all* before plural nouns: **A lot of/All/Few/Nearly all** families are small. Use *no one* before a verb: **No one** gets married before the age of 18.
>
> ▶ *Nearly all* means "almost all."

Read the sentences about the small town of Monroe. Rewrite the sentences using the quantifiers in the box. Use each quantifier only once.

a lot of	all	few	nearly all	✓ no one

1. In Monroe, 0% of the people drive before the age of 16.
   <u>In Monroe, no one drives before the age of 16.</u>
2. Ninety-eight percent of students finish high school.
   ....
3. One hundred percent of children start school by the age of six.
   ....
4. Eighty-nine percent of couples have more than one child.
   ....
5. Twenty-three percent of families have more than four children.
   ....

Unit 6

1 Adverbs of frequency (page 37)

> ▶ Adverbs of frequency (*always, almost always, usually, often, sometimes, hardly ever, almost never, never*) usually come before the main verb: She **never plays** tennis. I **almost always eat** breakfast. BUT Adverbs of frequency usually come after the verb *be*: I**'m always** late.
>
> ▶ *Usually* and *sometimes* can begin a sentence: **Usually** I walk to work. **Sometimes** I exercise in the morning.
>
> ▶ Some frequency expressions usually come at the end of a sentence: *every day, once a week, twice a month, three times a year:* Do you exercise **every day**? I exercise **three times a week**.

Put the words in order to make questions. Then complete the answers with the words in parentheses.

1. you   what   weekends   usually   do   do   on
   Q: *What do you usually do on weekends?* ....
   A: I .... (often / play sports)
2. ever   you   go jogging   do   with a friend
   Q: ....
   A: No, ... (always / alone)
3. you   play   do   tennis   how often
   Q: ....
   A: I .... (four times a week)
4. do   you   what   in the evening   usually   do
   Q: ....
   A: My family and I .... (almost always / watch TV)
5. go   how often   you   do   to the gym
   Q: ....
   A: I .... (never)

2 Questions with *how*; short answers (page 40)

> ▶ Don't confuse *good* and *well*. Use the adjective *good* with *be* and the adverb *well* with other verbs: How **good** are you at soccer? BUT How **well** do you play soccer?

Complete the questions with *How* and a word from the box. Then match the questions and the answers.

> good   long   often   well

1. .... do you lift weights? ....   a. Not very well, but I love it.
2. .... do you play tennis? ....   b. About six hours a week.
3. .... are you at aerobics? ....   c. Not very often. I prefer aerobics.
4. .... do you spend at the gym? ....   d. Pretty good, but I hate it.

Unit 7

1 Simple past (page 45)

> ▶ Use *did* with the base form – not the past form – of the main verb in questions: How
> **did** you **spend** the weekend? (NOT: How did you spent . . .?)
> ▶ Use *didn't* with the base form in negative statements: We **didn't go** shopping.
> (NOT: . . . we didn't went shopping.)

Complete the conversation.

A: ....Did.... you ...have... (have) a good weekend?

B: Yes, I .... I .... (have) a great time. My sister and I .... (go) shopping
on Saturday. We .... (spend) all day at the mall.

A: .... you .... (buy) anything special?

B: I .... (buy) a new laptop. And I .... (get) some new clothes, too.

A: Lucky you! What clothes .... you .... (buy)?

B: Well, I .... (need) some new boots. I .... (find) some great ones at Luff's
Department Store.

A: What about you? What .... you .... (do) on Saturday?

B: I .... (not do) anything special. I .... (stay) home and .... (work)
around the house. Oh, but I .... (see) a really good movie on TV. And then I
.... (make) dinner with my mother. I actually .... (enjoy) the day.

2 Past of *be* (page 47)

> ▶ Present   Past
> am/is   →   **was**
> are   →   **were**

Rewrite the sentences. Find another way to write each sentence using *was, wasn't,*
were, or *weren't* and the words in parentheses.

1. Tony didn't come to class yesterday. (in class)
   Tony wasn't in class yesterday.

2. He worked all day. (at work)
   ....

3. Tony and his co-workers worked on Saturday, too. (at work)
   ....

4. They didn't go to work on Sunday. (at work)
   ....

5. Did Tony stay home on Sunday? (at home)
   ....

6. Where did Tony go on Sunday? (on Sunday)
   ....

7. He and his brother went to a baseball game. (at a baseball game)
   ....

8. They stayed at the park until 7:00. (at the park)
   ....

Unit 8

1 *There is, there are; one, any, some* (page 51)

▶ Don't use a contraction in a short answer with *Yes*: Is there a hotel near here? Yes, **there is**. (NOT: ~~Yes, there's.~~)

▶ Use *some* in affirmative statements and *any* in negative statements: There are **some** grocery stores in my neighborhood, but there aren't **any** restaurants. Use *any* in most questions: Are there **any** nice stores around here?

Complete the conversations. Circle the correct words.

1. A: **Is / Are** there any supermarkets in this neighborhood?
   B: No, there **isn't / aren't**, but there are **one / some** on Main Street.
   A: And **is / are** there a post office near here?
   B: Yes, **there's / there is**. It's across from the bank.
2. A: **Is / Are** there a gas station around here?
   B: Yes, **there's / there are** one behind the shopping center.
   A: Great! And are there **a / any** coffee shops nearby?
   B: Yes, there's a good **one / some** in the shopping center.

2 Quantifiers; *how many* and *how much* (page 54)

▶ Use *a lot* with both count and noncount nouns: Are there many traffic lights on First Avenue? Yes, there are **a lot**. Is there much traffic? Yes, there's **a lot**.

▶ Use *any* – not *none* – in negative statements: How much traffic is there on your street? There **isn't any**. = There**'s none**. (NOT: ~~There isn't none.~~)

▶ Use *How many* with count nouns: **How many books** do you have?

▶ Use *How much* with noncount nouns: **How much traffic** is there?

A Complete the conversations. Circle the correct words.

1. A: Is there **many / much** traffic in your city?
   B: Well, there's **a few / a little**.
2. A: Are there **many / much** public telephones around here?
   B: No, there aren't **many / none**.
3. A: **How many / How much** restaurants are there in your neighborhood?
   B: There **is / are** a lot.
4. A: **How many / How much** noise **is / are** there in your city?
   B: There's **much / none**. It's very quiet.

B Write questions with the words in parentheses. Use *much* or *many*.

1. A: Is there much pollution in your neighborhood? .... (pollution)
   B: No, there isn't. My neighborhood is very clean.
2. A: .... (parks)
   B: Yes, there are. They're great for families.
3. A: .... (crime)
   B: There's none. It's a very safe part of the city.
4. A: .... (laundromats)
   B: There aren't any. A lot of people have their own washing machines.

Unit 9

1 Describing people (page 59)

> ▶ Use *have* or *is* to describe eye and hair color: I **have** brown hair. = My hair **is** brown. He **has** blue eyes. = His eyes **are** blue.
> ▶ Don't confuse *How* and *What* in questions: **How** tall are you? (NOT: ~~What tall are you?~~) **What** color is your hair? (NOT: ~~How color is your hair?~~)

Unscramble the questions. Then write answers using the phrases in the box.

blond	brown eyes	contact lenses
✓ tall and good-looking	5 feet 11	26 – two years older than me

A: brother   like   look   what   your   does
 What does your brother look like?
B: *He's tall and good-looking.*
A: tall   is   how   he
 ....

B: ....
A: he   does   glasses   wear

B: ....
A: what   hair   color   his   is

B: ....
A: he   does   blue   have   eyes

B: ....
A: old   he   how   and   is

B: ....

2 Modifiers with participles and prepositions (page 62)

> ▶ Don't use a form of *be* in modifiers with participles: Sylvia is the woman **standing** near the window. (NOT: ~~Sylvia is the woman is standing near the window.~~)

Rewrite the conversations. Use the words in parentheses and *one* or *ones*.

1. A: Who's Carla?   A: *Which one is Carla?* .... (which)
   B: She's the woman in the red dress.   B: .... (wearing)
2. A: Who are your neighbors?   A: .... (which)
   B: They're the people with the baby.   B: .... (walking)
3. A: Who's Jeff?   A: .... (which)
   B: He's the man wearing glasses.   B: .... (with)

Unit 10

1 Present perfect; *already, yet* (page 65)

▶ Use the present perfect for actions that happened some time in the past.
▶ Use *yet* in questions and negative statements: Have you checked your email **yet**? No, I haven't turned on my computer **yet**. Use *already* in affirmative statements: I've **already** checked my email.

A Complete the conversations with the present perfect of the verbs in parentheses and short answers.

1. A: ....Has........ Leslie ......called........ (call) you lately?
   B: No, she .... (not call) me, but I .... (get) some emails from her.
2. A: .... you and Jan .... (have) lunch yet?
   B: No, we .... We're thinking of going to Tony's. .... you .... (try) it yet? Come with us.
   A: Thanks. I .... (not eat) there yet, but I .... (hear) it's pretty good.

B Look at things Matt said. Put the adverb in the correct place in the second sentence.

1. I'm very hungry. I haven't eaten. ^{yet}⌃ (yet)
2. I don't need any groceries. I've ⌃gone shopping. (already)
3. What have you done? Have you been to the zoo? (yet)
4. I called my parents before dinner. I've talked to them. (already)

2 Present perfect vs. simple past (page 66)

▶ Don't mention a specific time with the present perfect: I'**ve been** to a jazz club. Use the simple past to say when a past action happened: I **went** to a jazz club **last night**.

Complete the conversation using the present perfect or the simple past of the verbs in parentheses and short answers.

1. A: ....Did.... you ....see.... (see) the game last night? I really .... (enjoy) it.
   B: Yes, I .... It .... (be) an amazing game. .... you ever .... (go) to a game?
   A: No, I .... I .... never .... (be) to the stadium. But I'd love to go! Maybe we can go to a game next year.
2. A: .... you ever .... (be) to Franco's Restaurant?
   B: Yes, I .... My friend and I .... (eat) there last weekend. How about you?
   A: No, I .... But I .... (hear) it's very good.
   B: Oh, yes – it's excellent!

3 *For* and *since* (page 67)

▶ Use *for* + a period of time to describe how long a present condition has been true: We've been in New York **for two months**. (= We arrived two months ago.)
▶ Use *since* + a point in time to describe when a present condition started: We've been here **since August**. (= We've been here from August to now.)

Circle the correct word.

1. I bought my car almost 10 years ago. I've had it **for / since** almost 10 years.
2. The Carters moved to Seattle six months ago. They've lived there **for / since** six months.
3. I've wanted to see that movie **for / since** a long time. It's been in theaters **for / since** March.

Unit 11

1 Adverbs before adjectives (page 73)

> ▶ Use *a/an* with (adverb) + adjective + singular noun: It's a **very modern city**.
> It's **an expensive city**. Don't use *a/an* with (adverb) + adjective:
> It's **really interesting**. (NOT: ~~It's a really interesting.~~)

Read the sentences. Add *a* or *an* where it's necessary to complete the sentences.

1. Brasília is ˄*an* extremely modern city.

2. Seoul is very interesting place.

3. Santiago is pretty exciting city to visit.

4. Montreal is beautiful city, and it's fairly old.

5. London has really busy airport.

2 Conjunctions (page 74)

> ▶ Use *and* for additional information: The food is delicious, **and** it's not expensive.
> ▶ Use *but*, *though*, and *however* for contrasting information: The food is delicious, **but**
> it's very expensive. / The food is delicious. It's expensive, **though/however**.

Circle the correct word.

1. Spring in my city is pretty nice, **and / but** it gets extremely hot in summer.
2. There are some great museums. They're always crowded, **and / however**.
3. There are a lot of interesting stores, **and / but** many of them aren't expensive.
4. There are many amazing restaurants, **and / but** some are closed in August.
5. My city is a great place to visit. Don't come in summer **but / though**!

3 Modal verbs *can* and *should* (page 75)

> ▶ Use *can* to talk about things that are possible: Where **can** I get some nice souvenirs?
> Use *should* to suggest things that are good to do: You **should** try the local
> restaurants.
> ▶ Use the base form with *can* and *should* – not the infinitive: Where **can** I ~~to~~ get some
> nice souvenirs? You **should** ~~to~~ try the local restaurants.

Complete the conversation with *can, can't, should,* or *shouldn't*.

A: I ....*can't*.......... decide where to go on vacation. .... I go to Costa Rica
or Hawaii?
B: You .... definitely visit Costa Rica.
A: Really? What can I see there?
B: Well, San Jose is an exciting city. You .... miss the Museo del Oro. That's
the gold museum, and you .... see beautiful animals made of gold.
A: OK. What else can I do there?
B: Well, you .... visit the museum on Mondays. It's closed then. But you
.... definitely visit the rain forest. It's amazing!

Unit 12

1 Adjective + infinitive; infinitive + noun (page 79)

▶ In negative statements, *not* comes before the infinitive: With a cold, it's important **not to exercise** too hard. (NOT: With a cold, it's important **to not exercise** too hard.)

Rewrite the sentences using the words in parentheses. Add *not* when necessary.

1. For a bad headache, you should relax and close your eyes. (a good idea)
   It's a good idea to relax and close your eyes when you have a headache.
2. You should put some cold tea on that sunburn. (sometimes helpful)
   ....
3. For a fever, you should take some aspirin. (important)
   ....
4. For a cough, you shouldn't drink milk. (important)
   ....
5. For sore muscles, you should take a hot bath. (sometimes helpful)
   ....
6. When you feel stressed, you shouldn't drink a lot of coffee. (a good idea)
   ....

2 Modal verbs *can, could, may* for requests; suggestions (page 81)

▶ In requests, *can, could,* and *may* have the same meaning. *May* is a little more formal than *can* and *could*.

Number the lines of the conversation. Then write the conversation below.

.... Yes, please. What do you suggest for itchy skin?
.... Here you are. Can I help you with anything else?
.... Sure I can. You should see a dentist!
...1.... Hello. May I help you?
.... You should try this lotion.
.... Yes. Can you suggest something for a toothache?
.... OK. And could I have a bottle of aspirin?

A: Hello. May I help you? ....
B: ....
A: ....
B: ....
A: ....
B: ....
A: ....

Unit 13

1 *So, too, neither, either* (page 87)

> ▶ Use *so* or *too* after an affirmative statement: I'm crazy about sushi. **So** am I./I am, **too**.
> ▶ Use *neither* or *not either* after a negative statement: I don't like fast food. **Neither** do I./I don't **either**.
> ▶ With *so* and *neither*, the verb comes before the subject: **So am I.** (NOT: ~~So I am.~~)
> **Neither do I.** (NOT: ~~Neither I do.~~)

A Choose the correct response to show that B agrees with A.

1. A: I'm in the mood for something salty.
   B: (**I am, too.**) / **I do, too.**
2. A: I can't stand fast food.
   B: **Neither do I. / I can't either.**
3. A: I really like Korean food.
   B: **So do I. / I am, too.**
4. A: I don't eat Italian food very often.
   B: **I do, too. / I don't either.**
5. A: I'm not crazy about pizza.
   B: **I am, too. / Neither am I.**

B Write responses to show agreement with these statements.

1. A: I'm not a very good cook.
   B: ....
2. A: I love french fries.
   B: ....
3. A: I can't eat very spicy food.
   B: ....
4. A: I never eat bland food.
   B: ....
5. A: I can make delicious desserts.
   B: ....

2 Modal verbs *would* and *will* for requests (page 89)

> ▶ Don't confuse *like* and *would like*. *Would like* means "want."
> ▶ You can also use *I'll have* . . . when ordering in a restaurant to mean *I will have* . . . .

Complete the conversation with *would, I'd,* or *I'll*.

A: .....Would.............. you like to order now?
B: Yes, please. .... have the shrimp curry.
A: .... you like noodles or rice with that?
B: Hmm, ... have rice.
A: And .... you like a salad, too?
B: No, thanks.
A: .... you like anything else?
B: Yes, ... like a cup of green tea.

Unit 14

1 Comparisons with adjectives (page 93)

> ▶ Use the comparative form (adjective + -er or more + adjective) to compare two people, places, or things: Which river is **longer**, the Nile or the Amazon? The Nile is **longer than** the Amazon. Use the superlative form (the + adjective + -est or the most + adjective) to compare three or more people, places, or things: Which river is **the longest**: the Nile, the Amazon, or the Mississippi? The Nile is **the longest** river in the world.
>
> ▶ You can use a comparative or superlative without repeating the noun: Which country is **larger**, Canada or China? Canada is **larger**. What's the highest waterfall in the world? Angel Falls is **the highest**.

Write questions with the words. Then look at the underlined words, and write the answers.

1. Which desert / dry / the Sahara or <u>the Atacama</u>?
   Q: <u>Which desert is drier, the Sahara or the Atacama?</u>
   A: <u>The Atacama is drier than the Sahara.</u>
2. Which island / large / <u>Greenland</u>, New Guinea, or Honshu?
   Q: ....
   A: ....
3. Which island / small / New Guinea or <u>Honshu</u>?
   Q: ....
   A: ....
4. Which U.S. city / large / Los Angeles, Chicago, or <u>New York</u>?
   Q: ....
   A: ....
5. Who / older / your father or your <u>grandfather</u>?
   Q: ....
   A: ....

2 Questions with *how* (page 96)

> ▶ Use *high* to describe mountains and waterfalls: How **high** is Mount Fuji? Angel Falls is 979 meters **high**. Use *tall* to describe buildings: How **tall** is the Empire State Building? (NOT: How high is the Empire State Building?)

Complete the questions with the phrases in the box. There is one extra phrase.

How big	How cold	✓ How deep	How high	How tall

1. Q: <u>How deep</u> is Lake Baikal?   A: It's 1,642 meters (5,387 feet) at its deepest point.
2. Q: .... is Alaska?   A: It's 586,412 square miles (1,518,800 kilometers).
3. Q: .... is Mount McKinley?   A: It's 20,300 feet (6,194 meters) high.
4. Q: .... is the CN Tower?   A: It is 553 meters (1,814 feet) tall.

Unit 15

1 Future with present continuous and *be going to* (page 101)

> Use the present continuous to talk about something that is happening now:
> What **are** you **doing**? I'm **studying**. You can also use the present continuous
> with time expressions to talk about the future: What **are** you **doing tomorrow**?
> I'm **working**.

A Read the sentences. Are they present or future? Write P or F.

1. Why are you wearing shorts? It's cold. ....P....
2. What are you wearing to the party on Friday? ....
3. Where are you going this weekend? ....
4. Where are you going? ....
5. Are you going to watch TV tonight? ....

B Complete the conversations. Use the present continuous and *be going to.*

1. A: What ....are........... you and Tony ....doing........... (do) tonight?
   B: We .... (try) the new Chinese restaurant. Would you like to come?
   A: I'd love to. What time .... you .... (go)?
   B: We .... (meet) at Tony's house at 7:00. And don't forget an umbrella.
      It .... (rain) tonight.
2. A: Where .... you .... (go) on vacation this year?
   B: I .... (visit) my cousins in Paris. It .... (be) great!
   A: Well, I .... (not go) anywhere this year. I .... (stay) home.
   B: That's not so bad. Just think about all the money you .... (save)!

2 Messages with *tell* and *ask* (page 103)

> ▶ In messages with a request, use the infinitive of the verb: Please ask her **to meet** me
>   at noon. (NOT: ~~Please ask her meet me at noon.~~)
> ▶ In messages with negative infinitives, *not* goes before to in the infinitive: Could you
>   ask him **not to be** late? (NOT: ~~Could you ask him to not be late?~~)

Read the messages. Ask someone to pass them on. Use the words in parentheses.

1. Message: Patrick – We don't have class tomorrow. (please)
   Please tell Patrick that we don't have class tomorrow. ....
2. Message: Ana – Call me tonight on my cell phone. (would)
   ....
3. Message: Alex – The concert on Saturday is canceled. (would)
   ....
4. Message: Sarah – Don't forget to return the book to the library. (could)
   ....

Unit 16

1 Describing change (page 107)

▶ You can use several tenses to describe change – present tense, past tense, and present perfect.

A Complete the sentences with the information in the box. Use the present perfect of the verbs given.

> buy a house   change her hairstyle   join a gym   start looking for a new job

1. Pedro and Debbie .... Their apartment was too small.
2. Allen .... The one he has now is too stressful.
3. Sandra .... Everyone says it's more stylish.
4. Kevin .... He feels healthier now.

B Rewrite the sentences using the present tense and the words in parentheses.

1. Joy doesn't wear jeans anymore. <u>She wears dresses</u> .... (dresses)
2. They don't live in the city anymore. .... (suburbs)
3. Carol isn't shy anymore. .... (outgoing)
4. I quit eating greasy food. .... (healthier)

2 Verb + infinitive (page 109)

▶ Use the infinitive after a verb to describe future plans or things you want to happen: I **want to learn** Spanish.

Complete the conversation with the words in parentheses and a verb from the box. You can use some verbs more than once.

> be   do   drive   go   live   make   stay   work

A: Hey, Steven. What .....<u>are you going to do</u>..... (go) after graduation?
B: Well, I .... (plan) here in the city for a few months.
A: Really? I .... (want) home. I'm ready for my mom's cooking.
B: I understand that, but my boss says I can keep my job for the summer. So I .... (want) a lot of hours because I .... (hope) enough money for a new car.
A: But you don't need a car in the city.
B: I .... (not plan) here for very long. In the fall, I .... (go) across the country. I really .... (want) in California.
A: California? Where in California .... (like)?
B: In Hollywood, of course. I .... (go) a movie star!

Grammar plus answer key

Unit 1

1 Statements with *be*; possessive adjectives

1. This **is** Delia Rios. **She's** a new student from Peru.
2. My name **is** Sergio. **I'm** from Brazil.
3. My brother and I **are** students here. **Our** names are Dave and Jeff.
4. **He's** Yoshi. **He's** 19 years old.
5. **They're** in my English class. **It's** a very big class.

2 Wh-questions with *be*

1. f
2. e
3. a
4. b
5. c
6. d

3 Yes/No questions and short answers with *be*

1. B: No, **they're not / they aren't**. They're in English 2.
2. A: Hi! **Are you** in this class?
   B: Yes, **I am**. I'm a new student here.
3. A: **Are you** from the United States?
   B: No, **we're not / we aren't**. We're from Montreal, Canada.
4. A: Hi, Sonia. **Are you** free?
   B: No, **I'm not**. I'm on my way to class.
5. A: That's the new student. **Is he** from Puerto Rico?
   B: No, **he's not / he isn't**. he's from Costa Rica.
6. A: **Is she** from Thailand?
   B: Yes, **she is**. She's from Bangkok.

Unit 2

1 Simple present Wh-questions and statements

1. A: I **have** good news! Dani **has** a new job.
   B: How **does** she **like** it?
   A: She **loves** it. The hours are great.
   B: What time **does** she **start**?
   A: She **starts** at nine and **finishes** at five.
2. A: What **do** you **do**?
   B: I'm a teacher.
   A: What **do** you **teach**?
   B: I **teach** Spanish, and English.
   A: Really? My sister **teaches** English, too.

2 Time expressions

B: I love it, but the hours are difficult. I start work **at** 7:30 A.M., and I work **until** 3:30.
A: That's interesting! I work the same hours, but I work **at** night. I start **at** 7:30 **in** the evening and finish **at** 3:30 **in** the morning.
B: Wow! What time do you get up?
A: Well, I get home **at** 4:30 and go to bed **at** 5:30. And I sleep **until** 2:00. But I only work **on** weekends, so it's OK. What about you?
B: Oh, I work **on** Monday, Wednesday, and Friday. And I get up **early** – around 6:00 A.M.

Unit 3

1 Demonstratives; *one, ones*

1. A: Excuse me. How much are **these** shoes?
   B: **They're** $279.
   A: And how much is **that** bag over there?
   B: **It's** only $129.
   A: And are the two gray **ones** $129, too?
   B: No. **Those** are only $119.
   A: Oh! **This** store is really expensive.
2. A: Can I help you?
   B: Yes, please. I really like **those** jeans over there. How much **are they**?
   A: Which **ones**? Do you mean **these**?
   B: No, the black **ones**.
   A: Let me look. Oh, **they're** $35.99.
   B: That's not bad. And how much is **this** sweater here?
   A: **It's** only $9.99.

2 Preferences; comparisons with adjectives

A
2. more boring
3. more exciting
4. friendlier
5. more interesting
6. more reasonable
7. sadder
8. warmer

B
2. I like the silver one (better). It's more interesting.
3. I prefer the silk one. It's prettier.
4. I like the purple ones (more). They're more exciting.

Unit 4

1 Simple present questions; short answers

A

2. A: **Does Joe like** Taylor Swift?
   B: No, **he doesn't**.
3. A: **Does Lisa like** talk shows?
   B: Yes, **she does**.
4. A: **Do you / you and Bob watch** the news on TV?
   B: Yes, **we do**.
5. A: **Do you like** hip-hop?
   B: No, **I don't**.
6. A: **Do your parents listen to** jazz?
   B: No, **they don't**.

B

2. us   3. them   4. him   5. her

2 *Would*; verb + *to* + verb

A: Would you like to see a movie with me tonight?
B: Yes, I would. What would you like to see?
A: I'd like to see the new Halle Berry movie.

Unit 5

1 Present continuous

1. A: **Is she living abroad?**
   B: Yes, **she is**. She**'s living / is living** in South Korea.
2. A: **How are you spending your summer?**
   B: I**'m working** part-time. I**'m taking** two classes also.
   A: **What are you taking?**
   B: My friend and I **are studying** photography and Japanese. We like our classes a lot.

2 Quantifiers

2. Nearly all students finish high school.
3. All children start school by the age of six.
4. A lot of couples have more than one child.
5. Few families have more than four children.

Unit 6

1 Adverbs of frequency

1. A: **I often play sports.**
2. Q: **Do you ever go jogging with a friend?**
   A: No, **I always jog / go jogging alone.**
3. Q: **How often do you play tennis?**
   A: I **play four times a week.**
4. Q: **What do you usually do in the evening?**
   A: My family and I almost always watch TV.
5. Q: **How often do you go to the gym?**
   A: I **never go (to the gym).**

2 Questions with *how*; short answers

1. **How often** do you lift weights? c
2. **How well** do you play tennis? a
3. **How good** are you at aerobics? d
4. **How long** do you spend at the gym? b

Unit 7

1 Simple past

B: Yes, I **did**. I **had** a great time. My sister and I **went** shopping on Saturday. We **spent** all day at the mall.
A: **Did** you **buy** anything special?
B: I **bought** a new laptop. And I **got** some new clothes, too.
A: Lucky you! What clothes **did** you **buy**?
B: Well, I **needed** some new boots. I **found** some great ones at Luff's Department Store.
A: What about you? What **did** you **do** on Saturday?
B: I **didn't do** anything special. I **stayed** home and **worked** around the house. Oh, but I **saw** a really good movie on TV. And then I **made** dinner with my mother. I actually **enjoyed** the day.

2 Past of *be*

2. He was at work all day.
3. Tony and his co-workers were at work on Saturday, too.
4. They weren't at work on Sunday.
5. Was Tony at home on Sunday?
6. Where was Tony on Sunday?
7. He and his brother were at a baseball game.
8. They were at the park until 7:00.

Unit 8

1 *There is, there are; one, any, some*

1. A: **Are** there any supermarkets in this neighborhood?
   B: No, there **aren't**, but there are **some** on Main Street.
   A: And **is** there a post office near here?
   B: Yes, **there is**. It's across from the bank.
2. A: **Is** there a gas station around here?
   B: Yes, **there's** one behind the shopping center.
   A: Great! And are there **any** coffee shops nearby?
   B: Yes, there's a good **one** in the shopping center.

2 Quantifiers; *how many* and *how much*

A

1. A: much
   B: a little
2. A: many
   B: many
3. A: How many
   B: are
4. A: How much is
   B: none

B

2. A: Are there many parks?
3. A: Is there much crime?
4. A: Are there many laundromats?

Unit 9

1 Describing people

A: How tall is he?
B: He's 5 feet 11.
A: Does he wear glasses?
B: No, he doesn't. He wears contact lenses.
A: What color is his hair?
B: He has blond hair.
A: Does he have blue eyes?
B: No, he has brown eyes.
A: And how old is he?
B: He's 26 – two years older than me.

2 Modifiers with participles and prepositions

1. B: She's the one wearing a red dress.
2. A: Which ones are your neighbors?
   B: They're the ones walking with the baby.
3. A: Which one is Jeff?
   B: He's the one with glasses.

Unit 10

1 Present perfect; *already, yet*

A

2. B: No, she **hasn't called** me, but I**'ve gotten** some emails from her.
3. A: **Have** you and Jan **had** lunch yet?
   B: No, we **haven't**. We're thinking of going to Tony's. **Have** you **tried** it yet? Come with us.
   A: Thanks. I **haven't eaten** there yet, but I**'ve heard** it's pretty good.

B

2. I've **already** gone shopping.
3. Have you been to the zoo **yet**?
4. I've **already** talked to them./I've talked to them **already**.

2 Present perfect vs. simple past

1. A: **Did** you **see** the game last night? I really **enjoyed** it.
   B: Yes, I **did**. It **was** an amazing game. **Have** you ever **gone** to a game?
   A: No, I **haven't**. I**'ve** never **been** to the stadium. But I'd love to go! Maybe we can go to a game next year.
2. A: **Have** you ever **been** to Franco's Restaurant?
   B: Yes, I **have**. My friend and I **ate** there last weekend. How about you?
   A: No, I **haven't**. But I've **heard** it's very good.
   B: Oh, yes – it's excellent!

3 *For* and *since*

1. I've had it **for** almost 10 years.
2. They've lived there **for** six months.
3. I've wanted to see that movie **for** a long time. It's been in theaters **since** March.

Unit 11

1 Adverbs before adjectives

2. Seoul is **a** very interesting place.
3. Santiago is **a** pretty exciting city to visit.
4. Montreal is **a** beautiful city, and it's fairly old.
5. London has **a** really busy airport.

2 Conjunctions

1. Spring in my city is pretty nice, **but** it gets extremely hot in summer.
2. They're often crowded, **however**.
3. There are a lot of interesting stores, **and** many of them aren't expensive.
4. There are many amazing restaurants, **but** some are closed in August.
5. Don't come in summer, **though**!

3 Modal verbs *can* and *should*

A: I **can't** decide where to go on vacation. **Should** I go to Costa Rica or Hawaii?
B: You **should** definitely visit Costa Rica.
A: Really? What can I see there?
B: Well, San Jose is an exciting city. You **shouldn't** miss the Museo del Oro. That's the gold museum, and you **can** see beautiful animals made of gold.
A: OK. What else **can** I do there?
B: Well, you **can't** visit the museum on Mondays. It's closed then. But you **should** definitely visit the rain forest.

Unit 12

1 Adjective + infinitive; infinitive + noun

2. For a sunburn, **it's sometimes helpful to put** some cold tea on it.
3. For a fever, **it's important to take** some aspirin.
4. For a cough, **it's important not to drink** milk.
5. For sore muscles, **it's sometimes helpful to take** a hot bath.
6. When you feel stressed, **it's not a good idea to drink** a lot of coffee.

2 Modal verbs *can, could, may* for requests; suggestions

2. Yes, please. What do you suggest for itchy skin?
3. You should try this lotion.
4. OK. And could I have a bottle of aspirin?
5. Here you are. Can I help you with anything else?
6. Yes. Can you suggest something for a toothache?
7. Sure I can. You should see a dentist!

Unit 13

1 *So, too, neither, either*

A

2. B: I can't either.
3. B: So do I.
4. B: I don't either.
5. B: Neither am I.

B

1. B: I'm not either.
2. B: I do, too.
3. B: I can't either.
4. B: Neither do I.
5. B: So can I.

2 Modal verbs *would* and *will* for requests

B: I'll
A: Would
B: I'll
A: would
A: Would
B: I'd

Unit 14

1 Comparisons with adjectives

2. Q: Which island is the largest: Greenland, New Guinea, or Honshu?
   A: Greenland is the largest.
3. Q: Which island is smaller, New Guinea or Honshu?
   A: Honshu is smaller than New Guinea.
4. Q: Which U.S. city is the largest: Los Angeles, Chicago, or New York?
   A: New York is the largest.
5. Q: Who is older, your father or your grandfather?
   A: Your / My grandfather is older.

2 Questions with *how*

2. How big
3. How high
4. How tall

Unit 15

1 Future with present continuous and *be going to*

A

2. F
3. F
4. P
5. F

B

1. B: We **we're going to try** the new Chinese restaurant. Would you like to come?
   A: I'd love to. What time **are** you are **you going to go**?
   B: We**'re going to meet** at Tony's house at 7:00. And don't forget an umbrella. It**'s going to rain** tonight.
2. A: Where **are** you **going to go** on vacation this year?
   B: I**'m going to visit** my cousins in Paris. It**'s going to be** great!
   A: Well, I**'m not going to go** anywhere this year. I**'m going to stay** home.
   B: That's not so bad. Just think about all the money you**'re going to save!**

2 Messages with *tell* and *ask*

2. Would you ask Ana to call me tonight on my cell phone?
3. Would you tell Alex (that) the concert on Saturday is canceled?
4. Could you tell Sarah not to forget to return the book to the library?

Unit 16

1 Describing change

A

1. Pedro and Debbie **have bought a house**.
2. Allen **has started looking for a new job**.
3. Sandra **has changed her hairstyle**.
4. Kevin **has joined a gym**.

B

Possible answers:
2. They live in the suburbs.
3. Carol / She is outgoing.
4. I eat healthier now.

2 Verb + infinitive

B: Well, I **plan to stay** here in the city for a few months.
A: Really? I **want to go** home. I'm ready for my mom's cooking.
B: I understand that, but my boss says I can keep my job for the summer. So I **want to work** a lot of hours because I **hope to make** enough money for a new car.
A: But you don't need a car in the city.
B: I **don't plan to be** here for very long. In the fall, I**'m going to drive** across the country. I really **want to live** in California.
A: California? Where in California **would you like to live**?
B: In Hollywood, of course. I**'m going to be** a movie star!

Credits

Illustrations

Photos

interchange

Jack C. Richards
Revised by Deborah B. Gordon

VIDEO ACTIVITY WORKSHEETS

1

CAMBRIDGE
UNIVERSITY PRESS

Credits

Illustration credits

Andrezzinho: 6 (*bottom*), 34; Mark Collins: 8 (*top*), 18, 30 (*bottom*), 58; Carlos Diaz: 4 (*center*), 48, 60, 62 (*bottom*); Chuck Gonzales: 2, 16 (*top*), 26, 54; Jim Haynes: 12 (*top*), 20, 24, 36, 46 (*top*), 57, 62 (*top*); Dan Hubig: 53, 61; Trevor Keen: 4 (*bottom*), 6 (*top*), 18 (*bottom*), 38, 65; Joanna Kerr: 12 (*bottom*), 30 (*top*), 32; KJA-artists.com: 23, 49, 64 (*bottom*); Monika Melnychuk/i2iart.com: 46 (*bottom*); Karen Minot: 50; Rob Schuster: 16 (*bottom*); James Yamasaki: 10 (*bottom*), 22 (*bottom*); Rose Zgodzinski: 22 (*top*)

Photography credits

14 (*top row, left to right*) ©Alex Staroseltsev/Shutterstock; ©Rafa Irusta/Shutterstock; ©Christophe Testi/Shutterstock; (*center*) ©Courtesy Everett Collection; (*bottom row, left to right*) ©Warner Bros/Everett Collection; ©Weinstein Company/Everett Collection; ©Dimension Films/Everett Collection; ©Warner Bros/Everett Collection; 20 ©UpperCut Images/SuperStock; 26 (*top row, left to right*) ©Worakit Sirijinda/Shutterstock; ©Maksym Gorpenyuk/Shutterstock; ©Etienne/Age Fotostock; (*bottom row, left to right*) ©Simon Gurney/Shutterstock; ©Simon James/Shutterstock; ©Samot/Shutterstock; 27 (*clockwise from top left*) ©Wright/Relax Images/Age Fotostock; ©Masterfile; ©C./Shutterstock; ©Julian Love/John Warburton-Lee Photography/Alamy; ©C./Shutterstock; 28 (*top row, left to right*) ©Maksym Gorpenyuk/Shutterstock; ©Worakit Sirijinda/Shutterstock; ©Simon Gurney/Shutterstock; (*bottom row, left to right*) ©Wright/Relax Image/Age Fotostock; ©Etienne/Age Fotostock; ©Travelshots/SuperStock; 42 (*Golden Gate Bridge*) ©Anna Shakina/Shutterstock; (*top row, left to right*) ©Hoberman Collection/SuperStock; ©Mitchell Funk/Photographer's Choice/Getty Images; ©Ruth Tomlinson/Robert Harding Picture Library/Age Fotostock; (*bottom row, left to right*) ©Ron Koeberer/Aurora Photos/Alamy; ©John Elk III/Lonely Planet Images/Getty Images; ©Novastock/F1online/Age Fotostock; 43 (*top row, left to right*) ©f Stop/SuperStock; ©Rafael Ramirez Lee/Shutterstock; (*cars on Golden Gate Bridge*) ©Pietro Scozzari/Age Fotostock; 44 (*top row, left to right*) ©Mitchell Funk/Photographer's Choice/Getty Images; ©Travel Division Images/Alamy; ©Ed Rhodes/Alamy; (*bottom row, left to right*) ©Lee Foster/Alamy; ©Roberta Allen/Alamy; ©Bob Thomason/Stone/Getty Images; 51 ©T.M.O.Buildings/Alamy; 52 © Image Source / Alamy; 53 (*pizza*) ©Comstock Images/Getty Images; (*sushi*) ©Kongsak//Shutterstock; 54 (*clockwise from top left*) ©Frédéric Soltan/Sygma/Corbis; ©Paul Harris/JAI/Corbis; ©Jochen Schlenker/Robert Harding World Imagery/Corbis; ©Corbis/SuperStock; 55 (*top, left to right*) ©David Sailors/Terra/Corbis; ©Hisham Ibrahim/Photographer's Choice/Getty Images; 64 (*left to right*) ©Beboy Ltd./iStockphoto; ©Seregam/Shutterstock; 65 ©Elena Yakusheva/Shutterstock

Plan of Video 1

1 Are you Evan Chu?

Preview

1 CULTURE

In North America, people go to conferences to learn more about their work, their hobbies, and other interests. At conferences, people usually don't know each other. They wear name tags to make it easier to meet each other and to help them remember new names. People at conferences usually use each other's first names.

Where do people wear name tags in your country?
When people meet new people at places like conferences, do they use first names or titles (Ms., Mrs., Mr., Professor) with last names?

2 VOCABULARY *At a conference*

PAIR WORK Here are some conference words and phrases.
Write the words and phrases under the pictures.

| clerk | name tag | introducing yourself | ✓participant |

1. participant   2. ....   3. ....   4. ....

3 GUESS THE STORY

Watch the first minute of the video with the sound off.
What do you think happens to Mike? Check (✓) your answer.

- [ ] Mike uses the wrong name tag.
- [ ] Mike changes his name to Evan Chu.
- [ ] Mike doesn't use any name tag.

☰ **Watch the video**

4 *GET THE PICTURE*

A Check your answer to Exercise 3. Did you guess correctly?

B Put the pictures in the correct order (1 to 4). Then write the correct sentence from the video under each picture. Compare with a partner.

"Excuse me. This isn't mine."
"Good to see you! How's it going?"
"Hi. I'm Evan Chu."
"Hi, Rachel. Good to meet you."

....

....

5 *WATCH FOR DETAILS*

Check (✓) the correct answers. Then compare with a partner.

1. Mike's last name is ....
   - ✓ O'Neill
   - ☐ Chu
   - ☐ Anderson

2. Linda and Mike are probably ....
   - ☐ friends
   - ☐ family
   - ☐ strangers

3. The clerk gives Evan ....
   - ☐ no name tag
   - ☐ a new name tag
   - ☐ Linda's name tag

4. Mike is wearing ....
   - ☐ his name tag
   - ☐ Bill's name tag
   - ☐ Evan's name tag

5. There are .... name tags for Evan Chu.
   - ☐ three
   - ☐ two
   - ☐ zero

6 WHAT'S YOUR OPINION?

Check (✓) your opinion. Then compare with a partner.

1. When the clerk can't find Evan's name tag, how does she feel?
   - [ ] angry
   - [ ] amused
   - [ ] confused

2. When Evan meets Rachel and Mike, how does he feel?
   - [ ] pleased
   - [ ] amused
   - [ ] surprised

3. When Mike realizes he has Evan's name tag, how does he feel?
   - [ ] angry
   - [ ] embarrassed
   - [ ] pleased

angry

confused

embarrassed

pleased

☰ Follow-up

7 ROLE PLAY *At a conference*

A Imagine you are at a conference. Choose your name, hometown, and job. Write them below. Make a name tag for yourself.

My name is ....

I am from ....

I am a/an ....

B **CLASS ACTIVITY** Now walk around the room and introduce yourself. Have conversations like this:

A: Hello, my name's Sidney.
B: Hi, I'm Michelle.
A: Where are you from, Michelle?
B: I'm from Paris, France. What about you?

Where are you from?

I'm from Ontario.

Language close-up

8 WHAT DID THEY SAY?

Watch the video and complete the conversation. Then practice it.

Mike, Bill, and Rachel introduce themselves.

Mike: Hi, ...I'm....... Mike ....O'Neill........ .
Bill: What did you say your name was .... ?
Mike: .... Mike. Mike O'Neill.
Bill: .... I'm Bill. Bill ....
.... to meet you, . . . Mike.
Mike: Good to .... you, ...
Rachel: Hi. ....
Bill: Hi. .... me.
Rachel: Hi, I'm Rachel Stevens. .... to the conference.
Mike: Hi, Rachel. .... to meet you. And, ...
do you do?
Rachel: I, um, I have .... own business. I'm an interior
.... , but I volunteer with the ....
History Association. Are you from .... here?
Mike: Oh, no. I'm .... Chicago.
Rachel: Chicago. Nice ....
Mike: .... you.

9 QUESTIONS WITH BE

A Complete the questions with **is** or **are**.

1. ....Is....... Mike's last name Chu?
2. .... Mike and Evan conference participants?
3. .... Evan and Bill friends?
4. .... Rachel a participant?
5. .... Mike an interior designer?

B PAIR WORK Take turns asking and answering the questions.

A: Is Mike's last name Chu?
B: No, it isn't. It's O'Neill.

10 WH-QUESTIONS *Getting to know people*

A Complete these questions with **is, are, do,** or **does**.

1. What ....is........ Evan's last name?
2. Where .... Mike from?
3. Who .... the participants?
4. What .... Rachel do?
5. Where .... Evan's first name tag?

B PAIR WORK Take turns asking and answering the questions above.

C CLASS ACTIVITY Now find out about your classmates. Write three more questions. Then go around the class and ask them.

1. What's your first name?
2. ....
3. ....
4. ....

2 I love my job!

Preview

1 *CULTURE*

In North America, people with full-time jobs usually work eight hours a day. The hours of a typical office job are 9:00 A.M. to 5:00 P.M. Many people also work part time. Some people work two or more part-time jobs. People in North America usually change jobs several times in their lives. The average person also changes careers – not just jobs – two or three times.

How many hours a day do people work in your country?
What are typical office hours? Do people also work part time?
Do people often change jobs or careers?

2 *VOCABULARY* Occupations

PAIR WORK Who works inside, who works outside, and who works in both places? Put the words in the chart. Can you add three more words?

chef

cab driver

Inside	Outside	Inside and Outside

dance instructor

construction worker

waiter

mover

3 GUESS THE STORY

Watch the first 25 seconds of the video.
Which jobs is Lisa going to focus on?

- ☐ cab driver
- ☐ chef
- ☐ construction worker
- ☐ dance instructor
- ☐ mover
- ☐ waiter

☰ Watch the video

4 GET THE PICTURE

Match the pictures of the people with their names and their jobs.

1. Sasha	2. Brian	3. Tim	4. Chris

waiter	mover	dance instructor	cab driver

5 WATCH FOR DETAILS

Check (✓) **True** or **False.** Then correct the false statements.
Compare with a partner.

	True	False	
1. Tim doesn't like his job.	☐	✓	Tim likes his job.
2. Tim doesn't drive the truck.	☐	☐	....
3. Sasha works five hours a day.	☐	☐	....
4. Chris works long hours.	☐	☐	....
5. Chris works at night.	☐	☐	....
6. Brian starts work at 9:00.	☐	☐	....

GIVING REASONS

PAIR WORK Read the sentences below. Then use them to complete the chart.

Reasons Tim likes his job	Reasons Chris doesn't like his job
....	....
....	....
....	....
....	....
Reasons Sasha likes her work	**Reasons Brian's job is important**
....	....
....	....
....	....
....	....

It helps people get fit and be healthy.

It's fun to drive a big truck.

It's necessary to work long hours.

It's fun to teach people new moves.

People are hungry.

People don't have time to cook.

There is traffic.

There are different problems to solve.

Follow-up

7 ROLE PLAY *Jobs*

PAIR WORK Imagine you are one of the people in the video.
Don't tell anyone who you are. Walk around the room and use these
questions to ask about each other's jobs. Guess people's jobs.

Do you like your job?
What do you like or not like about your job?

8 WHAT DID THEY SAY?

Watch the video and complete the conversation. Then practice it.

Lisa is talking to Chris.

Lisa: Hi. Do you ......*have*...... a minute?

Chris: ....

Lisa: What's your name, and what ....

.... ?

Chris: My name is Chris, and I ....

a ....

Lisa: .... you .... your job?

Chris: Most .... , yes.

Lisa: What .... you .... about your job?

Chris: I work .... I work ....

.... , too. And .... is the ....

9 QUESTIONS WITH DO; PRESENT TENSE VERBS

A Complete the *questions* in the present tense. Complete the *answers* with the correct verb. Then practice the conversation.

Tim: I'm a mover. I .... people .... their entire lives from their old home to their new home.

Lisa: How .... you .... about your job?

Tim: I really .... my job.

Lisa: How .... you .... your day?

Tim: I .... boxes, ... items, and .... the truck. Sometimes I .... the truck. That's the easy part.

B **PAIR WORK** Now have similar conversations using your own information. (If you don't work, choose a job from the book.)

10 ASKING ABOUT JOBS

PAIR WORK Brian's friend is a chef in his restaurant. Think of three different questions Lisa could ask him about his job. Then work with your partner to ask and answer these questions.

1. How do you like your job? ....
2. ....
3. ....
4. ....

3 Yard sale

Preview

1 CULTURE

In North America, people often sell old things like furniture, jewelry, or clothing at a garage sale or yard sale. They decide on prices, put the things on tables in their garage or yard, and then they put a sign in front of their house to advertise the sale. People come to look and maybe to buy. Some things at yard sales are antiques and are worth a lot of money.

GARAGE SALE
Saturday 9-5; children's clothes, books, toys, kitchen items, TV. 257 Maple Ave.

YARD SALE
Saturday/Sunday 8-4; exercise equipment, furniture, CDs, DVDs. 89 Oak St.

Do people have garage sales or yard sales in your country?
What old things do you have at home?
What things would you like to sell at a yard sale?

2 VOCABULARY Yard sale items

PAIR WORK Put the words in the chart. Can you add six more words? Add things from your home.

Kitchen items	Jewelry	Other
		books

snorkeling equipment

a bracelet

a watch

a necklace

books

dishes

cups and saucers

a camera

3 GUESS THE STORY

A *Watch the video with the sound off.* Which things from Exercise 2 do you see at the yard sale? Circle the things you see.

B What do you think the man wants to buy? What does the woman want to buy? Make a list.

....

....

....

....

....

....

....

....

Watch the video

4 WHAT'S YOUR OPINION?

In the end, do you think Todd and Mariela buy any of these things at the yard sale? Check (✓) **Yes** or **No**. Then compare your answers with a partner.

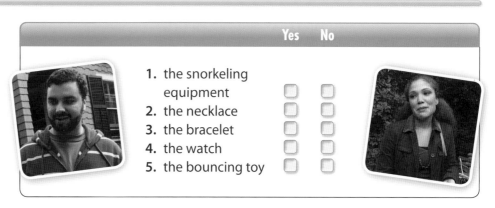

	Yes	No
1. the snorkeling equipment	☐	☐
2. the necklace	☐	☐
3. the bracelet	☐	☐
4. the watch	☐	☐
5. the bouncing toy	☐	☐

5 MAKING INFERENCES

PAIR WORK Check (✓) the best answers.

1. Mariela thinks Todd

   ....

   the snorkeling equipment.
   - ☐ really wants
   - ☐ really doesn't want

2. Todd thinks the snorkeling equipment is

   ....
   - ☐ cheap
   - ☐ expensive

3. Todd thinks the necklace and bracelet are

   ....
   - ☐ a good price
   - ☐ too expensive

4. Todd thinks the watch is

   ....
   - ☐ not very nice
   - ☐ too old

6 ROLE PLAY *Shop at a Yard Sale*

A PAIR WORK Imagine you are at a yard sale. Number the sentences (1 to 6) to make conversations. Then practice the conversations.

1. .... And how much are these earrings?
   ...1... Hello. Can I help you?
   .... It's twelve dollars.
   .... Yes, how much is this ring?
   .... They're twenty dollars.
   .... Thanks. I'll think about it.

2. .... Can I help you?
   .... Oh, that's pretty expensive.
   .... OK. I'll take it.
   .... Yes, how much is this MP3 player?
   .... Well, how about thirty dollars?
   .... It's forty dollars.

B CLASS ACTIVITY Plan a class yard sale. Form two groups.
Make a list of things your group will sell, and give each item a price.

Items for sale	Price

Now have the yard sale:

Group A: You are the sellers. Try to sell everything on your list to Group B. Then change roles and decide what to buy from Group B.

Group B: You are the buyers.
Ask questions and decide what to buy.
Then change roles and try to sell
everything on your list to Group A.

Language close-up

7 *WHAT DID THEY SAY?*

Watch the video and complete the conversation. Then practice it.

Mariela and Todd are looking at things at the yard sale.

Todd: Hey, Mariela, how do you ....like.......... this?

Mariela: Oh, ... , Todd.

Todd: Oh, come on. It's only a ....

Mariela: .... you really .... it, Todd?

Todd: No. I guess .... right.

Sarah: Hi. Can I .... you?

Todd: No, thanks .... We're just ....

Mariela: Oh! Todd, ... over here. Just look at this lovely old ....

Todd: Yeah, it's ....

Mariela: It's .... just "OK," Todd. It's very ....

8 *EXPRESSING OPINIONS*

Todd says these sentences. What do they mean in the video? Check (✓) the correct answer. Then compare with a partner.

1. How do you like this?
   ☐ Can you believe how little this costs?
   ☐ What do you think of this?

2. Oh, come on.
   ☐ Please let me [buy it].
   ☐ Are you kidding?

3. Yeah, it's OK.
   ☐ I like it a little.
   ☐ The price is reasonable.

4. That's not bad.
   ☐ It's nice.
   ☐ The price is reasonable.

5. Mariela, are you kidding?
   ☐ I don't believe it!
   ☐ Let's go!

9 HOW MUCH *AND* HOW OLD

A Complete the conversations with **how much is (are)** or **how old is (are)**.
Complete the answers with the correct verb.

1. A: How much is .... this necklace?
   B: It's only $10.
   A: .... it?
   B: It's 20 years old.

2. A: .... these books?
   B: They're $2 each.
   A: And .... they?
   B: They're about 10 years old.

3. A: .... these shoes?
   B: About two years old, I think.
   A: .... they?
   B: They're $20.

B **PAIR WORK** Practice the conversations in Exercise 9. Use items of your own.

Unit 3 ■ 13

Movies

Preview

 ## 1 CULTURE

In North America, most people live close to at least one movie theater. Movies are popular with people on dates, families, young people in groups, or just about anyone. Most movie theaters in North America have more than one screen. Some have as many as 20 or 25 screens! There are lots of different kinds of food and drinks to buy at movie theaters, but the most popular snack is popcorn.

Who likes to go to movies in your country?
What kinds of movies are popular?
What kinds of snacks do people buy?

Number of U.S. Movie Screens in 2009

Indoor 38,605   Drive-In 628

TOTAL 39,233

TICKET

2 VOCABULARY *Kinds of movies*

What kinds of movies or videos do you like? Check (✓) your opinions. Then compare answers in groups.

classic

WHAT'S YOUR OPINION?				
	I love them.	I like them.	I don't like them very much.	I don't like them at all.
romance movies	☐	☐	☐	☐
classic films	☐	☐	☐	☐
comedies	☐	☐	☐	☐
horror films	☐	☐	☐	☐
science-fiction movies	☐	☐	☐	☐
historical dramas	☐	☐	☐	☐

comedy

science fiction

historical drama

horror

3 GUESS THE STORY

Watch the first 45 seconds of the video.
Then answer these questions:

1. What different ways to watch movies does Lisa talk about?
2. What is Lisa's main question?
3. How many people is she going to interview?

Watch the video

4 GET THE PICTURE

A Circle the correct answers. Then compare with a partner.

	Person 1	Person 2	Person 3	Person 4
Favorite movie type	science fiction	thrillers	science fiction	horror
	thrillers	horror	historical drama	science fiction
	horror	comedies and romance	classics	foreign films
				classics
How often he or she watches a movie at home or on a mobile device	two or three times a week	two or three times a month	once or twice a week	three or four times a week
	two or three times a month	five or six times a month	three or four times a month	once or twice a week

B Circle which people gave these opinions.

1. Special effects are better on the big screen.   Person 1   Person 2   Person 3   Person 4
2. All movies are better on the big screen.   Person 1   Person 2   Person 3   Person 4
3. It's a night on the town.   Person 1   Person 2   Person 3   Person 4
4. Watching movies is more fun in a group.   Person 1   Person 2   Person 3   Person 4

5 INTERVIEW QUESTIONS

A How often does Lisa ask each of these questions, or questions that are very similar to these? Make a slash mark (/) each time you hear one of these questions. Then compare with a partner.

.... 1. Do you like movies?
.... 2. What type of movies do you like?
.... 3. How often do you watch movies on your television, computer, or mobile device?
.... 4. How often do you go to a movie theater to watch a movie?
.... 5. What makes going to the movie theater so special for you?

B What other Wh-question word does Lisa use?

≡ Follow-up

6 CLASS INTERVIEW

A **CLASS ACTIVITY** Use the questions in Exercise 5 to interview at least three classmates. Have conversations like this:

A: What types of movies do you like?
B: (*movie types*)
A: How often do you watch movies on your computer?
B: About twice a week.

B Now report the results of your interviews. What types of movies are the most popular? Least popular? How often do your classmates go to movie theaters? How often do they watch movies at home or on their mobile devices?

7 MAKING PLANS

GROUP WORK Plan to see a movie with your group. Also decide where to watch the movie. Give your opinions with statements and questions like these:

There's a great movie on tonight at ....
Do you really like .... ?
That sounds good. How about you, ... ?
I don't really like ....
Well, what kind of .... do you like?

☰ Language close-up

8 WHAT DID THEY SAY?

Watch the video and complete the conversation. Then practice it.

Lisa is interviewing Person 4.

Lisa: What ......*type*...... of movies ....*do*.......... you like?

Woman: I like .... films. I like to see ....
in other cultures.

Lisa: Do you like .... movies?

Woman: Yes, I do.

Lisa: .... ?

Woman: I like to see the .... black-and-white movies.

Lisa: How often .... you watch movies on your
television, computer, or .... device?

Woman: I watch movies on my .... quite frequently ....
I take the train to work. I probably see one or two a ....

Lisa: And how .... do you go to the theater to .... a movie?

Woman: I go pretty frequently. I would probably say, ... or twice a month.

Lisa: .... makes the theater so .... for you?

Woman: The special effects are much .... in the movie theater.

9 OBJECT PRONOUNS

A Fill in the blanks with **him**, **her**, **it**, or **them**.

1. A: Do you like horror films?
   B: No, I can't stand .....*them*..... .

2. A: Who's your favorite actor?
   B: Leonardo DiCaprio. I liked ....
   in *Inception*.

3. A: What do you think of Keira Knightley?
   B: I don't know .... What was
   she in?

4. A: What do you think of science fiction?
   B: I like .... a lot, too.

5. A: What do you think about romantic comedies?
   B: I like .... because they make
   me laugh.

6. A: Do you like 3-D?
   B: Yes, I like .... a lot, especially in
   action movies.

B Take turns asking and answering the questions above. Give your own opinions.

10 GIVING REASONS

PAIR WORK Take turns giving your opinions about movies, actors, and actresses.
Use these sentences to start your conversations.

1. A: I don't like historical dramas.
   B: Why not?
   A: I think they're dull.

2. A: I love horror movies.
   B: Really? Why?
   A: I like feeling scared.

3. A: I don't like thrillers at all.
   B: Why not?
   A: Because I don't like to feel scared.

4. A: I love going to movie theaters.
   B: What makes movie theaters so special for you?
   A: Because the special effects are better on a big screen.

5 A family picnic

1 CULTURE

In North America, 97 percent of people say that their family is the most important part of their life. But people in North America move often, and many children leave home at age 18. Many families only see each other on important holidays or at family parties.

- Six percent of all families move every year.
- On an average day, 116,438 people move.
- People often live far away from their parents and grandparents.
- Only 36 percent of families see their relatives once a week.

In your country, when do children leave home?
Do families move often?
How often do families see each other?

2 VOCABULARY *Family*

PAIR WORK How are these people related to Jane? Fill in the blanks in her family tree.

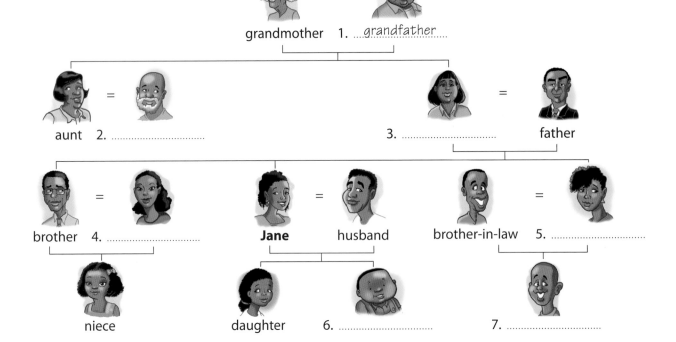

grandmother 1. *grandfather*

aunt 2. ....

3. .... father

brother 4. ....

Jane husband

brother-in-law 5. ....

niece

daughter 6. ....

7. ....

GUESS THE STORY

Watch the first 45 seconds of the video with the sound off.
The young woman is Beth. Who do you think these people are?

1.  Beth's husband

2. ....

3. ....

4. ....

Watch the video

4 GET THE PICTURE

Who's at the picnic? Check (✓) **Yes** or **No**. Then compare with a partner.

	Yes	No
Beth's parents	☐	☐
Beth's uncle and aunt	☐	☐
Beth's brother	☐	☐
Beth's sister	☐	☐
Beth's nephew	☐	☐
Beth's brother-in-law	☐	☐
Beth's niece	☐	☐
Beth's cousin	☐	☐
Beth's grandparents	☐	☐

5 WATCH FOR DETAILS

Check (✓) the correct answer. Then compare with a partner.

1. Kathleen and Jerry are Beth's .... parents.
   - ☐ mother's
   - ☐ father's

2. .... likes to fish.
   - ☐ Beth's father
   - ☐ Beth's brother-in-law

3. Kathleen and Jerry are looking for ....
   - ☐ birds
   - ☐ Ted

4. Beth's mother, aunt, and uncle are getting ready to ....
   - ☐ play a game
   - ☐ cook lunch

5. Beth's niece is ....
   - ☐ Kimberley
   - ☐ Megan

6. At every family picnic, Beth's husband ....
   - ☐ walks in the woods
   - ☐ takes a photograph

Unit 5 ■ **19**

6 WHAT'S YOUR OPINION?

PAIR WORK Read the culture note on page 18 again. Do you think Beth's family is like most families in North America? How is it the same and how is it different?

Follow-up

7 YOUR FAMILY

A **PAIR WORK** Is your family like Beth's? Tell about your family and find out about your partner's. Ask questions like these:

Are you living with your parents right now?
    If not, do you live near your parents?
Do you live near or far from your brothers, sisters,
    aunts, uncles, and grandparents?
Are you married?
Do you have children? If so, how old are they?
Do you have brothers and sisters?
Are they going to school or working?

B Draw a simple picture (or show your partner a photo) of your family. Your partner will ask questions about each person.

Is this your sister?
What does she do?
Is she studying English, too?

8 AN INTERESTING PERSON

A **PAIR WORK** Find out about your partner's most interesting relative or friend. Ask questions like these:

Who's your most interesting relative or friend?
What's his or her name?
What does he or she do?
Where is he or she living now?
How old is he or she?
Is he or she married?

B Now tell another classmate about your partner's relative like this:

Yong-su has an interesting cousin.
Her name is Son-hee.
She works at a zoo.
She's from Seoul.
She's working in New York now.
She's 30 years old.

Language close-up

9 WHAT DID SHE SAY?

Watch the video and complete Beth's description. Then practice it.

Beth describes her family members.

Hi, I'm Beth, and ....this........... is my husband, Chris. We're
.... for a family picnic. ....
the picnic in the country.

That's my .... , Ted. He .... to fish.
And .... my mom, Angela, ...
.... She's talking to my Aunt Helen and
Uncle James. Helen .... my mom's sister, and
James is Helen's ....

And that's my sister, Kimberley. Jake's .... in
the woods. He's .... years old and very
....

Kimberley .... Jake's mom. So Jake is my ....

10 PRESENT CONTINUOUS VS. SIMPLE PRESENT

A Complete the conversation using the present continuous
or simple present. Then practice with a partner.

1. A: Do all of your relatives live in the United States?
   B: No, I ......have...... (have) relatives in Mexico. My grandparents and older sister
   .... (live) there.

2. A: What does your sister do? Does she have a job?
   B: No, she .... (work) right now. She .... (go) to school.

3. A: What is she studying?
   B: She .... (study) English literature. She .... (love) it.

4. A: What about your grandparents? Do they still work or are they retired?
   B: They .... (work) anymore, but they love to travel. Right now, they're
   .... (visit) China!

B CLASS ACTIVITY Write similar questions of your own. Then go
around the class and interview your classmates about their families.
Write some of your questions below.

1. Do your parents live in . . . ? ....
2. ....
3. ....
4. ....

6 I like to stay in shape.

☰ Preview

1 CULTURE

In North America, most people think regular exercise is important, although not everyone does it. People exercise outdoors, at home, or at a gym or health club. Many people play sports after school, after work, or on weekends. They also bicycle, walk, swim, or jog. People exercise for different reasons: to lose weight, to stay in shape, or just to relax.

Do you exercise or play sports?
What sports are popular in your country?
What percentage of people in your country do you think exercise regularly?

In the U.S. and Canada

Thirty-five percent of people exercise every day.

Eighteen percent of people play team sports regularly.

2 VOCABULARY *Sports and exercise*

A **PAIR WORK** Write the activities under the correct pictures.

| stretching | basketball | ✓jogging | soccer | weight lifting | volleyball |

1. jogging
2. ....
3. ....
4. ....
5. ....
6. ....

B Write the words from part A in the chart. Can you add two more words?

Individual activities		Team sports	
jogging	....	....	....
....	....	....	....

3 GUESS THE STORY

Watch the first 40 seconds of the video.
What do you think happens next?

- ☐ The man talks about his exercise routine.
- ☐ The woman talks about her exercise routine.
- ☐ The man and woman compare their exercise routines.

▤ Watch the video

4 GET THE PICTURE

Check (✓) **True** or **False**. Correct the false statements. Then compare with a partner.

	True	False	
1. Tim and Anne are friends.	☐	☐	....
2. Tim really likes to exercise.	☐	☐	....
3. Anne is more energetic and fit than Tim.	☐	☐	....

5 WATCH FOR DETAILS

A Check (✓) the activities Tim talks about doing.

B Circle the activities you think he *really* does. Then compare your responses with a partner.

☐ jogging

☐ stretching

☐ bicycling

☐ lifting weights

☐ swimming

☐ sit-ups

☐ taking walks

☐ playing tennis

☐ team sports

Unit 6 ▪ **23**

6 WHAT'S YOUR OPINION?

PAIR WORK What kind of person is Anne? What kind of person is Tim? Choose at least one word for each person.

Anne	Tim
....	....
....	....
....	....

friendly

intelligent

polite

lazy

≡ Follow-up

 ## 7 INTERVIEW

A Add three questions to the list about sports and exercise.

1. What kinds of sports do you play?
2. What kinds of exercise do you do?
3. Are you in good shape?

4. ....
5. ....
6. ....

B **PAIR WORK** Take turns asking and answering your questions. Your partner will answer playing the role of the woman or the man in the video.

8 HOW ABOUT YOU?

A Complete the chart. Then compare with a partner.

Things you sometimes do	Things you don't usually do
I sometimes . . . after school.	I don't usually . . . on the weekend.
....	....
....	....
Things you never do	**Things you would like to start doing**
I never go . . . in the morning.	I'd like to start . . .
....	....
....	....

B **CLASS ACTIVITY** Who in the class likes to exercise? Who doesn't? Make a class chart.

☰ Language close-up

9 WHAT DID THEY SAY?

Watch the video and complete the conversation. Then practice it.

Anne stops to tie her shoe and talks to Tim.

Tim: It's a ......beautiful...... morning, huh? ....
always come out here this early?

Anne: Yes, I .... I .... get up around
.... o'clock. What about you? Do you come
.... a lot?

Tim: Yeah, I do. I .... stay in shape.

Anne: You .... ?

Tim: Yes.

Anne: How often do you .... ?

Tim: .... day.

Anne: .... ?

Tim: Yeah, I usually .... my day with ....
stretches. Then, I .... do some .... ,
lift .... , and, when the weather's .... ,
my .... and I are never too far apart.

10 ADVERBS OF FREQUENCY

A Rewrite the sentences with the adverbs in the correct place.

1. I get up before 5 A.M. (never)
   I never get up before 5 A.M.

2. I don't have a big breakfast. (usually)
   ....

3. I play tennis after work. (sometimes)
   ....

4. I take a long walk on the weekend. (often)
   ....

5. I watch TV. (never)
   ....

6. I jog in the morning. (always)
   ....

B Imagine you are the man in the video. Change the frequency adverbs in the sentences where necessary. Compare with a partner.

C How often do you do these things? Use the phrases below or your own ideas. Then compare with a partner.

every evening	twice a week	very often
once a year	about three times a month	every day

1. go to sleep by 10 P.M.
   ....

2. work late
   ....

3. ride a bicycle
   ....

4. lift weights
   ....

7 My trip to London

1 CULTURE

Each year, 27 million people visit London, England. London is one of the most popular tourist destinations in the world. London is famous for its beautiful historic buildings, parks and gardens, museums, multinational restaurants, double-decker buses, and shops. London is also famous for rainy weather and fog. It rains more than 100 days a year.

Do you know anything else about London?
Would you like to visit London?
What cities in the world would you like to visit?

There are more than 5,500 restaurants in London!

2 VOCABULARY *Places in London*

PAIR WORK How much do you know about London? Write the captions under the correct pictures.

| a boat trip on the River Thames | Buckingham Palace | St. Paul's Cathedral |
| the Tower of London | ✓ the London Eye | Big Ben |

1

.... the London Eye ....

....

....

3 GUESS THE STORY

Watch the video with the sound off. Then look at the pictures in Exercise 2.
Number them in the order the woman talks about them.

Watch the video

4 GET THE PICTURE

In the video, Melissa mentions three more places she saw in London. Look at the
pictures and cross out the place that she did NOT see.

Westminster Bridge

Westminster Abbey

The British Museum

The Houses of Parliament

5 WATCH FOR DETAILS

A What did Melissa say about these places? Check (✓) the correct answers.
Then compare with a partner.

1. The London Eye
   - ☐ The views were great.
   - ☐ The ride was fun.

2. The boat trip on the River Thames
   - ☐ The weather was rainy.
   - ☐ It was interesting.

3. Buckingham Palace
   - ☐ She took a tour.
   - ☐ The queen wasn't there.

4. The guards at Buckingham Palace
   - ☐ The guards ignore tourists.
   - ☐ The guards like the tourists.

B What did Melissa do on Sunday? Number the statements in the correct order.

.... She saw Westminster Abbey.

.... She saw Big Ben and Parliament.

.... She went to the airport.

.... She walked around.

.... She walked across Westminster Bridge.

6 *A DAY IN LONDON*

A `GROUP WORK` Which London sights are most interesting to you?
Number them from 1 to 6 (1 = the most interesting).

St. Paul's Cathedral   The London Eye   The Tower of London

Westminster Bridge   A boat on the River Thames   Buckingham Palace

B `PAIR WORK` Tell another person why two of these places interest you.

7 *WHAT'S YOUR OPINION?*

A `PAIR WORK` What do you like to do when you visit a new city? Add three
more things to the list. Then number them from 1 to 8.

.... go sightseeing

.... eat at local restaurants

.... buy souvenirs

.... take photographs

.... go shopping

....

....

....

B `PAIR WORK` Now compare answers with another person. Have conversations like this:
A: Do you like to go shopping?
B: No, I don't. I prefer sightseeing.

☰ Language close-up

8 *WHAT DID THEY SAY?*

Watch the video and complete the conversation. Then practice it.

Melissa is telling Lili about her trip.

Lili: How was your ....*trip*......... to London? Did you have
.... free time between meetings?

Melissa: London was .... We were very ....
all week, but I had some .... on Saturday and
Sunday morning. I flew .... on Sunday evening.

Lili: Did you .... any pictures?

Melissa: Better than .... I have ....

Lili: Excellent!

Melissa: I did .... on Saturday. First, I ....
to the London Eye. Here it ....

Lili: Did you .... on .... ?

Melissa: Yes, I .... The .... were fantastic.
Then, I went .... a boat .... the
River Thames.

Lili: What was the weather .... ? Doesn't it rain a lot in
England?

Melissa: The weather was .... It didn't .... all the time.

9 *PAST TENSE* *Describing a trip*

A Fill in the blanks with the correct past tense of the verbs in parentheses.
Then practice the conversation.

Lili: Tell me about your trip to London.

Melissa: Well, I ......*did*...... (do) a lot of interesting things. I .... (go) on the London Eye and
I .... (take) a boat trip on the Thames.

Lili: What .... (do) you see on the boat trip?

Melissa: It .... (be) really interesting. I .... (see) Tower Bridge and the Tower of London.

Lili: .... (do) you go in the Tower of London?

Melissa: No, I .... (do / not) have time. But after the boat trip, I .... (go) to Buckingham Palace.

Lili: .... (be) the Queen there?

Melissa: No, she .... (be / not).

Lili: .... (do) you take a tour?

Melissa: No, I .... (do / not). But I .... (see) many other places!

B **PAIR WORK** Have similar conversations about a real or an imaginary trip of your own.
Start like this:

A: I went to . . .
B: Really! Tell me about your trip.

Nice neighborhood

Preview

1 CULTURE

People in North America move often. When they look for a new home, they consider many factors. People with children, for example, think about the quality of the local schools. Others consider the number of restaurants, shops, and supermarkets nearby, the availability of public transportation, and how quiet the neighborhood is. People can use real estate agents to help them find a new home, or they can look in the newspaper or online for available places to live. Most people walk around the neighborhood and talk to the neighbors before they make a decision.

For Rent
Call Adams Realty
913-555-3434

In your country, do people use real estate agents to help them find new homes?
Do they talk to the neighbors before deciding on an apartment or house in a new neighborhood?
What else do people think about before they decide on a new home?

2 VOCABULARY *Questions about neighborhoods*

PAIR WORK Write the correct question under each picture.

Is it noisy?
Are there places to eat nearby?

✓ Is there any crime?
  Is there shopping nearby?

Is there public transportation nearby?
Is there enough street parking?

1. Is there any crime?

2. ....

3. ....

4. ....

5. ....

6. ....

3 GUESS THE STORY

Watch the first minute of the video with the sound off.
Then answer the questions:

1. Who is the woman with the couple?
   - ☐ a friend
   - ☐ a real estate agent
   - ☐ a neighbor

2. What do you think the couple is going to do?
   - ☐ go back into the apartment building
   - ☐ go with the woman
   - ☐ look around the neighborhood

☰ Watch the video

4 GET THE PICTURE

A Look at your answers to Exercise 3. Did you guess correctly?

B Check (✓) **True** or **False**. Then correct the false statements. Compare with a partner.

	True	False	
1. The neighborhood is quiet and safe now.	☐	☐	....
2. The neighborhood is far from downtown.	☐	☐	....
3. There aren't many restaurants.	☐	☐	....
4. They like the neighborhood.	☐	☐	....

5 MAKING INFERENCES

Check (✓) the best answers. Compare with a partner.

1. Carmen likes the apartment ....
   - ☐ more than Luis likes it
   - ☐ as much as Luis likes it

2. .... is happy to find a good bookstore.
   - ☐ Carmen
   - ☐ Luis

3. Luis likes the neighborhood because of the ....
   - ☐ different types of restaurants
   - ☐ music store

4. Luis and Carmen decide to ....
   - ☐ keep looking at apartments
   - ☐ take the apartment

6 A GOOD NEIGHBORHOOD

GROUP WORK What do you look for in a neighborhood? Number these neighborhood features from 1 to 6 (1 = the most important).

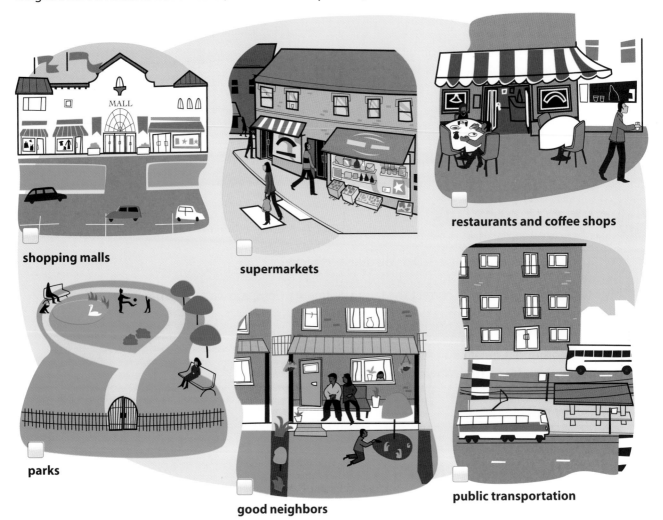

shopping malls

supermarkets

restaurants and coffee shops

parks

good neighbors

public transportation

7 WHAT'S YOUR OPINION?

A **PAIR WORK** List three more features of a good neighborhood.

1. ....

2. ....

3. ....

B Now think about your own neighborhood. Put a check (✓) beside the features in Exercises 6 and 7 that are true for your neighborhood. Then compare with a partner. Have conversations like this:

A: My neighborhood has a great grocery store. Does yours?
B: No, it doesn't. And the supermarket is far away. My neighborhood has . . .

8 *WHAT DID THEY SAY?*

Watch the video and complete the conversation. Then practice it.

Carmen and Luis explore the neighborhood.

Carmen: ....There's........ a furniture store.

Luis: Uh-huh. ....

Carmen: And .... a jewelry store.

My .... coming up . . .

Both: . . . . month.

Luis: Yeah, I ....

Carmen: .... , Luis. .... a really nice grocery store.

Luis: Yeah, that's a nice .... store.

Carmen: And .... are a lot of really good .... shops.

I .... like this neighborhood!

Luis: Yes, it's really .... Wow! .... an amazing guitar!

Carmen: So, ... we .... the apartment?

Luis: .... Why .... ? Let's go for it.

9 *QUANTIFIERS* *Describing a neighborhood*

A Fill in the blanks with **many** or **much**. Then practice the conversation.

A: Is there .... crime in this neighborhood?

B: Oh no. There isn't .... crime at all. Not anymore.

A: How about noise? How .... street noise is there?

B: Well, there aren't .... major roads in this neighborhood.

A: Are there .... students in the neighborhood?

B: Yes. It's very close to the university, so .... students live here.

A: I see. How .... parking spaces come with the apartment?

B: I'm afraid there aren't any parking spaces. You have to park on the street.

A: How about supermarkets? Is there .... shopping nearby?

B: Oh, yes. There's a big supermarket just down the street. And there

are .... other shops nearby, too.

A: OK. I'll have a look around and call you later. Thanks!

B **PAIR WORK** Practice the conversation again, but this time use neighborhood features of your own. Be sure to include sentences with the words *many* and *much*.

Suspicious visitors

1 *CULTURE*

To protect their homes against crime, people in North America sometimes do one or more of the following:

- keep their doors locked
- leave lights on when they go out
- have a "peephole" (or hole in the door) to see who's outside
- have an alarm system that makes noise if someone tries to open a door or window
- buy a dog to guard their home

Which types of neighborhoods have more crime in your country: suburbs, rural areas, or cities?

How do people protect their homes in your country?

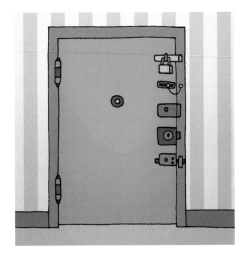

2 *VOCABULARY* *Physical appearance*

A **PAIR WORK** Write the words and phrases in the chart. (One word can go in two places.) Can you add two more words or phrases?

| average | blond | ✓early forties | late thirties | middle-aged | tall |
| bald | curly | elderly | long | short | teens |

Age	Height	Hair
early forties		

B List two words or phrases that describe the man and the woman.

The man	The woman
late forties	

3 GUESS THE STORY

Watch the first minute of the video with the sound off.
Answer the questions.

1. Who do you think is in the car?
2. Do you think the couple is expecting visitors?

☰ Watch the video

4 GET THE PICTURE

A Look at your answers to Exercise 3. Did you guess correctly?

B What really happens? Check (✓) your answer.
Then compare with a partner.

- ☐ Sarah is afraid of the police.
- ☐ The people in the car are escaped prisoners.
- ☐ The people outside are driving Sarah's car.
- ☐ The people outside are George's relatives.

5 WATCH FOR DETAILS

Put the pictures in order (1 to 6). Then write the correct sentence under each picture.
Compare with a partner.

George is calling the police.
Sarah and George are greeting their visitors.
Sarah is looking at the SUV.

✓ Sarah is writing, and George is pouring coffee.
The visitors are getting out of the SUV.
The visitors are standing outside their SUV.

....
....
....
....
....
....

Sarah is writing, and George is
pouring coffee.

....
....
....
....

6 DESCRIBING SOMEONE

A Circle the correct answers. Then compare with a partner.

1. Age	twenties	forties	twenties	forties
2. Hair color	light	dark	light	dark
3. Hair description	short	long	short	long
	straight	curly	straight	curly
4. Height	tall	short	tall	short
5. Other	baseball cap	no hat	baseball cap	no hat
	glasses	no glasses	glasses	no glasses

B What else can you add about Harry and Alexis? Compare your descriptions.

☰ Follow-up

7 THE RIGHT DECISION?

PAIR WORK Sarah and George decide to call the police. What do you think is the best thing to do in a situation like this?

☐ Call the police.
☐ Don't open the door, but ask, "Who is it?"
☐ Run and hide.
☐ other ....

8 WHAT HAPPENS NEXT?

A **GROUP WORK** What do you think happens when the police arrive? Write out the conversation between Sarah, George, Harry, Alexis, and the police. Start like this:

Officer: Is there a problem here?
George: Well, actually, . . .

B **CLASS ACTIVITY** Act out your conversation for the class.

☰ Language close-up

9 WHAT DID THEY SAY?

Watch the video and complete the conversation. Then practice it.

Sarah describes the visitors to George.

George: Sarah, would you ...._like_....... another cup of .... ?

Sarah: .... thanks. . . . Honey, ...
we know .... who has an SUV?

George: An SUV? The Thompsons .... an
SUV. A .... one.

Sarah: This .... not green.

George: .... not? What .... is it?

Sarah: I .... tell. It's red, or brown. It's ....

George: .... is it?

Sarah: It's parked in front of the ....
And .... are two .... inside.

George: .... ?

Sarah: Uh-huh. .... now they're getting out of it.

George: .... do they .... like?

Sarah: One man's .... , and he's got ....
hair, and he's .... sunglasses.

George: And .... about the .... one?

10 MODIFIERS WITH PARTICIPLES AND PREPOSITIONS

A Look at the picture. Match the information in columns A, B, and C.

A	B	C
Sarah	is the heavier man	wearing an open jacket.
George	is the young one	wearing a red sweater.
Harry	is the older woman	wearing a blue shirt.
Alexis	is the tall one	wearing a baseball cap.

B **PAIR WORK** What else do you remember about the people in the video?
Write sentences of your own.

1. ....   3. ....

2. ....   4. ....

11 DESCRIBING SOMEONE

A **PAIR WORK** Take turns asking and
answering questions about a classmate.
Try to guess who the person is.

A: Is it a tall person with curly hair?
B: No, the person is short and has . . .

B Write five sentences describing your classmates. Two of your
sentences should be false. Then read your sentences. Your partner
should say "True" or "False" and correct the false sentences.

A: Steve's the tall guy wearing a blue shirt.
B: False. He's wearing a white shirt.

10 What took you so long?

Preview

1 CULTURE

In North America, people usually like others to be on time, but for some occasions it's OK to be a little late. For example, people should always arrive on time or a little early for a business appointment, work, or a class. However, when they meet a friend or when someone invites them to dinner, it's OK to arrive 5 to 10 minutes late. For an informal party, it's OK to arrive 15 to 30 minutes late.

Are people usually on time for appointments, work, or a class in your country?

Is it OK to arrive late when you meet a friend for dinner or go to an informal party?

When are some other times when it is OK to arrive a little late? How late is too late?

2 VOCABULARY *Past tense of verbs*

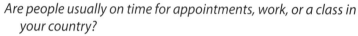

PAIR WORK Complete the chart with the past tense of these verbs.

Present	Past	Present	Past
call	called	lock	....
cost	cost	open	....
do	....	pay	....
find	....	put	....
get	....	remember	....
go	....	see	....
have	....	take	....
leave	....	try	....

3 GUESS THE STORY

Watch the first 30 seconds of the video with the sound off.
What do you think happened? Check (✓) your answer.

☐ The woman arrived very early.
☐ The man arrived very late.

Watch the video

4 GET THE PICTURE

What really happened? Check (✓) the correct answers. Then compare with a partner.

1. What was the problem with Jacob's car?
   - ☐ It didn't start.
   - ☐ He locked his keys in it.
   - ☐ It was the wrong car.

2. What was the problem with Jacob's wallet?
   - ☐ He left it in the car.
   - ☐ He lost it.
   - ☐ He had no money in it.

3. What did Jacob forget?
   - ☐ He forgot his cell phone.
   - ☐ He forgot to bring his neighbor.
   - ☐ He forgot where he parked.

5 WATCH FOR DETAILS

A Put the pictures in order (1 to 6). Then write the correct sentence under each picture. Compare with a partner.

✓Jacob noticed that his neighbor needed help.
Jacob paid the locksmith.
Jacob realized he didn't have his wallet.

Jacob saw his keys inside the car.
Jacob told Linda the story.
Jacob tried to call Linda.

....

....

Jacob noticed that his neighbor
needed help.

....

....

B PAIR WORK What else happened in the video? Can you add two things?

1. ....

2. ....

6 WHAT'S YOUR OPINION?

PAIR WORK Complete the chart. Check (✓) the words that describe Jacob and Linda.

	Forgetful	Upset	Helpful	Embarrassed	Understanding	Worried
Jacob	☐	☐	☐	☐	☐	☐
Linda	☐	☐	☐	☐	☐	☐

☰ Follow-up

7 QUESTION GAME

A Write three more questions about the story. Use the past tense and *how, why, how much, who,* or *where*.

1. Why did Jacob get out of his car?
2. When did Jacob lock his keys in the car?
3. ....
4. ....
5. ....

B **PAIR WORK** Answer your partner's questions. If you don't think the answer was in the video, say, "It didn't say."

8 TELL THE STORY

PAIR WORK Write out the story using *first, after that, next, then,* and *finally*. Include one mistake. Then read your story to another pair. Can they find the mistake?

First, Jacob was late, so he ran to his car. ....

....

....

....

....

....

....

....

....

....

☰ Language close-up

9 *WHAT DID THEY SAY?*

Watch the video and complete the conversation. Then practice it.

Jacob has just arrived at the restaurant.

Jacob: Linda, I'm really ....sorry........... .

Linda: It's ...., Jacob. I've only .... here
for a little .... Is .... all right?

Jacob: Yes, it is .... , but you won't ....
what just happened to me.

Linda: .... happened?

Jacob: Well, ... of all, I was .... leaving
my apartment, so I had to .... Then, just
.... I got in my car, I .... my
neighbor, Mrs. Flanagan. She had a heavy trash
.... , and she couldn't move it very easily.
So, I .... her.

Linda: That was .... of you.

Jacob: Yeah, but, ... after, there was a problem.
.... I went back to my .... ,
I couldn't get ....

Linda: Did you lock your .... in the car?

Jacob: .... you believe it?

Linda: Oh, no. What happened .... ?

Jacob: First, I .... to call you, but I got your
voicemail. Then, I called a locksmith.

10 *PRESENT PERFECT*

A **PAIR WORK** Write questions using **Have you ever...?** and the correct
forms of the verbs in parentheses. Can you add three questions to the list?

1. *Have you ever locked* .... (lock) your keys in the car?
2. .... (call) a locksmith?
3. .... (leave) your wallet in the car?
4. .... (arrive) late for an important appointment?
5. .... (go) to a restaurant without money?
6. .... (wait) a long time for someone in a restaurant?
7. ....
8. ....
9. ....

B **CLASS ACTIVITY** Go around the class and interview at least three classmates.
Try to find out who answered "yes" to the most questions.

11 San Francisco!

Preview

1 CULTURE

San Francisco attracts more than sixteen million visitors a year. There are many things to do in the city, from shopping at Fisherman's Wharf to walking over the Golden Gate Bridge. While visitors come all year, the summer is the most popular time. It never gets extremely cold or hot in San Francisco, but it can be fairly cool much of the time.

Have you heard of any other interesting places to visit in or around San Francisco?
What is one of the most interesting cities to visit in your country?
What do tourists do there?

2 VOCABULARY *Taking a trip*

PAIR WORK Match the pictures with the words in the glossary below.

1. architectural details

2. ....

3. ....

4. ....

5. ....

6. ....

aquarium a museum for fish and other animals and plants that live under or near water
✓**architectural details** the things that make buildings special
bay an area of water that is partly enclosed by land, but is open to the sea

cable car a type of public transportation that is pulled by a moving cable under a track on the street
monuments buildings or structures built to remember an important person or event in history
wharf a structure that is built on the water for boats, fishing, business, or tourism

3 GUESS THE STORY

Watch the video with the sound off. What do you think Dr. Smith is most interested in seeing?

1. Alamo Square
2. Golden Gate Bridge
3. Japanese Tea Garden

Watch the video

4 GET THE PICTURE

What places does the hotel clerk tell Dr. and Mrs. Smith about? Circle them.
Then compare with a partner.

Alamo Square	Fisherman's Wharf	Japanese Tea Garden
Alcatraz	Ghirardelli Square	Lombard Street
Coit Tower	Golden Gate Park	Muir Woods

5 WATCH FOR DETAILS

Why does the clerk say the Smiths should go to the places below? Complete the sentences.
Then compare with a partner.

1. You should visit Fisherman's ....
You can find a little bit of .... there.

2. Alamo Square is a small .... surrounded by really wonderful ....
We call them Painted ....

3. Lombard Street is a very steep ....
with a lot of ....

4. The most .... way to drive to San Francisco is across the .... Bridge.

6 COMPLETE THE STORY

Complete the paragraph below. Choose words from the list.
Then compare with a partner.

Alamo Square	Fisherman's Wharf	Lombard Street
Alcatraz Island	Golden Gate Bridge	✓ Northern California
boat ride	Golden Gate Park	Painted Ladies
cable car	Highway 101	Tea Garden

The Smiths arrived in San Francisco from ..Northern California.. . They entered the city by driving over the .... They decided to start their visit with a ride on a .... Next, they took a boat ride to .... Then, they walked through .... and saw the Japanese .... After that, they went to .... to do some shopping. The next day, they drove down curvy .... very slowly, and then they went to .... to see the colorful Victorian Houses.

Follow-up

7 SAN FRANCISCO

GROUP WORK Imagine you have two days in San Francisco. Plan your itinerary.
You can use these tourist attractions and any other places from this unit.

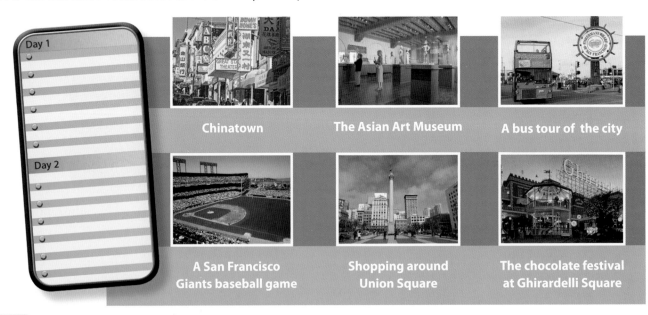

Chinatown

The Asian Art Museum

A bus tour of the city

A San Francisco
Giants baseball game

Shopping around
Union Square

The chocolate festival
at Ghirardelli Square

8 YOUR CITY

A **GROUP WORK** Now, imagine the Smiths are visiting your city. Plan their itinerary. Give at least six suggestions, like this:

A: First, I think they should go to . . .
B: Yes, and they should also visit the . . .

B **CLASS ACTIVITY** Share your information with the class.

≣ Language close-up

9 WHAT DID THEY SAY?

Watch the video and complete the conversation. Then practice it.

The Smiths are checking out of their Northern California hotel.

Clerk: Thank you. ....Here........... is your card and a copy of
the ....

Mrs. Smith: ....

Clerk: .... you enjoy your stay with .... ?

Dr. Smith: Yeah, it was .... , thank you.

Clerk: .... are you traveling to .... ?

Dr. Smith: We're heading .... , to San Francisco.

Clerk: San Francisco is .... !

Mrs. Smith: We're going to .... there for just a couple of
....

Clerk: .... you .... there before?

Dr. Smith: Well, I've been .... once, when I was a
.... , but Mona, she's .... been there.

Clerk: What are you .... to do .... you're there?

Mrs. Smith: No plans. We just want to .... I want to see all the ....

10 SHOULD AND SHOULDN'T *Giving advice*

A Complete these sentences with **should** or **shouldn't**. Then compare with a partner.

1. When you visit a foreign country, you ....should.... learn
a few words of the local language.

2. You .... find out about the weather before you travel.

3. To be safe, you .... carry a lot of cash when you travel.

4. You .... do some research on interesting places to visit.

5. You .... be afraid to ask local people questions.

B **PAIR WORK** Give advice for things visitors to your city should or
shouldn't do. Write three suggestions in each column.

They should . . .	They shouldn't . . .
1.	1. ....
2.	2. ....
3.	3. ....

12 Onion soup and chocolate

☰ Preview

1 CULTURE

In North America, people spend more on health care than in other parts of the world. In drugstores and health-food stores, people can buy over-the-counter medicines for colds, coughs, and sore throats, as well as vitamins and other supplements. Home remedies for common illnesses, such as colds and sore throats, are also popular.

What types of medicines are available over the counter for colds and sore throats in your country?

Do people usually take medicine or use home remedies when they have a cold?

2 VOCABULARY Cold remedies

PAIR WORK Write the remedies in the chart. Can you add two more to each category?

aspirin

chicken soup

steam

onions and garlic

cough medicine and sore throat lozenges

tea with lemon and honey

Home remedies		Over-the-counter drugs	
chicken soup			

3 GUESS THE STORY

Watch the video with the sound off.
What remedies in Exercise 2 does the host try?

☰ Watch the video

4 GET THE PICTURE

Answer the questions with the correct person's name. Then compare with a partner.

The host

Henry

Anna

Roberto

Kathleen

1. Who hates colds? ....

2. Who never gets a cold? ....

3. Who has a cold right now? ....

4. Who just caught a cold? ....

5 WATCH FOR DETAILS

Match the person with the remedy he or she suggests. Then compare with a partner.

.... Henry   A. Rest.

.... Anna   B. Drink hot lemon and honey, and rest.

.... Kathleen   C. Take vitamin C and drink coffee.

.... Roberto   D. Eat onion soup and chocolate, and keep warm.

6 WHAT'S YOUR OPINION?

PAIR WORK Answer these questions.

1. Which of the remedies have you tried?
2. Which of the remedies do you think works best?
3. Are there any remedies from the video that you will try in the future?
   If so, which ones?
4. What other home or drugstore remedies for a cold do you know about?
   Do you use them?

☰ Follow-up

7 HEALTH PROBLEMS

A **GROUP WORK** What do you do for these problems? Add two more remedies for each one. Then compare around the class. Who has the best remedies?

1. a backache

It's a good idea to lie
on the floor. Also, get
some . . .
....
....
....
....

2. a headache

Take some aspirin. It's
also helpful to . . .
....
....
....
....
....

3. a stomachache

You should eat some
yogurt. Also, try
some . . .
....
....
....
....

4. the flu

You should stay home
from school or work. It's
also important to . . .
....
....
....
....

B **PAIR WORK** Take turns role-playing a person with one of the problems in part A and a friend giving advice.

A: Hi, ... How are you?
B: I'm not doing too well. I have . . .
A: That's terrible! Listen. I've got the perfect remedy . . .

C Do you need advice for a problem of your own? Have a similar conversation, using personal information and asking for someone else's home remedies.

8 WHAT DID THEY SAY?

Watch the video and complete the conversation. Then practice it.

The host is interviewing Kathleen about what to do for a cold.

Host: What should you do .... *when* .... you get a cold?

Kathleen: Oh, I .... get a cold.

Host: .... ?

Kathleen: Yes, ... when I feel a cold coming
.... , I know it's .... to eat lots of
homemade .... soup.

Host: ....

Kathleen: Oh, and it's a good idea to eat .... of
.... , too!

Host: At the .... as the onion soup?

Kathleen: No, ... The onion soup ....
you vitamins, and the chocolate gives you ....
That .... the cold virus. Oh, uh, it's a good
.... to keep very .... , too. It's not
a good idea to hang around on the street.

Host: OK. ....

Kathleen: Bye!

9 REQUESTS AND SUGGESTIONS

A Complete the conversations with **may** or **could** to make requests and **should**, **try**, or
suggest to give suggestions. Then compare with a partner.

1. *At work*

A: Here's the perfect cold remedy: garlic juice, onions,
and carrots. You ...*should*.... drink a cup every two hours.

B: But I don't like carrots.

A: Well, then I .... an old-fashioned bowl of chicken
soup! And .... to get some rest, too.

2. *At a drugstore*

A: .... I help you?

B: Yes. .... I have something for a cold? It's a bad one.

A: Yes. I have these pills. They're a little strong. Just don't drive
after you take them.

B: Hmm. I drive to work. .... I have something else?

A: Well, ... these other pills then. They won't
make you sleepy.

B (PAIR WORK) Act out the conversations. First, act them out as written. Then, change the
problems and the remedies.

How about a pizza?

≣ Preview

1 CULTURE

Most U.S. and Canadian cities have restaurants that serve food from many different countries and cultures. Chinese, Italian, and Mexican restaurants have been very popular in North America for a long time, but now there are also Japanese, Thai, and Indian restaurants in most cities and small towns. Many people like to order food from restaurants for delivery to their homes. Chinese food and pizza are common home-delivery types of food.

What types of foreign food are available in your town?
Which ones are the most popular with you and your friends and family?

2 VOCABULARY *Food*

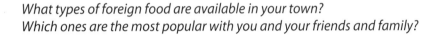

PAIR WORK Here are some foods from several different cultures. Where can you find these foods? Write the foods under the pictures.

egg rolls	prawns in coconut milk	tacos
✓pizza	sushi	vegetable curry

1. ....pizza.................

2. ....

3. ....

4. ....

5. ....

6. ....

3 GUESS THE STORY

Watch the first minute of the video with the sound off. Which type of restaurant do you think they choose?

☰ Watch the video

4 GET THE PICTURE

A Put the restaurants in the order that Carmen and Luis see them (1–4). Then compare with a partner.

B **PAIR WORK** Which two types of food do Carmen and Luis say they *don't* want?

5 WATCH FOR DETAILS

A Complete the names of the foods in the video with words from the list. Then circle the items Carmen and Luis order. Compare with a partner.

coconut milk	ginger	smoothie
✓ curry	pizza	tea

1. Seafood or green ....curry...........

2. Prawns in ....

3. Chicken with ....

4. Thai ....

5. Ginger and honey ....

6. Jasmine ....

B What items do both Carmen and Luis say they like?

....

6 *HOW ABOUT YOU?*

GROUP WORK   Answer these questions.

1. How often do you eat in restaurants?
2. What's your favorite kind of restaurant?
3. What do you usually order?
4. When is the last time you ate something for the first time? Describe it. Did you like it?
5. Which of the foods and drinks from the video have you tried or would you like to try?

7 IN A RESTAURANT

GROUP WORK   Role-play ordering lunch at one of the restaurants in the video. Two students order, while the third student plays the waiter or waitress. Then switch roles until each student has been the waiter or waitress. Use this model:

A: Do you have any questions about the menu?
B: . . .
A: Oh, that's very good. It's one of the most popular dishes.
    Are you ready to order?
C: . . .
A: OK. What would you like?
B: . . .
C: . . .
A: What do you want to drink?
B: . . .
C: . . .
A: OK. I'll be right back with your food
    and your drinks.

☰ Language close-up

8 WHAT DID THEY SAY?

Watch the video and complete the conversation. Then practice it.

Carmen and Luis are trying to decide what to eat.

Luis: You know, I'm beginning to ......feel...... hungry.

Carmen: .... am I. I really could eat ....

Luis: .... pizza?

Carmen: Hmm. I'm not .... I'm not really in the

.... for a pizza.

Luis: You know, ... am I.

Carmen: OK. Let's .... for something ....

But I want to eat. .... !

Luis: No .... I do, too.

Carmen: I .... Japanese food a ....

Luis: .... do I, but . . .

Carmen: We .... get some sushi.

Luis: Yeah, I'm just not .... that's ....

I want.

Carmen: But Luis, I'm ....

9 WOULD AND WILL *Ordering food*

A Rewrite these questions using **Would you like . . . ?**
Then compare with a partner.

1. What do you want to eat?

   <u>What would you like to eat?</u> ....

2. Do you want salad or soup with that?

   ....

3. Do you want something to drink?

   ....

4. What do you want for dessert?

   ....

B **PAIR WORK** Now answer the questions with **I'll have . . .**
A: What would you like to eat?
B: I'll have . . .

Around the World

Preview

1 CULTURE

In North America, game shows are one of the most popular types of TV programs. There are several different game shows on at various times of the day. In most game shows, players test their knowledge on different subjects. Sometimes the questions are quite easy, and sometimes they are very difficult. But other game shows are games of chance. The winner must be lucky, but doesn't have to know a lot of facts.

What are some game shows on TV in your country?
Which ones are the most popular?
Which ones do you like to watch?

2 GUESS THE FACTS

PAIR WORK How is your knowledge of geography? Check (✓) the correct answers.

1. Which is longer?
   - ☐ the Nile River
   - ☐ the Amazon River

2. Which is higher?
   - ☐ Mt. McKinley
   - ☐ Mt. Kilimanjaro

3. What's the largest desert in Asia?
   - ☐ the Great Indian Desert
   - ☐ the Gobi Desert

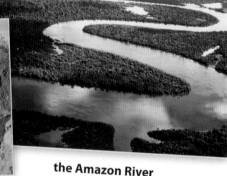

the Amazon River

the Nile River

Mt. McKinley

Mt. Kilimanjaro

4. Which is the largest city in North America?
    Los Angeles
    Mexico City

5. Which country is called the "island continent"?
    Antarctica
    Australia

Los Angeles

Mexico City

3 GUESS THE STORY

Watch the first minute of the video. Which contestant do you think is going to win?

Watch the video

4 CHECK THE FACTS

Correct your answers to Exercise 2. Did you guess correctly? Compare with a partner.

5 WATCH FOR DETAILS

Check (✓) the correct answers. Then compare with a partner.

1. Marlene is from
   ☐ Seattle, Washington.
   ☐ Washington, D.C.

2. Marlene is a
   ☐ computer programmer.
   ☐ computer engineer.

3. Ted is from
   ☐ Cambridge, Massachusetts.
   ☐ Boston, Massachusetts.

4. Ted is a
   ☐ high school teacher.
   ☐ college teacher.

5. Lili is from
   ☐ Vero Beach, Florida.
   ☐ Miami Beach, Florida.

6. Lili is a
   ☐ café owner.
   ☐ chef.

6 WHO WINS THE GAME?

A What is each person's score at the end of the game? Write the number.
Then compare with a partner.

Marlene ....   Ted ....   Lili ....

B Is the winner happy with the prize? Why or why not?

Follow-up

7 AROUND THE WORLD

A GROUP WORK Write three questions in each category for the game
"Around the World." Give one question 25 points, one question 50 points,
and one question 75 points. (You can also add categories of your own.)

Mountains	Islands
....	....
....	....
....	....
Rivers	**Cities**
....	....
....	....
....	....

B CLASS ACTIVITY Now play "Around the World." Half the class
is in Group A. The other half is in Group B.

Group A: Choose one student to be the host.

Group B: Take turns choosing a category for 25, 50, or 75 points.
Then answer the host's questions. Play for five minutes.

Begin your conversation like this:

A: Are you ready?
B: Yes, I'll try (*name of category*) for 25 points.
A: OK. (*Asks question.*)
B: (*Answers question.*)
A: That's right! **or** Sorry, that's not correct.

Now change roles. Group B should choose a host and Group A
should answer the questions. Play for five more minutes.
Which group wins the game?

☰ Language close-up

8 WHAT DID HE SAY?

Watch the video and complete the host's comments. Then practice it.

The host introduces the contestants.

Hi, ...again........ , folks. And .... back to the Final Round of our

show. I'm your host, Richard Darien, and .... are our contestants:

A computer .... from Seattle, Washington: Marlene Miller!

Marlene has .... points.

And next to you we have a high school .... from Boston,

Massachusetts: Ted Simmons! Ted currently has .... points,

and he is .... the .... !

And our .... contestant is a café .... from Vero Beach,

Florida: Lili Chen! Lili has .... points, so she's currently .... with Marlene.

Oh boy, this is going to be an .... game, ... get on to the Final

Round. Our .... are Cities, Deserts, ... , Mountains, and ....

9 COMPARISONS WITH ADJECTIVES

A Write questions using the comparative or superlative form of each
adjective in parentheses. Then add three questions of your own.

1. city: New York – Tokyo? (cold)
   <u>Which city is colder, New York or Tokyo?</u>

2. planet: Earth – Saturn – Mars? (big)
   ....

3. structure: the Eiffel Tower – the Statue of Liberty? (tall)
   ....

4. building: the Houses of Parliament – the Empire
   State Building? (old)
   ....
   ....

5. country: Brazil – Canada – Argentina? (large)
   ....

6. ....
7. ....
8. ....

B PAIR WORK Take turns asking and answering the questions.
Who answered the most questions correctly?

15 String cheese

 1 CULTURE

Many people in the United States and Canada celebrate their birthdays with a party. These parties can be dinner parties, dance parties, or just parties where people have snacks and chat with one another. Typical snacks at parties include chips and dip, cheese and crackers, nuts, cookies, and other snacks that people eat with their fingers.

Are birthday parties common for adults as well as for children in your country?
What kinds of foods do you often have at birthday parties?

 2 VOCABULARY *Asking for favors*

Match the requests for favors with the responses.

.... 1. May I ask you for a favor?

.... 2. Could you please pick me up on your way to the party?

.... 3. Could you bring some soda to the party?

.... 4. Would you ask Claire to call me when she gets home?

.... 5. Would you please call me when your class is finished?

a. Sorry, but I won't be able to. I'm riding with someone else.

b. Sure. That should be about 9:30.

c. No problem. I'll leave her a message.

d. Sure. What is it?

e. I'd be happy to. How many bottles should I get?

3 GUESS THE STORY

Watch the first 30 seconds of the video with the sound off.
Answer the questions.

1. What is Mariela doing?
2. Why do you think Mariela is upset?
3. What do you think Olivia does to help her?

 Watch the video

4 CHECK YOUR GUESSES

Now check your answers to the questions in Exercise 3. Did you guess correctly? Compare with a partner.

5 WATCH FOR DETAILS

Answer the questions with a number. Then compare with a partner.

How many . . .

1. people does Olivia call? ....

2. messages does Olivia leave? ....

3. people does Olivia talk to on the phone? ....

4. people does Olivia ask to bring cheese to the party? ....

5. people bring cheese to the party? ....

6 MAKING INFERENCES

Check (✓) the best answers. Then complete the last item
with your opinion. Check with a partner.

1. .... cheese is necessary for the party.
   - ☐ Both Mariela and Olivia think
   - ☐ Only Mariela thinks
   - ☐ Only Olivia thinks

2. Olivia asks everyone to get different kinds of cheese
   because ....
   - ☐ she can't remember the kinds Mariela mentioned
   - ☐ she wants everyone to buy different kinds of cheese
   - ☐ Todd likes all kinds of cheese

3. In the end, there is probably .... cheese at the party.
   - ☐ too much
   - ☐ the right amount of
   - ☐ not enough

4. Melanie gives Todd a ball of string because ....

☰ Follow-up

7 HAVING A PARTY

A **GROUP WORK** Use this chart to plan a party. Then make invitations for your party.

Choose an occasion.	Choose a location and time.
....	....
....	....
Choose things to do at the party.	**Choose the foods and drinks you want at the party.**
....	....
....	....

B **CLASS ACTIVITY** Walk around the class inviting students to
your party. Show them your invitation.

Begin your conversations like this:

A: Hi, would you like to come to my party? It's (*say a date and time*).
B: Thanks. I'd love to. What's the occasion?
A: It's for (*give a reason for the party*).
B: That sounds fun. Can I bring anything?
A: Thanks for offering. You could bring (*suggest something*).
B: OK. See you then.
A: Bye.

Language close-up

8 *WHAT DID THEY SAY?*

Watch the video and complete the conversation. Then practice it.

Olivia is asking Carlos for a favor.

Olivia: Hi, Carlos? ....It's............ Olivia. How are you?

Carlos: Olivia, hi. I'm .... , thanks. ....
seeing you at Todd's .... party, ... ?

Olivia: Yeah, that's right. .... , Carlos, could you
.... some cheese to the party?

Carlos: Cheese?

Olivia: Todd really .... cheese, and Mariela didn't get
.... , and now she's in a panic .... it.

Carlos: Yeah, sure. What .... of cheese?

Olivia: Camembert, I .... , or Roquefort, and some
Gorgonzola. Oh, and some .... cheese.

Carlos: OK, Olivia. .... do it. Don't ....

Olivia: Thanks, Carlos. It's so .... of you
to .... us.

9 *REQUESTING A FAVOR*

PAIR WORK Practice the conversation in Exercise 8 again. This time make a request
for something different. Then switch roles and ask for other things. Choose from the
list below or use your own ideas.

Things for the party:

1. different types of music
2. different types of drinks
3. different types of decorations
4. different types of desserts
5. different types of snack food

16 Life changes

☰ Preview

1 CULTURE

> After high school, many students in the United States and Canada don't go straight to college. They get a job or take time off to travel before continuing their education. Most students are not sure what they want to do with their lives just after high school. Their goals and plans become clearer as they gain more life experience.

What were your goals and plans when you were younger?
How have they changed over the years?

2 VOCABULARY *Career goals*

A Here are some people's dreams for their future. What does each person hope to do or be? Write the sentences under the pictures.

   I'm going to be a chef.   I'd like to be a reporter.
   I'd really love to perform on Broadway.   I plan to practice law.
✓ I hope to have a family.   I hope to be a teacher.

1. I hope to have a family.   2. ....   3. ....

4. ....   5. ....   6. ....

B **CLASS ACTIVITY** Walk around the room talking to people. Use these expressions to talk about what you hope to do or be.

Begin your conversation like this:

A: I'd love to be a (*occupation*). How about you?
B: I plan to (*work verb*).

3 GUESS THE STORY

Watch the video with the sound off. What do you think each person does for a living?

1. Reza is a / an ....
2. Kim is a / an ....
3. Robert is a / an ....

Reza

Kim

Robert

☰ Watch the video

4 CHECK YOUR GUESSES

A Check your answers to Exercise 3. Did you guess correctly? Compare with a partner.

B Check (✓) the level of education each person finished.

	High School	College	Graduate School
1. Reza	☐	☐	☐
2. Kim	☐	☐	☐
3. Robert	☐	☐	☐

5 WATCH FOR DETAILS

Check (✓) **True** or **False**. Correct the false statements. Then compare with a partner.

	True	False	
1. Reza worked in politics before going to law school.	☐	☐	....
2. Reza is married and has children.	☐	☐	....
3. Kim always hoped to be a reporter.	☐	☐	....
4. Kim was interested in writing about theater.	☐	☐	....
5. Kim works for a large newspaper.	☐	☐	....
6. Robert didn't go to college.	☐	☐	....
7. Robert teaches and performs comedy.	☐	☐	....
8. Robert would love to own a comedy club.	☐	☐	....

6 A JOB QUIZ

A Check (✓) five things you like to do or you are good at.

What do you like to do?

.... work with people
.... work alone
.... build or create things
.... fix things
.... help people
.... listen to people

.... talk to people
.... solve problems
.... work with my hands
.... work with my mind
.... work inside
.... work outside

.... work with numbers
.... with ideas
.... work with children
.... work with animals
.... my idea:
....

B CLASS ACTIVITY Walk around the room and find another student who checked at least three of the same things as you did. Sit down with the student or students and make a list of jobs that might be good for these categories.

1. ....

2. ....

3. ....

7 CAREER AND LIFE ADVICE

PAIR WORK Take turns being a career or life coach for each other. What advice would you give? Use the information in Exercise 6 and phrases in the box. You can begin your conversations like this:

A: I'd love to work with children.
B: What else do you like to do?
A: I like . . .
B: And what are you good at?
A: I'm good at . . .
B: Well, I think you should . . .

> You could . . .
> You should . . .
> It would be a good idea/useful for you to . . .

8 WHAT DID HE SAY?

Watch the video and complete the description.

Reza is talking about his life before and after law school.

In ....college........ , I was a political science major. And ....
college, I went to Washington, D.C., to .... in ....
I worked on Capitol Hill for .... two years, which is ....
the government is, and it's also the .... of the ....

.... in government, I .... more about the law.
And I .... to get more .... in the law. I decided
I wanted to come .... and go to law school ....
Boston. When I .... , I had a job .... for me, and I started
work right away at the ....

The .... level now is a lot .... than when I was
in .... school. In law school, you're stressing ....
your academics, but when you're .... law, as a lawyer, you're
.... about doing the best job you .... on those projects
you're working on for .... clients.

9 TELLING YOUR STORY

A Choose verbs from the box to complete the story.
Then compare with a partner.

bought	had	registered
✓ finished	knew	save
found	looked for	started
got	moved back	wanted

1. When I ....finished....... high school, I didn't know what I
   .... to do.
2. I .... I wanted to improve my English, so I went online
   and .... an English school in an English-speaking country.
3. I .... a great school in London, England.
4. To .... money, I .... a job and
   .... home with my parents.
5. After six months, I .... enough money.
6. I .... a plane ticket, and I .... at the school.
   I .... taking classes the day after I arrived.

B Change the sentences in part A so they tell your story. Then tell your
story to another student.

interchange
FOURTH EDITION

Jack C. Richards
With Jonathan Hull and Susan Proctor
Series Editor: David Bohlke

CAMBRIDGE
UNIVERSITY PRESS

WORKBOOK **1**

Contents

Credits

Illustrations

Andrezzinho: 42; **Illias Arahovitis**: 13 (*bottom*); **Rob De Bank**: 48;
Carlos Diaz: 1; **Jada Fitch**: 2, 21; **Tim Foley**: 52 (*top*); **Travis Foster**: 16, 70;
Dylan Gibson: 3; **Chuck Gonzales**: 49, 90; **Jim Haynes**: 9, 72;
Dan Hubig: 13 (top); **Randy Jones**: 36, 46, 47, 51, 66, 78; **Trevor Keen**: 55;
Jim Kelly: 16 (*bottom right*)

Kja-artists: 53; **Greg Lawhun**: 15, 52 (*bottom*); **Karen Minot**: 10, 29,
64, 82; **Rob Schuster**: 12, 22, 40, 58, 88; **Ben Shannon**: 35, 50;
Daniel Vasconcellos: 11, 14, 25, 91, 92; **Sam Viviano**: 69;
James Yamasaki: 5, 54; **Rose Zgodzinski**: 28, 63, 75, 85, 87;
Carol Zuber-Mallison: 4, 19, 34, 65, 69, 89

Photos

4 (*clockwise from top left*) (*Marlo*) © Brand X Pictures/Thinkstock; (*Su-yin*)
© iStockphoto/Thinkstock; (*Ahmed*) © Photos.com/Thinkstock; (*Charlotte*)
© Westend61/The Agency Collection/Getty Images
6 © Reggie Casagrande/Photographer's Choice/Getty Images
7 (*middle left*) © Stefanie Grewel/Cultura/Age Fotostock; (*middle
right*) © Hemera/Thinkstock; (*bottom left*) © Michael Melford/National
Geographic/Getty Images; (*bottom right*) © Jeff Greenberg/Alamy
8 (*clockwise from top left*) © Sculpies/Shutterstock; © Exactostock/
SuperStock; © Stockbyte/Getty Images; © John Lund/Marc Romanelli/
Blend Images/Getty Images; © Radius Images/Alamy
10 (*top left*) © Asia Images Group/Getty Images; (*top right*) © Images-
USA/Alamy; (*bottom right*) © Larry Gatz/The Image Bank/Getty Images
12 © Syracuse Newspapers/M. Klicker/The Image Works
17 (*all*) (*black sunglass, leather cap*) © Hemera/Thinkstock; (*wool cap,
laptop*) © iStockphoto/Thinkstock; (*shoes*) © Daniel Diebel/Getty Images;
(*silver necklace*) © PhotoObjects.net/Thinkstock; (*gold necklace*)
© Eye-Stock/Alamy; (*desktop computer*) © Photodisc/Thinkstock; (*sandals*)
© Oksana Shufrich/iStockphoto; (*white sunglass*) © Ruslan MediaGFX/
Alamy
18 (*clockwise from top left*) © Hemera/Thinkstock; © Clover/SuperStock;
© Sam Dao/Alamy; © Art Stock Photos/Alamy
19 (*middle right*) © AP Photo/Mark Duncan; (*bottom right*) © Marilyn
Kingwill/ArenaPAL/Topham/The Image Works
20 (*top left*) © Bryan Bedder/Getty Images; (*top right*) © AP Photo/Frank
Micelotta; (*middle left*) © Photos 12/Alamy; (*middle right*) © AP Photo/
Armando Franca; (*bottom right*) © AP Photo/Wade Payne
23 (*top right*) © Clinton Gilders/FilmMagic/Getty Images; (*bottom right*)
© Jose Luis Pelaez Inc/Blend Images/Getty Images
24 (*top right*) © AP Photo/Chris Pizzello; (*middle right*) © Jesse D.
Garrabrant/NBAE/Getty Images
26 (*middle left*) © Travelpix Ltd/Photographer's Choice/Getty Images;
(*middle right*) © Monica and Michael Sweet/Flickr/Getty Images
27 (*from top to bottom*) Rick Gomez/Age Fotostock; © John Anthony
Rizzo/UpperCut Images/Alamy; © Photos.com/Thinkstock; © Gualtiero
Boffi/Shutterstock; © Beyond Fotomedia GmbH/Alamy
30 (*top left*) © Exotica.im 2/Alamy; (*top right*) © Amana Images Inc./Alamy
31 (*top right*) © David Madison/Stone/Getty Images; (*middle left to right*)
© BananaStock/Thinkstock; © Pixland/Thinkstock
33 © iStockphoto/Thinkstock
34 (*top left*) © Galyna Andrushko/Shutterstock; (*top right*) © Denkou
Images/Alamy; (*middle*) © Rich Legg/iStockphoto
37 © Tony Kurdzuk/The Star-Ledger/The Image Works
38 (*top left*) © Creatas/Thinkstock; (*top right*) © Jupiterimages/Comstock
Images/Getty Images
40 (*middle left*) © Kevin Miller/iStockphoto; (*middle right*) © Melvyn
Longhurst/Alamy
41 (*top right*) © peruvianpictures.com/Alamy; (*middle right*) © A
Liedmann/Blickwinkel/age fotostock
55 (*top left to right*) © Jan Greune/LOOK Die Bildagentur der Fotografen
GmbH/Alamy; © Manchan/Digital Vision/Getty Images
56 © StockShot/Alamy

57 (*top left to right*) © Rodolfo Arpia/Shutterstock; © David Maung/
Bloomberg/Getty Images; (*middle left to right*) © Valentina Kristeva/
Alamy; © Directphoto.org/Alamy; (*bottom left to right*) © David Muscroft/
Alamy; © Neil Tingle/Alamy
58 (*middle left to right*) © International Photobank/Alamy; © Image100/
SuperStock
59 (*top, left to right*) © K. & H. Benser /Photolibrary ; © Darby Sawchuk/
Alamy; © Bork/Shutterstock; © John Greim/Age Fotostock
60 © Amana Images Inc./Alamy
61 (*top right*) © Sandra Baker/Alamy; (*middle right*) © Brian A Jackson/
Shutterstock
62 (*top, left to right*) © Adalberto Ríos Szalay/Age Fotostock; © Iain
Masterton/Alamy; © WorldTravel/Alamy
63 (*middle right*) © Fotohunter/Shutterstock; (*bottom*) © Tibor Bognar/
Alamy
64 (*top, left to right*) © Jon Sparks/Alamy; © Islemount Images/Alamy;
© Mark Hannaford/John Warburton-Lee Photography/Alamy
65 © Olga Khoroshunova/iStockphoto
68 © Chris Rout/Bubbles Photolibrary/Alamy
71 © Guy Cali/Corbis/Alamy
73 (*top, left to right*) © Johann Helgason/Shutterstock; © iStockphoto/
Thinkstock; (*middle, left to right*) © Chas/Shutterstock; © Diensen
Pamben/Newsteam/Getty Images; (*bottom, left to right*) © GraÃ§a
Victoria/Shutterstock; © iStockphoto/Thinkstock
74 (*left, top to bottom*) © Hemera/Thinkstock; © Nayashkova Olga/
Shutterstock; © Igor Dutina/Shutterstock; © HomeStudio/Shutterstock;
© JTB Photo Communications, Inc./Alamy
76 (*top to bottom*) © Hiroshi Higuchi/Photographer's Choice/Getty
Images; © Liquidlibrary/Thinkstock; © Lew Robertson/FoodPix/Getty
Images
77 © Exactostock/SuperStock
79 (*right, top to bottom*) © Brand X Pictures/Thinkstock; © Beboy/
Shutterstock; © Apdesign/Shutterstock
80 © Peter Forsberg/Alamy
81 (*top, left to right*) © Gavin Hellier/Alamy; © Megapress/Alamy;
© Spacetrek Images/NASAPicade LLC/Alamy
82 © Volodymyr Goinyk/iStockphoto
83 (*top left*) © JTB Photo/SuperStock; (*middle left*) © Jakrit Jiraratwaro/
Shutterstock; (*middle right*) © Fredy Thuerig/Shutterstock; (*bottom left*)
© Roy Hsu/Photographer's Choice/Getty Images; (*bottom right*)
© Tom Hirtreiter/Shutterstock
86 © AP Photo/Matt Sayles
87 (*bottom, left to right*) © Comstock/Thinkstock; © James Quine/Alamy;
© Eyecandy Images/Alamy; © Paul Doyle/Alamy; © Imagebroker.net/
SuperStock; © Sozaijiten/Datacraft/Getty Images
93 (*top, left to right*) © iStockphoto/Thinkstock; © Picturenet/Blend
Images/Getty Images; © Jupiterimages/Comstock Images/Getty Images
94 © iStockphoto/Thinkstock
95 (*right, top to bottom*) ©Ace Stock Limited/Alamy; © BEW Authors/
BE&W/Age Fotostock; © Hartphotography/Shutterstock
96 © Exactostock/SuperStock

1 Please call me Beth.

1 Write about yourself.

My first name is _____ .

My last name is _____ .

Please call me _____ .

I'm from _____ .

2 Put the words in order to make questions. Then answer the questions.

A: *Who's that?*

B: *Oh, that's my teacher.*

1. name   what's   last   her

   A: What's her last name _____ ?

   B: Her last name is _____ .

2. name   her   what's   first

   A: _____ ?

   B: _____ .

3. from   your   teacher   where   is

   A: _____ ?

   B: _____ .

4. class   your   how   English   is

   A: _____ ?

   B: _____ .

5. classmates   what   your   are   like

   A: _____ ?

   B: _____ .

3 | *Choose the correct responses.*

1. A: Hi, I'm Nicole.

   B: <u>Oh, hi. I'm Michael.</u>
   - Oh, hi. I'm Michael.
   - What do people call you?

2. A: My name is Young-hoon Park.

   B: _____
   - Nice to meet you, Young-hoon.
   - Let's go and say hello.

3. A: Hello. I'm a new club member.

   B: _____
   - Thanks.
   - Welcome.

4. A: I'm sorry. What's your name again?

   B: _____
   - K-I-N-G.
   - Joe King.

5. A: How do you spell your first name?

   B: _____
   - I'm Antonio.
   - A-N-T-O-N-I-O.

6. A: What do people call you?

   B: _____
   - It's Ken Tanaka.
   - Everyone calls me Ken.

4 | *Look at the answers. What are the questions?*

1. Jim: What <u>'s your first name?</u>

   Bob: My first name's Bob.

2. Jim: What _____

   Bob: My last name's Hayes.

3. Jim: Who _____

   Bob: That's my wife.

4. Jim: What _____

   Bob: Her name is Rosa.

5. Jim: Where _____

   Bob: She's from Mexico.

6. Jim: Who _____

   Bob: They're my wife's parents.

5 Choose the correct words.

1. They're my classmates. _____Their_____ names are Kate and Noriko. (They / Their)

2. We're students. _____ classroom number is 108-C. (Our / We)

3. Excuse me. What's _____ last name again? (you / your)

4. That's Ji-won. _____ is in my class. (He / His)

5. _____ name is Elizabeth. Please call me Liz. (I / My)

6. This is Paul's wife. _____ name is Jennifer. (His / Her)

7. My parents are on vacation. _____ are in South Korea. (We / They)

8. I'm from Venice, Italy. _____ is a beautiful city. (It / It's)

6 Complete this conversation with am, are, or is.

Lisa: Who _____are_____ the men over there, Amy?

Amy: Oh, they _____ on the volleyball team. Let me introduce you.
Hi, Surachai, this _____ Lisa Neil.

Surachai: Nice to meet you, Lisa.

Lisa: Nice to meet you, too. Where _____ you from?

Surachai: I _____ from Thailand.

Amy: And this _____ Mario. He _____ from Brazil.

Lisa: Hi, Mario.

7 | *Hello and welcome!*

A Read these four student biographies. Then complete the chart below.

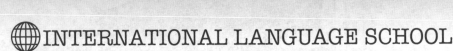

⊕INTERNATIONAL LANGUAGE SCHOOL

Every month, we introduce new students to the school. This month, we want to introduce four new students to you. Please say "hello" to them!

 Mario is in English 101. He is from Cali, Colombia. His first language is Spanish, and he also speaks a little French. He wants to be on the school volleyball team. He says he doesn't play very well, but he wants to learn!

Su-yin is in English 102. She is from Wuhan, China. She says she writes and reads English pretty well, but she needs a lot of practice speaking English. Her first language is Chinese. She wants to play volleyball on the school team.

Charlotte is in English 103. She is from Brussels, Belgium. She speaks French and Dutch. She is an engineering student. She wants to be an engineer. She says she doesn't play any sports. She wants to make a lot of new friends in her class.

Finally, meet Ahmed. He is in Charlotte's class. He says he speaks English well, but his writing isn't very good! Ahmed is from Luxor in Egypt, and his first language is Arabic. He is a soccer player, and he wants to be on the school soccer team.

Name	Where from	Languages	Sports
1. Mario			
2.	Brussels, Belgium		
3.		Chinese and English	
4.			soccer

B Write a short biography of a classmate.

_____

_____

_____

_____

8 Choose the correct sentences to complete this conversation.

- ☐ What are your classmates like?
- ☐ No, she's not. She's my sister!
- ☑ Hi, Sarah. I'm Rich. How are you?
- ☐ Oh, really? Is Susan Miller in your class?
- ☐ No, I'm not. I'm on vacation. Are you a student?

Sarah: Hello, I'm Sarah.

Rich: <u>Hi, Sarah. I'm Rich. How are you?</u>

Sarah: Pretty good, thanks. Are you a student here?

Rich: _____

Sarah: Yes, I am.

Rich: _____

Sarah: They're really interesting.

Rich: _____

Sarah: Yes, she is. Is she your friend?

Rich: _____

9 Complete this conversation. Use contractions where possible.

> ### Grammar note: Contractions
>
> **Do not use contractions for short answers with Yes.**
>
> Are you from Argentina? Is he from Greece?
>   Yes, I am. (*not* Yes, I'm.)   Yes, he is. (*not* Yes, he's.)

Alex: Hello. _____I'm_____ Alex Lam. And this
is my sister Amy.

Tina: Hi. _____ Tina Fernandez.

Amy: Are you from South America, Tina?

Tina: Yes, _____ . _____ from Argentina.
Where are you and your sister from, Alex?

Alex: _____ from Taiwan.

Tina: Are you from Taipei?

Alex: No, _____ . _____ from Tainan.
Say, are you in English 101?

Tina: No, _____ . I'm in English 102.

10 **Look at the answers. What are the questions?**

1. A: <u>Are you on vacation here?</u>

   B: No, I'm not on vacation. I'm a student here.

2. A: _____

   B: No, I'm not. I'm very busy now.

3. A: _____

   B: No, we're not from Spain. We're from Mexico.

4. A: _____

   B: No, my teacher isn't Mr. Brown. I'm in Ms. West's class.

5. A: _____

   B: Yes, Natalie and Mika are in my class.

6. A: _____

   B: Yes, it's an interesting class.

7. A: _____

   B: No, they're not on the same baseball team. They're on the same volleyball team.

11 **Read the expressions in the box. Which ones say "hello" and which ones say "good-bye"?**

	Hello	Good-bye
1. How are you?	☑	☐
2. See you tomorrow.	☐	☐
3. Good night.	☐	☐
4. Good morning.	☐	☐
5. Talk to you later.	☐	☐
6. How's it going?	☐	☐
7. Have a good day.	☐	☐
8. What's up?	☐	☐

12 **Answer these questions about yourself. Use contractions where possible.**

1. Are you from South America? _____

2. Are you on vacation? _____

3. Are you a student at a university? _____

4. Is your English class in the morning? _____

5. Is your teacher from England? _____

6. Is your first name popular? _____

2 What do you do?

1 *Match the words in columns A and B. Write the names of the jobs.*

A	B	
☑ English	☐ attendant	1. <u>English teacher</u>
☐ fitness	☐ designer	2. _____
☐ flight	☐ instructor	3. _____
☐ newspaper	☐ guide	4. _____
☐ tour	☐ reporter	5. _____
☐ website	☑ teacher	6. _____

2 *Write sentences using* **He** *or* **She.**

1. I'm a website designer. I work in an office. I like computers a lot.

   <u>He</u> _____

   _____

2. I work in a gym. I'm a fitness instructor. I teach aerobics.

   <u>She</u> _____

   _____

3. I'm a tour guide. I take people on tours. I travel a lot.

   <u>He</u> _____

   _____

4. I work for an airline. I assist passengers. I'm a flight attendant.

   <u>She</u> _____

   _____

7

3 *Write* a *or* an *in the correct places.*

> ### Grammar note: Articles a and an
>
> **Use a + singular noun before a consonant sound.**
> **Use an + singular noun before a vowel sound.**
>
> He is **a c**arpenter.   He is **an a**ccountant.
> He is **a g**ood carpenter.   He is **an e**xpensive accountant.
> **Do not use a or an + plural nouns.**
> They are good carpenter**s**.   They are expensive accountant**s**.

       a   a

1. He's carpenter. He works for construction company. He builds schools and houses.

2. She works for travel company. She arranges tours. She's travel agent.

3. He has difficult job. He's cashier. He works in supermarket.

4. She's architect. She works for large company. She designs houses. It's interesting job.

5. He works with cars in garage. He's mechanic. He's also part-time student. He takes business class in the evening.

4 *Choose someone in your family. Write about his or her job.*

_____

_____

_____

_____

5 **Complete this conversation with the correct words.**

Tom: What ___does___ your husband _____ , exactly?
          (do / does)   (do / does)

Liz: He _____ for a department store. He's a store manager.
     (work / works)

Tom: How _____ he _____ it?
        (do / does)   (like / likes)

Liz: It's an interesting job. He _____ it very much.
                     (like / likes)

      But he _____ long hours. And what _____ you _____ ?
         (work / works)   (do / does)   (do / does)

Tom: I'm a student. I _____ architecture.
              (study / studies)

Liz: Oh, really? Where _____ you _____ to school?
              (do / does)   (go / goes)

Tom: I _____ to Lincoln University. My girlfriend _____ there, too.
    (go / goes)   (go / goes)

Liz: Really? And what _____ she _____ ?
            (do / does)   (study / studies)

Tom: She _____ hotel management.
     (study / studies)

Liz: That sounds interesting.

6 **Complete the questions in this conversation.**

Mark: Where _do you work?_ _____

Victor: I work for Cybotics Industries.

Mark: And what _____ there?

Victor: I'm in management.

Mark: How _____

Victor: It's a great job. And what _____

Mark: I'm a salesperson.

Victor: Really? What _____

Mark: I sell computers. Do you want to buy one?

7 *Read these two interviews. Answer the questions.*

Today,

JOB Talk

interviews two people with interesting jobs.

Job Talk: Felix, where do you work?
Felix: I work at home, and I work in Southeast Asia.

Job Talk: Really? Well, what do you do at home?
Felix: I'm a chef. I practice cooking new things, and then I write cookbooks.

Job Talk: That sounds interesting. And what do you do in Southeast Asia?
Felix: I make TV programs about Thai cooking.

Job Talk: You have an interesting life, Felix.
Felix: Yes, but it's hard work!

Job Talk: What do you do, Keisha?
Keisha: I'm a lifeguard. And I give swimming lessons.

Job Talk: That's interesting. Do you work at the beach?
Keisha: No, I work at the city pool.

Job Talk: How do you like your job?
Keisha: I love it. I work outdoors, and I get lots of exercise.

Job Talk: Do you work all day?
Keisha: No, I work from nine o'clock in the morning until noon.

Job Talk: What do you do in the afternoon?
Keisha: I swim!

1. What does Felix do? He _____

2. What does he do at home? _____

3. What does he do in Southeast Asia? _____

4. What does Keisha do? She _____

5. Where does she work? _____

6. When does she finish work? _____

8 *Meet Pat. Write questions about him using* **What, Where, When,** *and* **How.**

1. What does he do? _____

2. _____

3. _____

4. _____

MERCY HOSPITAL

Patrick Kennedy

Registered Nurse/Night Shift

9 *How does Pat spend his weekends? Complete this paragraph with the words from the list.*

☐ around ☐ at ☐ before ☐ early ☐ in ☐ late ☑ on ☐ until

Everyone knows Pat at the hospital. Pat is a part-time nurse. He works at night on weekends. _____On_____ Saturdays and Sundays, Pat sleeps most of the day and wakes up a little _____ nine _____ the evening, usually at 8:45 or 8:50. He has breakfast very late, _____ 9:30 or 10:00 P.M.! He watches television _____ eleven o'clock, and then starts work _____ midnight. _____ in the morning, usually around 5:00 A.M., he leaves work, has a little snack, goes home, goes to bed, and sleeps _____ . It's a perfect schedule for Pat. He's a pre-med student on weekdays at a local college.

10 *Use these words to complete the crossword puzzle.*

☐ answers ☐ sells ☐ types
☐ does ☐ serves ☐ works
☐ gets ☑ starts ☐ writes
☐ goes ☐ takes

Across

1 Lauren _____ work at 5:00 P.M.

4 Karen _____ in a hospital.

5 Ellen _____ up early in the morning.

7 Seoul Garden _____ good Korean food.

9 Rodney _____ to bed after midnight.

10 Andrea is a receptionist. She _____ the phone and greets people.

Down

2 Linda is a tour guide. She _____ people on tours.

3 Dan _____ 100 words a minute on his new computer.

4 Mei-li _____ about 30 text messages a day.

6 My father works in a bookstore. He _____ books and magazines.

8 What _____ your sister do?

11 *Choose the sentences in the box that have the same meaning as the sentences below.*

- ☐ He goes to the university.
- ☐ She fixes cars.
- ☐ She stays up late.
- ☐ What does he do?
- ☑ He's a dance teacher.
- ☐ He works part time.

1. He teaches dance.

   He's a dance teacher.

2. What's his job?

   _____

3. She's a mechanic.

   _____

4. He's a student.

   _____

5. She goes to bed at midnight.

   _____

6. He works four hours every day.

   _____

12 *Fill in the missing words or phrases from these job advertisements.*

1. ☐ at night
   ☐ part time
   ☐ weekends
   ☑ nurses

2. ☐ Interesting
   ☐ Spanish
   ☐ tours
   ☐ student

3. ☐ manager
   ☐ long hours
   ☐ restaurant
   ☐ until

New York Hospital needs

____nurses____. Work during

the day or _____,

weekdays or _____,

full time or _____.

Call
614-555-1191

_____ job for a

language _____.

Mornings only. Take

people on _____.

Need good English and

_____ skills.

Email Dave at dave189@cup.org

No need to work _____!

Only work from 6:00 _____

11:00 four evenings a week.

Our _____ serves

great food! Work as our

_____.

Call 308-555-6845.

3 How much is it?

1 Choose the correct sentences to complete this conversation.

- ☐ Which one?
- ☑ Which ones?
- ☐ Oh, Sam. Thank you very much.
- ☐ Well, I like it, but it's expensive.
- ☐ Yes. But I don't really like light blue.

Sam: Look at those pants, Rebecca.

Rebecca: _Which ones?_

Sam: The light blue ones over there. They're nice.

Rebecca: _____

Sam: Hmm. Well, what about that sweater? It's perfect for you.

Rebecca: _____

Sam: This red one.

Rebecca: _____

Sam: Hey, let me buy it for you. It's a present!

Rebecca: _____

2 Complete these conversations with How much is / are . . . ? and this, that, these, or those.

1. A: _How much is this_ _____ backpack?

   B: It's $31.99.

2. A: _____ bracelets?

   B: They're $29.

3. A: _____ shoes?

   B: They're $64.

4. A: _____ cat?

   B: That's *my* cat, and he's not for sale!

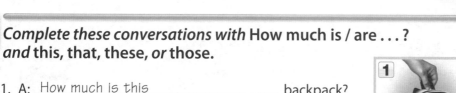
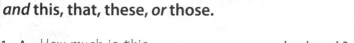

3 *Write the plurals of these words.*

Spelling note: Plural nouns

Most words		**Words ending in -ss, -sh, -ch, and -x**	
cap	cap**s**	glass	glass**es**
shoe	shoe**s**	dish	dish**es**
		watch	watch**es**

Words ending in -f and -fe		**Words ending in consonant + -y**	
shelf	shel**ves**	country	countr**ies**
knife	kni**ves**		

1. backpack   backpacks
2. box   _____
3. company   _____
4. day   _____
5. dress   _____
6. glove   _____

7. hairbrush   _____
8. necklace   _____
9. ring   _____
10. scarf   _____
11. sweater   _____
12. tie   _____

4 *What do you think of these prices? Write a response.*

| That's cheap. | That's not bad. | That's reasonable. | That's pretty expensive! |

1. $90 for a wool tie
   That's pretty expensive!   _____

2. $150 for gold earrings
   _____

3. $500 for a silk dress
   _____

4. $40 for leather gloves
   _____

5. $2,000 for a computer
   _____

6. $5 for two plastic hairbrushes
   _____

7. $15 for a silver necklace
   _____

5 Choose the correct words to complete the conversations.

1. Clerk: Good afternoon.

   Luis: Oh, hi. How much is ____this____ watch?
   (this / these)

   Clerk: _____ $195.
   (It's / They're)

   Luis: And how much is that _____ ?
   (one / ones)

   Clerk: _____ $255.
   (It's / They're)

   Luis: Oh, really? Well, thanks anyway.

2. Meg: Excuse me. How much are _____ jeans?
   (that / those)

   Clerk: _____ only $59.
   (It's / They're)

   Meg: And how much is _____ sweater?
   (this / these)

   Clerk: Which _____ ? They're all different.
   (one / ones)

   Meg: This green _____ .
   (one / ones)

   Clerk: _____ $34.
   (It's / They're)

3. Sonia: I like _____ sunglasses over there.
   (that / those)

   Clerk: Which _____ ?
   (one / ones)

   Sonia: The small brown _____ .
   (one / ones)

   Clerk: _____ $199.
   (It's / They're)

   Sonia: Oh, they're expensive!

6

What do you make out of these materials? Complete the chart using words from the list. (You will use words more than once.)

| boots | bracelet | gloves | jacket | necklace | pants | ring | shirt |

Cotton	Gold	Leather	Plastic	Silk	Wool
gloves					

7

Make comparisons using the words given. Add *than* **if necessary.**

cotton gloves

1. A: These cotton gloves are nice.

   B: Yes, but the leather ones are _____nicer_____ . (nice)

   A: They're also _____ . (expensive)

leather gloves

2. A: Those silk jackets look

   _____

   the wool ones. (attractive)

   B: Yes, but the wool ones are

   _____ . (warm)

silk jackets

wool jackets

purple shirt

3. A: This purple shirt is an interesting color!

   B: Yes, but the color is

   _____ the design. (pretty)

   A: The design isn't bad.

   B: I think the pattern on that red shirt

   is _____ the pattern on

   this purple one. (good)

red shirt

4. A: Hey, look at this silver ring! It's nice.

   And it's _____ that gold ring. (cheap)

   B: But it's _____ the gold one. (small)

   A: Well, yeah. The gold one is _____ the silver one. (big)

   But look at the price tag. One thousand dollars is a lot of money!

$1,000

gold ring

$650

silver ring

8 Complete the chart. Use the words from the list.

☑ boots ☐ DVD player ☐ ring
☐ bracelet ☐ earrings ☐ television
☐ cap ☐ MP3 player ☐ T-shirt
☐ dress ☐ necklace ☐ video camera

Clothing	Electronics	Jewelry
boots		

9 Answer these questions. Give your own information.

1	2	3	4	5
black sunglasses	wool cap	high-top shoes	laptop computer	silver necklace

| white sunglasses | leather cap | sandals | desktop computer | gold necklace |

1. Which sunglasses do you prefer, the black ones or the white ones?
   I prefer the black ones.

2. Which cap do you like more, the wool one or the leather one?

3. Which ones do you like more, the high-tops or the sandals?

4. Which one do you prefer, the laptop computer or the desktop computer?

5. Which necklace do you like better, the silver one or the gold one?

10 *Great gadgets!*

1 _____

2 _____

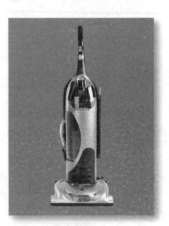

3 _____

A Read these ads. Match the pictures and descriptions.

a. Warning! This knife is very, very sharp! And it stays sharp forever because it's made of ceramic – hard like a diamond! What can it do? It can cut anything and everything. Only $34.49!

b. This machine cuts your house-cleaning time by 50%! Why? It's a very light vacuum cleaner. So it's easy to move from room to room. And it cleans everything in your home – even the air! Only $159.99. In dark gray or light blue.

4 _____

c. Are you always late in the morning? Are you tired of waiting at home while your phone charges? You need a solar backpack. The solar panels recharge mobile phones and other electrical devices. You can leave the house for school or work and charge while you go! No more lateness! And help the environment. Only $125.

d. Thirsty? Need to make your own fresh juice? You need a juicer. In seconds, it can blend fruits and vegetables for juice. In no time, you can prepare healthy juice drinks from apples, carrots, and other favorite foods. $85.

B Check (✓) True or False.

	True	False
1. The knife is made of diamonds.	☐	☐
2. The vacuum cleaner comes in two colors.	☐	☐
3. The solar backpack is more than $120.	☐	☐
4. The juicer can make fruit pies.	☐	☐

C What's special about a gadget you have? Write a paragraph about it.

_____

_____

_____

_____

4 I really like hip-hop.

1   Check (✓) the boxes to complete the survey about music and TV.

1 Do you like these types of music?			
	I love it!	**It's OK.**	**I don't like it.**
pop	☐	☐	☐
classical	☐	☐	☐
hip-hop	☐	☐	☐
rock	☐	☐	☐
jazz	☐	☐	☐

2 Do you like these types of TV shows?			
	I love them!	**They're OK.**	**I don't like them.**
talk shows	☐	☐	☐
reality shows	☐	☐	☐
sitcoms	☐	☐	☐
soap operas	☐	☐	☐
game shows	☐	☐	☐

2   What's your opinion? Answer the questions with the expressions and pronouns in the box.

Usher

Yes, I do.	**Object pronouns**
I love . . .	him
I like . . . a lot.	her
No, I don't.	it
I don't like . . . very much.	them
I can't stand . . .	

1. Do you like heavy metal music?
   <u>Yes, I do. I like it a lot.</u>

2. Do you like Usher?
   _____

3. Do you like romantic comedies?
   _____

4. Do you like Adele?
   _____

Adele

5. Do you like video games?
   _____

6. Do you like science fiction books?
   _____

3 *Choose the correct job for each picture.*

1. Katy Perry is _____
   _____

2. The Kings of Leon are _____
   _____

3. Colin Firth is _____

4. Nani is _____
   _____

4 *Complete these conversations.*

1. Ed: ___Do___ you ___like___ country music, Sarah?

   Sarah: Yes, I _____ it a lot. I'm a real fan of Keith Urban.

   Ed: Oh, _____ he play the guitar?

   Sarah: Yes, he _____ . He's my favorite musician.

2. Anne: _____ kind of music _____
   your parents _____ , Jason?

   Jason: They _____ classical music.

   Anne: Who _____ they _____ ? Mozart?

   Jason: No, they _____ like him very much. They prefer Beethoven.

3. Scott: Teresa, _____ you _____ Beyoncé?

   Teresa: No, I _____ . I can't stand her. I like Alicia Keys.

   Scott: I don't know her. What kind of music _____ she sing?

   Teresa: She _____ R&B. She's really great!

Keith Urban

5 Complete these questions and write answers.

1. <u>What kinds</u> of movies do you like? I like _____

2. _____ is your favorite movie? My favorite _____

3. _____ of movies do you dislike? _____

4. _____ of TV shows do you like? _____

5. _____ is your favorite actor or actress? _____

6. _____ is your favorite song? _____

7. _____ is your favorite rock band? _____

8. _____ is your favorite video game? _____

6 What do you think? Answer the questions.

1. Which movies are more interesting, musicals or science fiction films?

_____

2. Which films are scarier, horror films or thrillers?

_____

3. Which do you like more, animated films or historical dramas?

_____

4. Which do you prefer, romantic comedies or action films?

_____

5. Which films are more exciting, westerns or crime thrillers?

_____

7 Verbs and nouns

A Which nouns often go with these verbs? Complete the chart. Use each noun only once.

listen to	play	watch
jazz		

- ☐ the piano
- ☐ videos
- ☑ jazz
- ☐ a sports match
- ☐ music
- ☐ the guitar
- ☐ a movie
- ☐ the trumpet
- ☐ the radio

B Write a sentence using each verb in part A.

1. _____

2. _____

3. _____

8 Movie reviews

A Read these movie reviews. Choose a title from the box for each review.

House of Laughs	The Best Man Wins	Ahead of Time	Coming Up for Air

movie reviews

1. _____

What are high school kids like in the future? This movie answers that question. It's about a group of school kids in the year 2012. After class one day, they find a time machine behind the school. One of the teens sees a button marked "Year 2500" and clicks on it. They suddenly travel to the twenty-sixth century! Do they get back in time for school the next day? Watch and find out. ★★★★

2. _____

This movie is about a group of six young people in London. They live in the same house in a suburb far from the city center. They all come from different countries. They speak different languages, and their customs are different. The story is very funny, and the acting is very good. This movie is like a really good TV soap opera. There are lots and lots of laughs in this movie. ★★★★★

3. _____

The action never stops in this movie. Police officer Karen Montana wants to catch Mr. X, a gold thief. Mr. X is stealing gold from an old shipwreck at the bottom of the ocean. Before Ms. Montana can catch him, she has to learn how to scuba dive. But every time she goes underwater, he swims to the surface. She catches him, but not until the final minute of this very long film. ★★

B What kind of movie is each one in part A?

1. ☐ a horror film
   ☐ a science fiction film
   ☐ a historical drama

2. ☐ a travel film
   ☐ a western
   ☐ a comedy

3. ☐ a romantic comedy
   ☐ a crime thriller
   ☐ a documentary

9 Choose the correct responses.

1. A: What do you think of *Glee*?

   B: <u>I'm not a real fan of the show.</u>

   • How about you?
   • I'm not a real fan of the show.

2. A: Do you like country music?

   B: _____

   • I can't stand it.
   • I can't stand them.

3. A: There's a baseball game tonight.

   B: _____

   • Thanks. I'd love to.
   • Great. Let's go.

4. A: Would you like to see a movie this weekend?

   B: _____

   • That sounds great!
   • I don't agree.

the cast of *Glee*

10 Yes *or* no?

A Young-ha is inviting friends to a movie. Do they accept the invitation or not? Check (✓) Yes or No for each response.

Accept?	Yes	No
1. I'd love to. What time does it start?	✓	☐
2. Thanks, but I don't really like animated films.	☐	☐
3. That sounds great. Where is it?	☐	☐
4. I'd love to, but I have to work until midnight.	☐	☐
5. Thanks. I'd really like to. When do you want to meet?	☐	☐

B Respond to the invitations.

1. I have tickets to a hip-hop concert on Saturday. Would you like to go?

   _____

2. There's a soccer game tonight. Do you want to go with me?

   _____

3. Jason Mraz is performing tomorrow at the stadium. Would you like to see him?

   _____

I really like hip-hop. ▪ 23

11 *Choose the correct phrases to complete these conversations.*

1. Robin: <u>Do you like</u> rock music, Kate?
(Do you like / Would you like)

   Kate: Yes, I do. _____ it a lot.
(I like / I'd like)

   Robin: There's a Linkin Park concert on Friday.
_____ to go with me?
(Do you like / Would you like)

   Kate: Yes, _____ . Thanks.
(I love to / I'd love to)

2. Carlos: There is a basketball game on TV tonight.
_____ to come over and watch it?
(Do you like / Would you like)

   Phil: _____ , but I have to study tonight.
(I like to / I'd like to)

   Carlos: Well, _____ soccer?
(do you like / would you like)

   Phil: Yes, _____ . I love it!
(I do / I would)

   Carlos: There's a match on TV tomorrow at 3:00.
_____ to watch that with me?
(Do you like / Would you like)

   Phil: _____ . Thanks.
(I like to / I'd love to)

12 *Rewrite these sentences. Find another way to say each sentence using the words given.*

1. Do you like jazz?
<u>What do you think of jazz?</u> (think of)

2. Richard doesn't like classical music.
_____ (can't stand)

3. I think horror films are great!
_____ (love)

4. Celia doesn't like pop music.
_____ (be a fan of)

5. Do you want to go to a baseball game?
_____ (would like)

5 I come from a big family.

1 Which words are for males? Which are for females? Complete the chart.

- ☑ aunt
- ☑ brother
- ☐ daughter
- ☐ father
- ☐ husband
- ☐ mother
- ☐ nephew
- ☐ niece
- ☐ sister
- ☐ son
- ☐ uncle
- ☐ wife

Males			Females		
brother	♂		aunt	♀	

2 Complete this conversation. Use the present continuous of the verbs given.

Joel: You look tired, Don. _Are you studying_ (study)
      late at night these days?

Don: No, I'm not. My brother and sister _____ (stay)
     with me right now. We go to bed after midnight every night.

Joel: Really? What _____ (do) this
      summer? _____ (take) classes, too?

Don: No, they aren't. My brother is on vacation now, but he
     _____ (look) for a part-time job here.

Joel: What about your sister? _____ (work)?

Don: Yes, she is. She has a part-time job at the university.
     What about you, Joel? Are you in school this summer?

Joel: Yes, I am. I _____ (study) two languages.

Don: Oh, _____ (take) French and
     Spanish again?

Joel: Well, I'm taking Spanish again, but I
      _____ (start) Japanese.

Don: Really? That's exciting!

25

3 **Rewrite these sentences. Find another way to say each sentence using the words given.**

1. Joseph is Maria's uncle.

   <u>Maria is Joseph's niece.</u> (niece)

2. Liz is married to Peter.

   <u>Peter is</u> (husband)

3. Isabel is Frank's and Liza's granddaughter.

   _____ (grandparents)

4. We have two children.

   _____ (son and daughter)

5. My wife's father is a painter.

   _____ (father-in-law)

6. Michael does not have a job right now.

   _____ (look for)

4 **Choose the correct sentences to complete this conversation.**

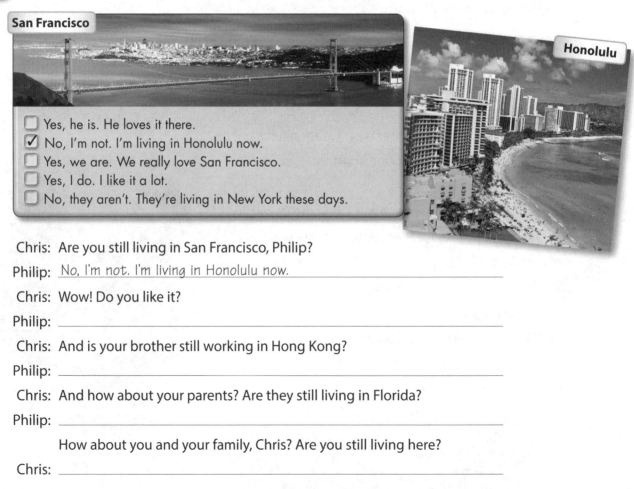

San Francisco

Honolulu

- ☐ Yes, he is. He loves it there.
- ☑ No, I'm not. I'm living in Honolulu now.
- ☐ Yes, we are. We really love San Francisco.
- ☐ Yes, I do. I like it a lot.
- ☐ No, they aren't. They're living in New York these days.

Chris: Are you still living in San Francisco, Philip?

Philip: <u>No, I'm not. I'm living in Honolulu now.</u>

Chris: Wow! Do you like it?

Philip: _____

Chris: And is your brother still working in Hong Kong?

Philip: _____

Chris: And how about your parents? Are they still living in Florida?

Philip: _____

How about you and your family, Chris? Are you still living here?

Chris: _____

5 Complete these sentences. Use the simple present or the present continuous of the verbs given.

1. This is my aunt Barbara.

   She _____lives_____ (live) in Rome, but

   she _____ (visit) Chile this summer.

   She _____ (take) some summer classes there.

2. And these are my parents.

   They _____ (work) in London.

   They _____ (be) on vacation right now.

3. And here you can see my grandparents.

   They _____ (not work) now.

   They _____ (be) retired.

4. This is my brother-in-law Edward.

   He _____ (want) to be a company

   director. He _____ (study) business

   in Canada right now.

5. And this is my niece Christina.

   She _____ (go) to high school.

   She _____ (like) mathematics, but

   she _____ (not like) English.

6 Choose a friend or a family member. Write about him or her using the simple present and present continuous.

_____

_____

_____

_____

A Answer these questions. Then read the passage.

1. At what age do most young people leave their parents' home in your country? _____

2. Do some young people live with their parents after they get married? _____

Leaving Home

Young people leave their parents' homes at different ages in different parts of the world. In the United States, a lot of college students do not live at home. They often choose to go to college in different cities – away from their parents. At college, many live in university housing. After college, most people prefer to live in their own homes. They often live alone, but some people rent apartments with others. These people are called *roommates*.

By the age of 22, few young people in the United States live with their parents. Families stay together longer in many Asian countries and cities. In Hong Kong, for example, nearly all university students live with their parents. Rents in the city are very expensive, and few students have the money to pay for their own apartments. Very few young people live alone or become roommates in a shared apartment. Many young people in Hong Kong continue to live with their parents even after they marry.

B Check (✓) True or False. For statements that are false, write the correct information.

In the United States	True	False
1. Very few students live in university housing. _____	☐	☐
2. Some young adults share apartments with roommates. _____	☐	☐
3. Nearly all young adults live with their parents. _____	☐	☐

In Hong Kong	True	False
4. Not many university students live with their parents. _____	☐	☐
5. Few young people live alone. _____	☐	☐
6. Most young married couples have enough money to live in their own apartments. _____	☐	☐

8 *Arrange the quantifiers from the most to the least.*

☑ all   ☐ nearly all
☐ a lot of   ☑ no
☐ few   ☐ not many
☐ many   ☐ some
☐ most

1. _all_
2. _____
3. _____
4. _____
5. _____
6. _____
7. _____
8. _____
9. _no_

9 *Rewrite these sentences about the United States using the quantifiers given.*

1. Eighty-five percent of children go to public schools. Fifteen percent of children go to private schools.

   Most _children go to public schools._

   Few _____

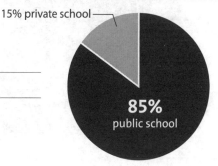

Where Children Go to School

15% private school

85% public school

2. Sixty-five percent of young people go to college after they finish high school. Thirty-one percent of young people look for work.

   Many _____

   Some _____

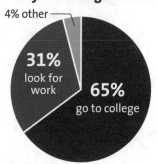

What People Do After They Finish High School

4% other

31% look for work

65% go to college

3. Ninety-five percent of people over 65 like to talk to family and friends. Forty-three percent like to spend time on a hobby. Eight percent of people over 65 like to spend time on the Internet.

   Not many _____

   A lot of _____

   Nearly all _____

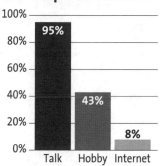

What People 65 and Over Do

100%
80%
60%
40%
20%
0%

95% Talk
43% Hobby
8% Internet

10 *Choose the correct words or phrases to complete this paragraph.*

In my country, some ___*couples*___ (couples / cousins / relatives) get married fairly young.
Not many marriages _____ (break up / get divorced / stay together), and nearly
all _____ (divorced / married / single) people remarry. Elderly couples often
_____ (divorce again / move away / live at home) and take
care of their grandchildren.

11 *Complete these sentences about your country. Use the words in the box.*

all	nearly all	most	a lot of	some	few	no

1. _____ young people go to college.
2. _____ people study English.
3. _____ married couples have more than five children.
4. _____ elderly people have part-time jobs.
5. _____ students have full-time jobs.
6. _____ children go to school on Saturdays.

6 How often do you exercise?

1 **Complete the chart. Use words from the box.**
(Some of the words can be both individual sports and exercise.)

aerobics	football	swimming
baseball	jogging	tennis
basketball	stretching	volleyball
bicycling	soccer	yoga

team sport

Team sports	Individual sports	Exercise
baseball		

individual sport

exercise

2 **Arrange these words to make sentences or questions.**

1. go   never   I   almost   bicycling

   I almost never go bicycling .

2. hardly   they   tennis   play   ever

   _____ .

3. go   do   often   jogging   how   you

   _____ ?

4. often   mornings   do   on   we   yoga   Sunday

   _____ .

5. ever   Charlie   do   does   aerobics

   _____ ?

6. do   on   you   what   usually   Saturdays   do

   _____ ?

31

3 *Use these questions to complete the conversations.*
How often do you . . . ? Do you ever . . . ? What do you usually . . . ?

1. A: <u>Do you ever exercise?</u>

   B: Yes, I often exercise on weekends.

2. A: _____

   B: Well, I usually do karate on Saturdays and yoga on Sundays.

3. A: _____

   B: No, I never go to the gym after work.

4. A: _____

   B: I don't exercise very often at all.

5. A: _____

   B: Yes, I sometimes play sports on weekends – usually baseball.

6. A: _____

   B: I usually play tennis in my free time.

4 *Keeping fit?*

A Check (✓) how often you do each of the things in the chart.

	Every day	Once or twice a week	Sometimes	Not very often	Never
do aerobics	☐	☐	☐	☐	☐
play basketball	☐	☐	☐	☐	☐
exercise	☐	☐	☐	☐	☐
go jogging	☐	☐	☐	☐	☐
do karate	☐	☐	☐	☐	☐
play soccer	☐	☐	☐	☐	☐
go swimming	☐	☐	☐	☐	☐
do weight training	☐	☐	☐	☐	☐

B Write about yourself using the information in the chart.

_____

_____

_____

_____

5 Complete this conversation.
Write the correct prepositions in the correct places.

Susan: What time do you go jogging ^in the morning? (around / in / on)

Jerry: I always go jogging 7:00. (at / for / on)

How about you, Susan?

Susan: I usually go jogging noon. (around / in / with)

I jog about an hour. (at / for / until)

Jerry: And do you also play sports your free time? (at / in / until)

Susan: No, I usually go out my classmates. (around / for / with)

What about you?

Jerry: I go to the gym Mondays and Wednesdays. (at / on / until)

And sometimes I go bicycling weekends. (for / in / on)

Susan: Wow! You really like to stay in shape.

6 Complete the crossword puzzle.

Across

4 Pierre never _____ . He's a real couch potato.

6 How often do you _____ yoga?

7 I like to stay in _____ . I play sports every day.

8 Jeff does weight _____ every evening. He lifts weights of 40 kilos.

10 Diana goes _____ twice a week. She usually runs about three miles.

Down

1 Andrew always watches TV in his _____ time.

2 Kate has a regular _____ program.

3 I do _____ at the gym three times a week. The teacher plays great music!

5 Paul is on the _____ team at his high school.

7 Marie never goes _____ when the water is cold.

9 Amy often _____ bicycling on weekends.

7 Fun activities

A Read these ads. How can someone get more information about the programs in each ad?

Hiking Club _____

Adult Education Program _____

Community Center _____

Do you enjoy the outdoors? Do you need exercise?
Do you like walking and meeting new people?

Join the Hiking Club!

🐾 See us online at myhikingclub.cup.org

🐾 We go on a different hike every weekend.

🐾 Sometimes we go on a two-day hike and camp overnight!

Join us the first of every month for volunteer trail cleanup!

Adult Education Program at Monroe High School
Mondays and Tuesdays, 6:00–9:00 P.M.

Fall classes: social networking; buying and selling online; cooking; salsa dancing; Spanish, Arabic, and Italian language classes

For more information, pick up our brochure at any Star Supermarket or the public library.

Come to the Community Center!

Check out our new activities!

◆ Aerobics, table tennis, and yoga!

◆ Friday night, teen disco. Saturday night, seniors night.

Singles, couples, and families welcome.

◆ For anyone from 9 to 90!

Call us at 888-555-9916.

B Where can you do these activities? Check (✓) the answers.

	Hiking Club	Adult Education Program	Community Center
play indoor sports	☐	☐	☐
do outdoor activities	☐	☐	☐
take evening classes	☐	☐	☐
go dancing	☐	☐	☐
learn to cook	☐	☐	☐
meet new people	☐	☐	☐

8 *Choose the correct responses.*

1. A: How often do you go swimming, Linda?

   B: *Once a week.*

   - I guess I'm OK.
   - Once a week.
   - About an hour.

2. A: How long do you spend in the pool?

   B: _____

   - About 45 minutes.
   - About average.
   - About three miles.

3. A: And how well do you swim?

   B: _____

   - I'm not very well.
   - I almost never do.
   - I'm about average.

4. A: How good are you at other sports?

   B: _____

   - Not very good, actually.
   - I sometimes play twice a week.
   - Pretty well, I guess.

9 *Look at the answers. Write questions using* how.

1. A: *How long do you spend exercising?*

   B: I don't spend any time at all. In fact, I don't exercise.

2. A: _____ for a walk?

   B: Almost every day. I really enjoy it.

3. A: _____

   B: I spend about an hour jogging.

4. A: _____ at soccer?

   B: I'm pretty good at it. I'm on the school team.

5. A: _____

   B: Basketball? Pretty well, I guess. I like it a lot.

10 Rewrite these sentences. Find another way to say each sentence using the words given.

1. I don't watch TV very much.
   <u>I hardly ever watch TV.</u> (hardly ever)

2. Tom exercises twice a month.
   _____ (not very often)

3. Philip tries to keep fit.
   _____ (stay in shape)

4. Jill often exercises at the gym.
   _____ (work out)

5. I go jogging with my wife all the time.
   _____ (always)

6. How good are you at tennis?
   _____ (play)

11 What do you think about sports? Answer these questions.

1. Do you like to exercise for a short time or a long time?
   _____

2. Do you prefer exercising in the morning or in the evening?
   _____

3. Which do you like better, walking or jogging?
   _____

4. Do you like to watch sports or play sports?
   _____

5. Which do you like better, team sports or individual sports?
   _____

6. How good are you at games like basketball or tennis?
   _____

7. What sport or game don't you like?
   _____

7 We had a great time!

1 *Past tense*

A Write the simple past of these regular verbs.

1. cook <u>cooked</u>
2. enjoy _____
3. invite _____

4. love _____
5. study _____
6. try _____

7. visit _____
8. wash _____
9. watch _____

B Write the simple form of these irregular simple past verbs.

1. <u>buy</u> bought
2. _____ gave
3. _____ met
4. _____ saw

5. _____ slept
6. _____ spent
7. _____ took
8. _____ went

C Use two of the verbs above and write sentences about the past.

Example: <u>We went to a rock concert last night.</u>

1. _____
2. _____

2 *Use the cues to answer these questions.*

1. Where did you go this weekend?

   <u>I went to a party.</u> _____ (to a party)

2. Who did you meet at the party?

   _____ (someone very interesting)

3. What time did you and Eva get home?

   _____ (a little after 1:00)

4. How did you and Bob like the art exhibition?

   _____ (a lot)

5. What did you buy?

   _____ (some new leather boots)

6. Where did Jeff and Joyce spend their vacation?

   _____ (in the country)

3 *What do you like to do alone? with other people? Complete the chart with activities from the box. Then add one more activity to each list.*

cook dinner
do homework
exercise
go shopping
go to a sports event
go to the movies
have a picnic
play video games
take a vacation
watch TV

Activities I like to do alone	Activities I like to do with other people
_____	_____
_____	_____
_____	_____
_____	_____
_____	_____
_____	_____
_____	_____

4 *Complete the questions in this conversation.*

A: How _did you spend your weekend?_____

B: I spent the weekend with Joe and Kathy.

A: What _____

B: Well, on Saturday, we went shopping.

A: And _____ in the evening?

B: No, nothing special.

A: Where _____ on Sunday?

B: We went to the amusement park.

A: How _____

B: We had a great time. In fact, we stayed there all day.

A: Really? What time _____

B: We got home very late, around midnight.

5

Answer these questions with negative statements. Then add a positive statement using the information in the box.

> ☑ have a boring time   ☐ finish our homework on Saturday   ☐ go out with friends
> ☐ watch it on TV   ☐ work all day until six o'clock   ☐ take the bus

1. A: We had a great time at Carrie's party. Did you and Jane enjoy it?

   B: _No, we didn't. We had a boring time._

2. A: I stayed home from work all day yesterday. Did you take the day off, too?

   B: _____

3. A: I worked all weekend on my research paper. Did you spend the weekend at home, too?

   B: _____

4. A: I studied all weekend. Did you and John have a lot of homework, too?

   B: _____

5. A: Carl drove me to work yesterday morning. Did you drive to work?

   B: _____

6. A: Kathy went to the baseball game last night. Did you and Bob go to the game?

   B: _____

6

Read about Andy's week. Match the sentences that have a similar meaning.

A	B
1. He was broke last week. __f__	a. He had people over.
2. He didn't work on Friday. _____	b. He had a good time.
3. He worked around the house. _____	c. He didn't do the laundry.
4. He didn't wash the clothes. _____	d. He took a day off.
5. He invited friends for dinner. _____	e. He did housework.
6. He had a lot of fun. _____	✓ f. He spent all his money.

7 *Did we take the same trip?*

A Read the postings. Who went to Bangkok for the first time?

William

We went to Thailand for our summer vacation. We spent a week in Bangkok and did something every day. We went to the floating market very early one morning. We didn't buy anything there – we just looked. Another day, we went to Wat Phra Kaew, the famous Temple of The Emerald Buddha. Check out my pic!

Then we saw two more temples nearby. We also went on a river trip somewhere outside Bangkok. The best thing about the trip was the food. The next time we have friends over for dinner, I'm going to cook Thai food.

Sue

Last summer, we spent our vacation in Thailand. We were very excited – it was our first trip there. We spent two days in Bangkok. Of course, we got a river taxi to the floating market. We bought some delicious fruit there. I'm posting a picture.

The next day we went to a very interesting temple called the Temple of the Emerald Buddha. We didn't have time to visit any other temples. However, we went to two historic cities – Ayutthaya and Sukhothai. Both have really interesting ruins. Everyting was great. It's impossible to say what was the best thing about the trip.

B Who did these things on their trip? Check (✓) the answers.

	William	Sue
1. stayed for two days in Bangkok	☐	✓
2. visited the floating market	☐	☐
3. bought fruit	☐	☐
4. saw some historic ruins	☐	☐
5. traveled on the river	☐	☐
6. loved the food the most	☐	☐
7. enjoyed everything	☐	☐

8 Complete this conversation with was, wasn't, were, or weren't.

A: How __was__ your vacation in Peru, Julia?

B: It _____ great. I really enjoyed it.

A: How long _____ you there?

B: We _____ there for two weeks.

A: _____ you in Lima all the time?

B: No, we _____. We _____ in the mountains for a few days.

A: And how _____ the weather? _____ it good?

B: No, it _____ good at all! In fact, it _____ terrible. The city _____ very hot, and the mountains _____ really cold!

9 Choose the correct questions to complete this conversation.

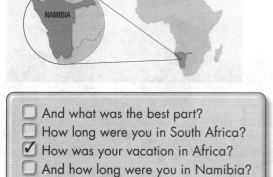

Namibian meerkats

- ☐ And what was the best part?
- ☐ How long were you in South Africa?
- ☑ How was your vacation in Africa?
- ☐ And how long were you in Namibia?
- ☐ How was the weather?

A: How was your vacation in Africa? _____

B: It was a great trip. I really enjoyed South Africa and Namibia.

A: _____

B: For ten days.

A: _____

B: I was in Namibia for about five days.

A: Wow, that's a long time! _____

B: It was hot and sunny the whole time.

A: _____

B: It was definitely the national parks and wildlife in Namibia. And we saw some meerkats!

10 Choose the correct words or phrases.

1. I'm sorry I was late. I had to _____ a phone call. (do / make / go)

2. My friends and I really enjoyed your party. We all had a _____ time.
   (boring / good / funny)

3. I stayed home last night and _____ the laundry.
   (did / went / made)

4. We didn't see very much in the mountains. The weather was pretty _____ .
   (cool / foggy / sunny)

5. I worked really hard in Switzerland last week. I was there _____ .
   (in my car / on business / on vacation)

11 My kind of vacation

A What do you like to do on vacation? Rank these activities from 1 (you like it the most) to 6 (you like it the least).

_____ go to the beach

_____ look at historical buildings

_____ go shopping

_____ visit museums

_____ spend time at home

_____ have good food

B Answer these questions about vacations.

1. How often do you go on vacation?

   _____

2. How long do you spend on vacation?

   _____

3. Who do you usually go with?

   _____

4. Where do you usually go?

   _____

5. What do you usually do on vacation?

   _____

What's your neighborhood like?

Places

A Match the words in columns A and B. Write the names of the places.

A	B	
☑ barber	☐ agency	1. <u>barbershop</u>
☐ gas	☐ bar	2. _____
☐ grocery	☐ café	3. _____
☐ Internet	☐ office	4. _____
☐ karaoke	☐ phone	5. _____
☐ movie	☑ shop	6. _____
☐ pay	☐ station	7. _____
☐ post	☐ store	8. _____
☐ travel	☐ theater	9. _____

B Write questions with "Is there a . . . ?" or "Are there any . . . ?" and the names of places from part A.

1. A: I need a haircut. <u>Is there a barbershop</u> near here?

   B: Yes, there's one on Elm Street.

2. A: I want to check my email. _____ near here?

   B: No, there aren't, but there are some near the university.

3. A: I want to mail this package. _____ around here?

   B: Yes, there's one next to the laundromat.

4. A: I need to make a phone call. _____ around here?

   B: Yes, there are some across from the library.

5. A: We need some gas. _____ on this street?

   B: No, there aren't, but there are a couple on Second Avenue.

6. A: We need to make a reservation for a trip. _____

   near here?

   B: Yes, there's one near the Prince Hotel.

2 *Look at these street maps of Avery and Bailey. There are ten differences between them. Find the other eight.*

> **Grammar note: There are; some *and* any**
>
> **Positive statement**
> There **are some** pay phones near the bank.
>
> **Negative statement**
> There **aren't any** pay phones near the bank.

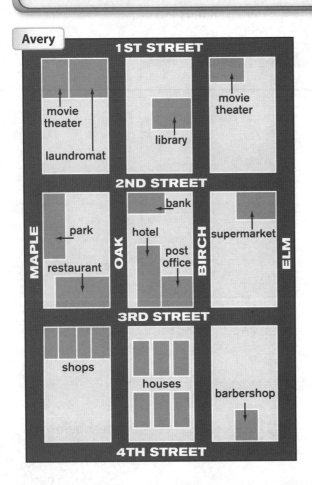

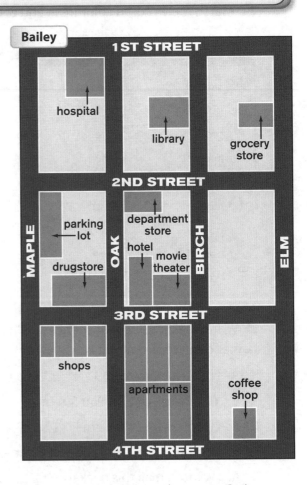

1. <u>There are some movie theaters on 1st Street in Avery, but there aren't any in Bailey.</u>

2. <u>There's a park on the corner of 2nd Street and Maple in Avery, but there isn't one in Bailey. There's a parking lot.</u>

3. _____

4. _____

5. _____

6. _____

7. _____

8. _____

9. _____

10. _____

3 *Answer these questions. Use the map and the prepositions in the box.*

> ☐ between   ☐ in front of   ☐ near
> ☑ next to   ☐ on the corner of   ☐ opposite

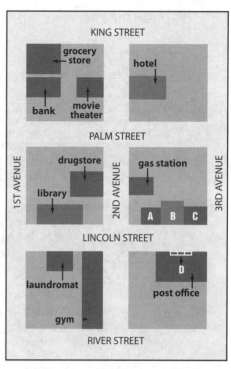

1. Where's the nearest bank?

   There's one next to the grocery store on 1st Avenue.

2. Is there a post office near here?

   Yes. There _____

   _____

3. I'm looking for a drugstore.

   _____

   _____

4. Is there a laundromat in this neighborhood?

   _____

   _____

5. Is there a department store on Lincoln Street?

   _____

   _____

6. Are there any pay phones around here?

   _____

   _____

> A = travel agency   C = gym
>
> B = department store   D = pay phones

4 *Answer these questions about your city or neighborhood.*
Use the expressions in the box and your own information.

> Yes, there is. There's one on . . .   Yes, there are. There are some on . . .
> No, there isn't.   No, there aren't.

1. Are there any cheap restaurants around the school?

   _____

2. Is there a police station near the school?

   _____

3. Are there any nice coffee shops in your neighborhood?

   _____

4. Is there a karaoke bar close to your home?

   _____

5 *The grass is always greener . . .*

A Read the interviews. Where would Diana like to live? Where would Victor like to live?

MODERN LIFE

Modern Life magazine asked two people about their neighborhoods.

Interview with Diana Towne

"My neighborhood is very convenient – it's near the shopping center and the bus station. It's also safe. But those are the only good things about living downtown. It's very noisy because the streets are always full of people! The traffic is terrible, and parking is a big problem! I can never park on my own street. I'd like to live in the suburbs."

Interview with Victor Bord

"My wife and I live in the suburbs, and it's just too quiet! There aren't many shops, and there are certainly no clubs or movie theaters. There are a lot of parks, good schools, and very little crime, but nothing ever really happens here. And it takes a long time to drive anywhere. I'd really love to live downtown."

B How do Diana and Victor feel about their neighborhoods?
Complete the chart.

	Advantages	Disadvantages
Downtown	near the shopping center	
Suburbs		

C How do you feel about your neighborhood? Write about it.

_____

_____

_____

_____

6 Complete the chart. Use words from the box.

☑ bank	☐ hospital	☐ noise	☐ people	☐ school	☐ traffic
☑ crime	☐ library	☐ parking	☐ pollution	☐ theater	☐ water

Count nouns		Noncount nouns	
bank	_____	crime	_____
_____	_____	_____	_____
_____	_____	_____	_____

7 Write questions using "How much . . . ?" or "How many . . . ?" Then look at the picture and write answers to the questions. Use the expressions in the box.

☑ a lot	☐ a couple	☐ many	☐ only a little	☐ not any	☐ a lot

1. (noise)   How much noise is there? _____   There's a lot. _____
2. (buses)   _____   _____
3. (traffic)   _____   _____
4. (banks)   _____   _____
5. (people)   _____   _____
6. (crime)   _____   _____

8 **Choose the correct words or phrases to complete this conversation.**

Luis: Are there _____any_____ (any / one / none) nightclubs around here, Alex?

Alex: Sure. There are _____ (any / one / a lot).

There's a great club _____ (across from / between / on)

the National Bank, but it's expensive.

Luis: Well, are there _____ (any / none / one) others?

Alex: Yeah, there are _____ (a few / a little / one).

There's a nice _____ (any / one / some) near here.

It's called Sounds of Brazil.

Luis: That's perfect! Where is it, exactly?

Alex: It's on Third Avenue, _____ (between / on / on the corner of)

the Royal Theater and May's Restaurant.

Luis: So let's go!

9 **Choose the correct words or phrases.**

1. I'm going to the stationery store to get a _____ .
    (birthday card / coffee / food)

2. We're taking a long drive. We need to go to the _____ .
    (laundromat / gas station / travel agency)

3. I live on the 8th floor of my _____ .
    (apartment building / neighborhood / theater)

4. Our apartment is in the center of the city. We live _____ .
    (downtown / in the neighborhood / in the suburbs)

What does she look like?

Write the opposites. Use the words in the box.

☐ light   ☑ straight   ☐ young   ☐ short   ☐ tall

1. curly / <u>straight</u>   4. long / _____

2. dark / _____   5. short / _____

3. elderly / _____

2 *Descriptions*

A Match the words in columns A and B. Write the descriptions.

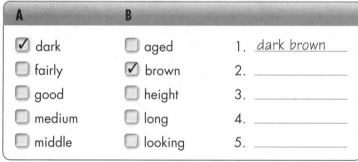

A	B	
☑ dark	☐ aged	1. <u>dark brown</u>
☐ fairly	☑ brown	2. _____
☐ good	☐ height	3. _____
☐ medium	☐ long	4. _____
☐ middle	☐ looking	5. _____

B Answer the questions using the descriptions from part A.

1. A: What does he look like?

   B: <u>He's good-looking.</u>

2. A: How long is his hair?

   B: _____

3. A: What color is his hair?

   B: _____

4. A: How old is he?

   B: _____

5. A: How tall is he?

   B: _____

3 *Complete this conversation with questions.*

Steve: Let's find Amy. I need to talk to her.

Jim: *What does she look like?*

Steve: She's very pretty, with straight black hair.

Jim: And _____

Steve: It's medium length.

Jim: _____

Steve: She's fairly tall.

Jim: And _____

Steve: She's in her early twenties.

Jim: _____

Steve: Sometimes. I think she's wearing them now.

Jim: I think I see her over there. Is that her?

4 *Describe yourself. How old are you? What do you look like?*
What are you wearing today?

_____

_____

_____

_____

_____

5 Circle two things in each description that do not match the picture.
Then correct the information.

George

1. George is in his (late sixties) He's pretty tall.

   He has a mustache, and he's bald.

   He's wearing a shirt, jeans, and boots.

   He isn't in his late sixties. He's in his twenties.

   _____

   _____

   _____

2. Sophie is about 25. She's very pretty.

   She's medium height. Her hair is long and blond.

   She's wearing a black sweater, a jacket, and sneakers.

   She's standing next to her motorcycle.

   _____

   _____

   _____

   _____

Sophie

Lucinda

3. Lucinda is in her early twenties.

   She's pretty serious-looking. She has glasses.

   She's fairly tall, and has curly dark hair.

   She's wearing a nice-looking jacket and jeans.

   _____

   _____

   _____

   _____

6 Which of these clothing items are more formal? Which are more casual? Complete the chart.

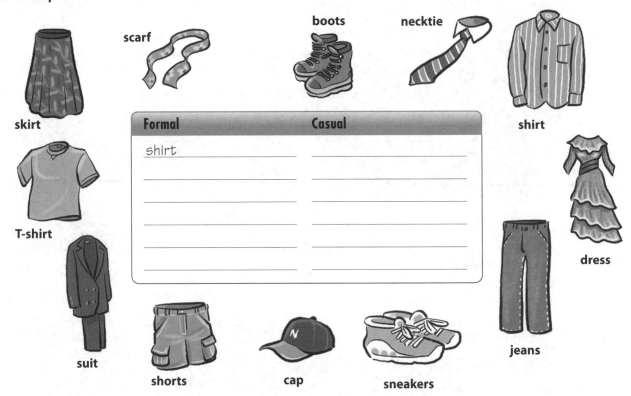

scarf

boots

necktie

skirt

shirt

Formal	Casual
shirt	

T-shirt

dress

suit

shorts

cap

sneakers

jeans

7 Write a sentence about each person. Use the words in the box and participles.

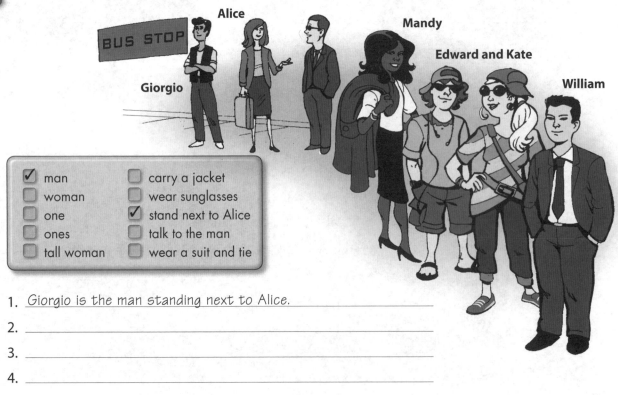

Alice

Mandy

Edward and Kate

Giorgio

William

BUS STOP

☑ man	☐ carry a jacket
☐ woman	☐ wear sunglasses
☐ one	☑ stand next to Alice
☐ ones	☐ talk to the man
☐ tall woman	☐ wear a suit and tie

1. Giorgio is the man standing next to Alice.

2. _____

3. _____

4. _____

5. _____

8 *Answer the questions. Use the words given.*

1. A: Which ones are Jake and Marie?

    B: <u>They're the ones playing chess.</u>　　　　　　　　 (playing chess)

2. A: Who's Carlos?

    B: _____ (couch)

3. A: Who are Dan and Cindy?

    B: _____ (dancing)

4. A: Which one is Angela?

    B: _____ (couch)

5. A: Who's Ken?

    B: _____ (short black hair)

9 *Rewrite these sentences and questions.*
Find another way to say them using the words given.

1. A: Who's Mika?

    <u>Which one's Mika?</u>　　　　　　　　　　　　　 (Which)

    B: She's the one in the black dress.

    <u>She's the one wearing the black dress.</u>　　　 (wearing)

2. A: Which ones are the teachers?

    _____ (Who)

    B: They're the ones on the couch.

    _____ (sitting)

3. A: Which one is Larry?

    _____ (Who)

    B: He's the guy wearing the coat.

    _____ (in)

What does she look like? ▪ **53**

10 Complete this description. Use the present continuous or the participle of the verbs in the box.

[ ] ask   [ ] carry   [✓] look   [ ] stand   [ ] use   [ ] wait   [ ] walk   [ ] wear

Yeah, classes start tomorrow. What am I doing? Let's see.... I _'m looking_ out my window right now. There's a middle aged _____ with her baby. Some people _____ at the bus stop. A serious-looking man _____ for directions. A young guy _____ his cell phone. Two people _____ next to him. Hey! The one _____ a baseball cap is my classmate! And hey, here comes a really cute girl _____ a backpack. Wait a minute! I know her. That's my old friend. I have to go now! Bye.

DORMITORY

BUS STOP

11 Choose the correct responses.

1. A: Where's Jan?

   B: _She couldn't make it._
   - I'd like to meet her.
   - She couldn't make it.

2. A: Who's Sam?

   B: _____
   - I'm afraid I missed him.
   - The handsome guy near the door.

3. A: Is she the one on the couch?

   B: _____
   - That's right.
   - My father is by the chair.

4. A: How tall is she?

   B: _____
   - Fairly long.
   - Pretty short.

10 Have you ever ridden a camel?

1 Match the verb forms in columns A and B.

A		B	
1. be	_d_	a.	gone
2. call	___	b.	done
3. do	___	c.	seen
4. eat	___	✓ d.	been
5. go	___	e.	called
6. have	___	f.	run
7. make	___	g.	made
8. run	___	h.	had
9. see	___	i.	tried
10. try	___	j.	eaten

2 Complete the questions in these conversations. Use the present perfect of the verbs in Exercise 1.

1. A: _Have you seen_ Lacey's new hairstyle?

   B: Yes, it's very . . . interesting.

2. A: _____ your homework yet?

   B: Yes, I have. I did it last night.

3. A: How many phone calls _____ today?

   B: I made only one – to call you!

4. A: How long _____ those sunglasses?

   B: I've had them for a few weeks.

5. A: _____ at Rio Café?

   B: Yes, we've already eaten there. It's very good but
   a little expensive.

6. A: How many times _____ shopping
   at the mall this month?

   B: Actually, I haven't gone at all. Why don't we go
   later today?

3 Already *and* yet

A Check (✓) the things you've already done. Put an ✗ next to the things you haven't done yet.

1. _____ graduated from high school
2. _____ learned to drive
3. _____ gone abroad
4. _____ been in an airplane
5. _____ tried skiing
6. _____ gotten married

B Write sentences about each thing in part A. Use *already* and *yet*.

> **Grammar note: Already *and* yet**
>
> **Already** *is used in positive statements with the present perfect.*
> I've **already** graduated from high school.
>
> **Yet** *is used in negative statements with the present perfect.*
> I haven't graduated from college **yet.**

1. _____
2. _____
3. _____
4. _____
5. _____
6. _____

4 *Complete these sentences with* for *or* since.

1. Damien has lived in Hong Kong _____ since _____ 2001.
2. I have been a nurse _____ several years.
3. Masayuki was an exchange student in Spain _____ a whole semester.
4. I'm so sleepy. I've been awake _____ 4:00 this morning.
5. Mr. and Mrs. Chang have been married _____ nearly 40 years.
6. Maggie has had the same hairstyle _____ high school.
7. How are you? I haven't seen you _____ your wedding.
8. Where have you been? I've been here _____ over an hour!
9. I haven't had this much fun _____ I was a kid.

5 *Look at these pictures. How often have you done these things?*
Write sentences using the expressions in the box.

> I've . . . many times   I've . . . once or twice.
> I've . . . three or four times.   I haven't . . . lately.
> I've . . . several times.   I've never . . .

ride a roller coaster

1. _____

go to a food festival

2. _____

go bungee jumping

3. _____
_____

hear live music

4. _____
_____

see an opera

5. _____
_____

play tennis

6. _____
_____

A Read the two stories. Where did each writer go? What activity did each writer want to do?

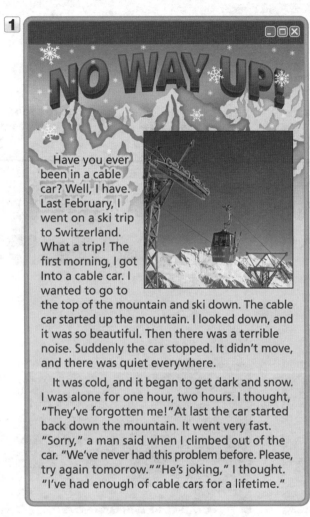

1 Have you ever been in a cable car? Well, I have. Last February, I went on a ski trip to Switzerland. What a trip! The first morning, I got Into a cable car. I wanted to go to the top of the mountain and ski down. The cable car started up the mountain. I looked down, and it was so beautiful. Then there was a terrible noise. Suddenly the car stopped. It didn't move, and there was quiet everywhere.

It was cold, and it began to get dark and snow. I was alone for one hour, two hours. I thought, "They've forgotten me!" At last the car started back down the mountain. It went very fast. "Sorry," a man said when I climbed out of the car. "We've never had this problem before. Please, try again tomorrow." "He's joking," I thought. "I've had enough of cable cars for a lifetime."

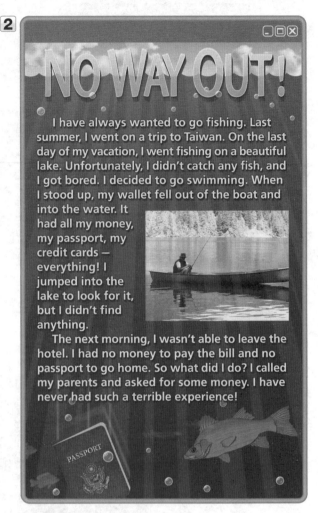

2 I have always wanted to go fishing. Last summer, I went on a trip to Taiwan. On the last day of my vacation, I went fishing on a beautiful lake. Unfortunately, I didn't catch any fish, and I got bored. I decided to go swimming. When I stood up, my wallet fell out of the boat and into the water. It had all my money, my passport, my credit cards — everything! I jumped into the lake to look for it, but I didn't find anything.

The next morning, I wasn't able to leave the hotel. I had no money to pay the bill and no passport to go home. So what did I do? I called my parents and asked for some money. I have never had such a terrible experience!

B In which story or stories did the writer(s) do these things? Write *1*, *2*, or *1* and *2*.

__1__ stayed in the mountains	_____ spent time on a boat
_____ lost a wallet	_____ waited for help
_____ enjoyed the view	_____ went swimming
_____ got no exercise	_____ had a terrible day

C Write about a terrible day you have had. What happened? What went wrong?

_____

_____

_____

_____

_____

7 *Look at the answers. Write questions using **Have you ever . . . ?***

flamenco dancing

sumo wrestling

oysters

wall climbing

1. A: <u>Have you ever watched flamenco dancing?</u>

 B: Yes, I have. I watched flamenco dancing last summer in Spain.

2. A: _____

 B: Actually, I saw a sumo wrestling match last month on TV. It was terrific!

3. A: _____

 B: No, I haven't. I've never eaten oysters.

4. A: _____

 B: No, I've never been wall climbing.

5. A: _____

 B: Yes, I rode in a sports car last month.

6. A: _____

 B: No, I haven't. I've never been camping.

7. A: _____

 B: Yes, I have. I once rode my brother's motorcycle.

8 *Write your own answers to the questions in Exercise 7.*
Use expressions like the ones from the list.

Yes, I have. I . . . yesterday.	No, I haven't. I've never . . .
I . . . on Monday.	I . . . yet.
I . . . last year.	
I . . . in August.	

1. _____

2. _____

3 _____

4. _____

5. _____

6. _____

7. _____

9 *Complete the conversation. Use the simple past or the present perfect of the words given.*

A: ___Have___ you ever ___lost___ (lose) anything valuable?

B: Yes, I _____ (lose) my cell phone last month.

A: _____ you _____ (find) it yet?

B: No. Actually, I _____ already _____ (buy) a new one. Look!

A: Oh, that's nice. Where _____ you _____ (buy) it?

B: I _____ (get) it at Tech Town last weekend. What about you? _____ you ever _____ (lose) anything valuable?

A: Well, I _____ (leave) my leather jacket in a coffee shop a couple of months ago.

B: Oh, no! _____ you _____ (go) back and look for it?

A: Well, I _____ (call) them, but it was gone.

10 *Choose the correct responses.*

1. A: Has Marie called her family lately?

   B: _No, she hasn't._
   - How many times?
   - No, she hasn't.

2. A: Are you having a good time?

   B: _____
   - Yes, in a long time.
   - Yes, really good.

3. A: How long did Joe stay at the party?

   B: _____
   - For two hours.
   - Since midnight.

4. A: Have you had lunch?

   B: _____
   - Yes, in a few minutes.
   - Yes, I've already eaten.

5. A: How many times has Gina lost her keys?

   B: _____
   - Twice.
   - Already.

6. A: What about a tour of the city?

   B: _____
   - I've never, have you?
   - Sure. I hear it's great.

7. A: Have you been here long?

   B: _____
   - No, not yet.
   - No, just a few minutes.

8. A: Have you seen Chad today?

   B: _____
   - Yes, I saw him this morning.
   - Yes, for 7:00.

11 It's a very exciting place!

1 Choose the correct words to complete the sentences.

New York City

Florence

1. Prices are high in New York City. Everything is very _____expensive_____ there.
   (cheap / expensive / stressful)

2. Florence is a beautiful old city. There are not many _____ buildings.
   (big / modern / small)

3. My hometown is not an exciting place. The nightlife there is pretty _____ .
   (boring / nice / interesting)

4. Some parts of our city are fairly dangerous. They're not very _____ late at night.
   (hot / interesting / safe)

5. Athens is a very quiet city in the winter. The streets are never _____ at that time of the year.
   (spacious / crowded / relaxing)

2 Choose the correct questions to complete this conversation.

☐ What's the weather like?
☐ Is it big?
☐ Is the nightlife exciting?
☑ What's your hometown like?

A: _What's your hometown like?_

B: My hometown? It's a pretty nice place, and the people are very friendly.

A: _____

B: No, it's fairly small, but it's not *too* small.

A: _____

B: The winter is wet and really cold. It's very nice in the summer, though.

A: _____

B: No! It's really boring. There are no good restaurants or nightclubs.

3 *Choose the correct conjunctions and rewrite the sentences.*

> **Grammar note:** **And, but, though,** *and* **however**
>
> ***Use*** **and** *for additional information.*
> It's an exciting city, **and** the weather is great.
>
> ***Use*** **but, though,** *and* **however** *for contrasting information.*
> It's very safe during the day, **but** it's pretty dangerous at night.
> The summers are hot. The evenings are fairly cold, **though**.
> It is a fairly large city. It's not too interesting, **however**.

São Paulo, Brazil

Sapporo, Japan

Marrakech, Morocco

1. São Paulo is a very busy place. The streets are always crowded. (and / but)

   <u>São Paulo is a very busy place, and the streets are always crowded.</u>

   _____

2. Sapporo is a very nice place. The winters are terribly cold. (and / though)

   _____

   _____

3. Marrakech is an exciting city. It's a fun place to sightsee. (and / however)

   _____

   _____

4. My hometown is a great place for a vacation. It's not too good for shopping. (and / but)

   _____

   _____

5. Our hometown is somewhat ugly. It has some beautiful old homes. (and / however)

   _____

   _____

4 Check (✓) if these sentences need **a** or **an**. *Then write* a or an *in the correct places.*

> **Grammar note: A and an**
>
> Use **a** or **an** with (adverb +) adjective + singular noun.
> It has **a fairly new park.** It's **an old city.**
> **Don't use a or an** with (adverb +) adjective.
> It's **fairly new**. It's **old**.

1. ☑ Beijing has ^*a* very modern airport.

2. ☐ Restaurants are very cheap in Ecuador.

3. ☐ Copenhagen is clean city.

4. ☐ The buildings in Paris are really beautiful.

5. ☐ Apartments are very expensive in Hong Kong.

6. ☐ Dubai is very hot city in the summer.

7. ☐ Mexico City has excellent museums.

8. ☐ Rio de Janeiro is exciting place to visit.

Beijing Capital International Airport

5 Complete this description of London with **is** or **has**.

Ever-Popular London

London _____ Britain's biggest city. It _____ a very old capital city and dates back to the Romans. It _____ a city of interesting buildings and churches, and it _____ many beautiful parks. It also _____ some of the best museums in the world. London _____ very crowded in the summer, but it _____ not too busy in the winter. It _____ a popular city with foreign tourists and _____ millions of visitors a year. The city _____ famous for its shopping and _____ many excellent department stores. London _____ convenient trains and buses that cross the city, so it _____ easy for tourists to get around.

6 *From city to city*

A Scan the webpage. Where is each city?

 **Helsinki**

 **Vancouver**

 **Salvador da Bahia**

Helsinki was founded in 1550 and became the capital city of Finland in 1812. It's a fairly small city, with a population of about 600,000. Helsinki is very beautiful, and it is a good city for walking and bicycling. It has lots of parks, and there are forests nearby. Cruises are popular. The city is on the Baltic Sea, and there are hundreds of small islands nearby. The best time to go is the summer because the Finnish winter is very cold. It has an average temperature in February of -3.6° Celsius.

A small community called Granville was founded on the west coast of Canada in the 1870s. It was renamed Vancouver in 1886. Today, Vancouver is a large city of over 2 million people. About 49 percent of the population speak English as a first language, and about 25 percent speak Chinese as a first language. The city has lots of really good restaurants that serve many kinds of food. Vancouver has fairly mild weather. It's not very hot or very cold. There is skiing nearby in the Coast Mountain Range.

Salvador da Bahia was founded in 1549. Since then, it has been a very important city in northeast Brazil. It was the country's first capital city. With about 2.6 million people, Salvador da Bahia is a popular tourist destination. Visitors come for its architecture and its beaches. People also come for the African heritage in the food and music. Capoeira, for example, is a popular mix of music, dancing, and martial arts. The weather is usually hot and humid, but sea breezes make it feel pleasant.

B Read the webpage and complete the chart.

City	Date founded	Population	Weather	Attractions
Helsinki	1550	_____	_____	_____
				_____
Vancouver	_____	_____	_____	_____
				_____
Salvador da Bahia	_____	_____	_____	_____
				_____

C Complete the sentences.

1. _Vancouver_____ changed its name in 1886.
2. _____ has many Chinese speakers.
3. _____ is the coldest of the three cities.
4. _____ were both founded in the mid-sixteenth century.

7 *Complete these sentences. Use phrases from the list.*

- ☐ shouldn't miss
- ☑ should see
- ☐ can get
- ☐ can take
- ☐ shouldn't stay
- ☐ shouldn't walk

1. You ___should see___ the new zoo. It's very interesting.
2. You _____ near the airport. It's too noisy.
3. You _____ the museum. It has some new exhibits.
4. You _____ a bus tour of the city if you like.
5. You _____ alone at night. It's too dangerous.
6. You _____ a taxi if you're out late.

8 *Complete this conversation with* **should** *or* **shouldn't** *and* **I** *or* **you.**

A: I'm taking my vacation in Indonesia.
What ___should I___ do there?

B: _____ miss Yogyakarta, the old capital city. There are a lot of beautiful old buildings. For example, _____ see the temple of Borobudur.

A: Sounds great. Bali is very popular, too. _____ go there?

B: Yes, _____ . It's very interesting.

A: _____ take a lot of money with me?

B: No, _____ . Indonesia is not an expensive country to visit.

A: So when _____ go there?

B: Anytime. The weather's always nice.

Yogyakarta, Indonesia

9 *Ask questions about a place you want to visit.*
Use **can, should,** *or* **shouldn't.**

1. the time to visit
   <u>What time of year should you visit?</u>

2. things to see and do there
   _____

3. things not to do
   _____

4. special foods to try
   _____

5. fun things to buy
   _____

6. other interesting things to do
   _____

10 *Rewrite these sentences. Find another way to say each sentence*
using the words given.

1. It's a stressful city.
   <u>It isn't a relaxing city.</u>   (not relaxing)

2. The streets are always full of people.
   _____   (crowded)

3. It's not a very beautiful city.
   _____   (fairly ugly)

4. When should we visit the city?
   _____   (a good time)

5. You really should visit the weekend market.
   _____   (not miss)

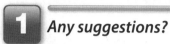

It really works!

1 Any suggestions?

A Check (✓) the best advice for each health problem.

1. a backache
- ✓ use a heating pad
- ☐ get some exercise
- ☐ drink herbal tea

2. a bad cold
- ☐ see a dentist
- ☐ go to bed and rest
- ☐ go swimming

3. a burn
- ☐ take a multivitamin
- ☐ put it under cold water
- ☐ drink warm milk

4. a headache
- ☐ take some vitamin C
- ☐ take some aspirin
- ☐ take a cough drop

5. an insect bite
- ☐ apply anti-itch cream
- ☐ use eyedrops
- ☐ drink lots of liquids

6. sore muscles
- ☐ drink lots of hot water
- ☐ take some cold medicine
- ☐ use some ointment

B Write a question about each problem in part A. Then write answers using the words from the box. Use the advice in part A or your own ideas.

> It's important . . .   It's sometimes helpful . . .   It's a good idea . . .

1. A: <u>What should you do for a backache?</u>
   B: <u>It's helpful to use a heating pad.</u>

2. A: _____
   B: _____

3. A: _____
   B: _____

4. A: _____
   B: _____

5. A: _____
   B: _____

6. A: _____
   B: _____

2 *Rewrite these sentences. Give advice using*
It's important . . . , It's a good idea . . . , or It's sometimes helpful . . . .

> ### Grammar note: Negative infinitives
>
> | Problem | Advice | Negative infinitive |
> |---------|--------|---------------------|
> | For the flu, | don't exercise a lot. | For the flu, it's a good idea **not to exercise** a lot. |

1. For a toothache, don't eat cold foods.

   For a toothache, it's important not to eat cold foods.

2. For a sore throat, don't talk too much.

   _____

3. For a burn, don't put ice on it.

   _____

4. For insomnia, don't drink coffee at night.

   _____

5. For a fever, don't get out of bed.

   _____

3 *Check (✓) three health problems you have had. Write what you
did for each one. Use the remedies below or your own remedies.*

Health problems

☐ a backache
☐ a headache
☐ a toothache
☐ a cold
☐ a sore throat
☐ the hiccups
☐ a sunburn
☐ stress

Some remedies

take some aspirin   get some medicine from the drugstore
use some lotion   put some ointment on it
take some cough drops   see my doctor/dentist
go to bed   do nothing

Example: Yesterday, I had a bad headache, so I took some aspirin.

1. _____

2. _____

3. _____

4 Getting to sleep

A Scan the article. Check (✓) the things that the article says may stop people from sleeping at night. Then read the article to check your answers.

☐ noisy neighbors ☐ some medicines ☐ a regular sleep schedule
☐ sleeping after lunch ☐ stress ☐ sheep

SLEEP

Most people need seven to eight hours of sleep a night. Some people need less than this, and some people need more.

According to sleep expert Dr. Robert Schachter, many people have difficulty sleeping, but they do not know why. Most people know it is important not to drink coffee or tea before they go to bed – both

beverages have caffeine. Caffeine keeps people awake. However, not everybody knows that some medicines, such as cold tablets, also have caffeine in them. Stress can cause insomnia, too. Busy people with stressful jobs may not be able to sleep at night.

Dr. Schachter suggests, "You shouldn't use your bedroom as a TV room or an exercise room. You should use it for sleeping only. It's a good idea to have a regular sleeping schedule. Get up and go to bed at the same time every day. It's also important not to eat before bedtime. Eating may keep you awake."

And if all this doesn't work, try counting sheep!

B Check (✓) True or False.

	True	False
1. Everyone needs eight hours of sleep a night.	☐	☐
2. Caffeine helps you fall asleep.	☐	☐
3. Cold tablets can keep you awake.	☐	☐
4. Busy people may have trouble falling asleep.	☐	☐
5. It is a good idea to have a TV near your bed.	☐	☐
6. You should have regular sleeping hours.	☐	☐
7. You shouldn't eat just before you go to bed.	☐	☐
8. Counting sheep may help people sleep.	☐	☐

5 *What do you suggest?*

A Complete the word map with medicines from the list.

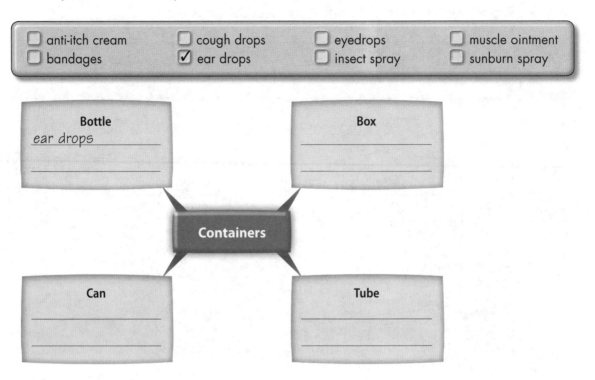

☐ anti-itch cream   ☐ cough drops   ☐ eyedrops   ☐ muscle ointment
☐ bandages   ☑ ear drops   ☐ insect spray   ☐ sunburn spray

Bottle
ear drops
_____

Box
_____
_____

Containers

Can
_____
_____

Tube
_____
_____

B What should these people buy? Give advice. Use the containers and medicine from part A.

1. Joe has very tired eyes.

   He should buy a bottle of eyedrops.

2. Mary has a bad cough.

   _____

3. David has a terrible earache.

   _____

4. There may be mosquitoes where Ed's camping.

   _____

5. Manuel has dry, itchy skin.

   _____

6. Susan has a cut on her hand.

   _____

7. Jin-sook and Brandy got sunburned at the beach.

   _____

8. Mark's shoulders are sore after his workout.

   _____

6 *Check (✓) the correct sentences to make conversations.*

1. Pharmacist: ☑ Can I help you?
   ☐ Should I help you?

   Customer: ☐ Yes. Can I have a bottle of aspirin?
   ☐ Yes. I suggest a bottle of aspirin.

   Pharmacist: Here you are.

   Customer: ☐ And what do you need for a sunburn?
   ☐ And what do you have for a sunburn?

   Pharmacist: ☐ Do you suggest this lotion?
   ☐ I suggest this lotion.

   Customer: Thanks.

2. Pharmacist: Hi. Can I help you?

   Customer: ☐ Yes. Can I suggest something for sore muscles?
   ☐ Yes. Could I have something for sore muscles?

   Pharmacist: ☐ Sure. Try this ointment.
   ☐ Sure. Could I try this ointment?

   Customer: ☐ Thanks. And what should you get for the flu?
   ☐ Thanks. And what do you suggest for the flu?

   Pharmacist: ☐ Can I have some of these tablets? They really work.
   ☐ Try some of these tablets. They really work.

   Customer: ☐ OK, thanks. I'll take them. And you should get a pack of tissues.
   ☐ OK, thanks. I'll take them. And could I have a pack of tissues?

   Pharmacist: Sure. Here you are.

7 Complete this conversation with the correct words.

A: Wow, you don't look very good! Do you feel OK?

B: No, I think I'm getting a cold. What should I do _____ it?
   (for / to / with)

A: You should stay _____ home and go _____ bed.
   (at / in / of)   (in / of / to)

B: You're probably right. I've got a really bad cough, too.

A: Try drinking some hot tea _____ honey. It really helps.
   (for / of / with)

B: Anything else?

A: Yeah, I suggest you get a big box _____ tissues!
   (at / in / of)

8 Give suggestions for these problems. Use words from the box.

> Try . . .   I suggest . . .   You should . . .

1. I have a very sore throat.

   Try some hot tea.

2. I think I'm getting a cold.

   _____

3. I can't stop sneezing.

   _____

4. I don't have any energy.

   _____

5. I'm stressed out!

   _____

6. I can't get to sleep.

   _____

13 May I take your order?

1 *Show that you agree. Write sentences with the words given.*

1. A: I don't want fast food tonight.

   B: <u>I don't either.</u> (either)

2. A: I really like Chinese food.

   B: _____ (so)

3. A: I'm in the mood for Italian food.

   B: _____ (too)

4. A: I can't stand spicy food.

   B: _____ (neither)

5. A: I don't like bland food very much.

   B: _____ (either)

6. A: I think Japanese food is delicious.

   B: _____ (too)

73

2 *What do you think?*

A Look at the pictures. Write sentences about the food.
Use the expressions in the box and the given words.

useful expressions
I love . . .   I'm not crazy about . . .
I'm crazy about . . .   I don't like . . . very much.
I like . . . a lot.   I can't stand . . .
It's a little too . . .

greasy

1. <u>It's a little too greasy.</u>

healthy

2. _____

salty

3. _____

bland

4. _____

rich

5. _____

B What are your three favorite kinds of food? Write about why you like them.

_____

_____

_____

_____

3 Online reviewers

A Skim the restaurant reviews. Match the reviewer with the number of stars.

1. Camille   ★★★★★   Fantastic!!
2. Luke   ★★★   Pretty good.
3. Adam   ★   Awful!

Restaurant Reviews

Search for (Indian, Mexican, cheap lunch)

Neighborhood (Address, City)

Trattoria Romana

Luke

Trattoria Romana is an excellent Italian restaurant. It has a quiet and relaxing atmosphere, and the service is very good. It's always crowded, so make a reservation early. The menu is not very big. There are only four entrées on the menu, but everything is fresh. The chicken with pasta is wonderful. Desserts are their specialty – rich and really delicious! You'll spend about $32 per person. It's my new favorite place to eat.

Dynasty

Camille

Last Saturday, I was the only customer at Dynasty, a new diner on 57th Street. It's not a nice place. The servers are slow and unfriendly. The atmosphere is boring, and so is the menu. The restaurant specializes in American food – mostly steak and potatoes. My steak was almost raw, and the fries were greasy. It isn't cheap either. It cost me $36. If you go there, you won't need a reservation. My advice, however, is simple: "Don't go!"

Beirut Café

Adam

Beirut Café is a new Lebanese restaurant located downtown on the corner of 12th and Maple. The specialty is *meze* – lots of different small dishes. The atmosphere is lively, and the service is pretty friendly. There's live Lebanese music and dancing on weekends. Beirut Café is not very expensive – about $18 a person. The food is good. If you go, you need a reservation.

B Read these reviews and complete the chart.

	Trattoria Romana	Dynasty	Beirut Café
Food	Italian	_____	_____
Atmosphere	quiet and relaxing	_____	_____
Specialties	_____	_____	_____
Service	_____	_____	_____
Price/person	_____	_____	_____
Reservation	☐ yes ☐ no	☐ yes ☐ no	☐ yes ☐ no

4 *Check (✓) the item that does not belong.*

1. ☐ beef
   ☑ fish
   ☐ lamb
2. ☐ strawberries
   ☐ grapes
   ☐ peas
3. ☐ octopus
   ☐ bread
   ☐ pasta
4. ☐ corn
   ☐ chicken
   ☐ potatoes
5. ☐ iced tea
   ☐ ice cream
   ☐ iced coffee
6. ☐ sushi
   ☐ a turkey sandwich
   ☐ a hamburger

5 *Use one or more words to complete this conversation between a server and a customer.*

Server: May I take your order?

Customer: <u>Yes, I'll have</u> the beef with potatoes.

Server: What kind of dressing _____ on your salad – French, blue cheese, or vinaigrette?

Customer: _____ like French, please.

Server: And would you like _____ to drink?

Customer: Yes, _____ have iced coffee.

Server: With milk and sugar?

Customer: Yes, _____ .

Server: Anything else?

Customer: No, _____ . That'll _____ all.

Server: OK. I'll bring it right away.

6 Choose the correct responses.

1. A: What would you like?

   B: <u>I'll have two cheeseburgers with everything.</u>

   - I'll be your server today.
   - Yes, I'd like to.
   - I'll have two cheeseburgers with everything.

2. A: Would you like french fries or salad?

   B: _____

   - I guess I will, thanks.
   - I'd like french fries, please.
   - Yes, please.

3. A: What kind of soda would you like?

   B: _____

   - I'll have a cola.
   - I'd like a pizza, please.
   - A small order, please.

4. A: Would you like anything to drink?

   B: _____

   - No, thanks.
   - Yes, a hamburger, please.
   - I'll have some noodles, please.

5. A: What flavor ice cream would you like?

   B: _____

   - Fresh, please.
   - Chocolate, please.
   - Ice cream, please.

6. A: Would you like anything else?

   B: _____

   - Yes, thank you very much.
   - Not at all, thanks.
   - That'll be all, thanks.

7 Choose the correct words.

1. Baked potatoes are less ____<u>greasy</u>____ than french fries. (greasy / healthy / spicy)

2. In a restaurant, the server takes your _____ . (menu / order / service)

3. Many people like _____ on their salad. (dessert / dressing / soda)

4. Some people rarely cook with spices. They prefer _____ food. (bland / hot / rich)

5. Strawberry is a popular ice cream _____ . (drink / flavor / meal)

8 *Complete the conversation. Use the words and expressions in the box.*

☐ am ☑ neither ☐ will ☐ can't stand them
☐ can ☐ so ☐ would ☐ favorite kind of food
☐ do ☐ too ☐ like it a lot

Sherry: I feel tired tonight. I really don't want to cook.

Whitney: ___Neither___ do I. Say, do you like Thai food?

Sherry: It's delicious! I _____ !

Whitney: I do, _____ . It's my _____ .
Let's call Chiang Mai restaurant for home delivery.

Sherry: Great idea! Their food is always good. I eat there a lot.

Whitney: _____ do I. Well, what _____ you like tonight?

Sherry: I'm in the mood for some soup.

Whitney: So _____ I. And I think I _____ have spicy
chicken and special Thai rice.

Sherry: OK, let's order. Oh, wait a minute, I don't have any money with me.

Whitney: Neither _____ I. What should we do?

Sherry: Well, let's look in the refrigerator. Hmm. Do you like boiled eggs?

Whitney: I _____ !

Sherry: Actually, neither _____ I.

14 The biggest and the best!

1 Geography

A Circle the correct word.

1. This is a stream of water occurring when a river falls from a high place.
   a. waterfall   b. ocean   c. hill

2. This is a large area of land that has lots of trees on it.
   a. desert   b. forest   c. river

3. This is a low area of land between mountains or hills.
   a. valley   b. river   c. beach

4. This is an area of water with land all around it.
   a. lake   b. ocean   c. island

5. This is a mountain with a hole on top. Smoke and lava sometimes come out, and it can be dangerous.
   a. hill   b. canyon   c. volcano

6. This is a dry, sandy place. It doesn't rain much here, and there aren't many plants.
   a. desert   b. sea   c. volcano

B Complete the names. Use words from the box.

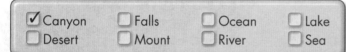

☑ Canyon   ☐ Falls   ☐ Ocean   ☐ Lake
☐ Desert   ☐ Mount   ☐ River   ☐ Sea

1. Grand ___Canyon___
2. Amazon _____
3. _____ Superior
4. _____ Fuji
5. Mediterranean _____
6. Angel _____
7. Pacific _____
8. Sahara _____

2 *Write the comparative and superlative of the words given.*

> **Spelling note: Comparatives and superlatives**
>
> | | Adjective | Comparative | Superlative |
> |---|---|---|---|
> | Add -er or -est to most words. | long | long**er** | the long**est** |
> | Add -r or -st to words ending in -e. | large | larg**er** | the larg**est** |
> | Drop the y and add -ier or -iest. | dry | dri**er** | the dri**est** |
> | Double the final consonant and add -er or -est. | big | bigg**er** | the bigg**est** |

1. busy   _busier_   _the busiest_
2. cool   _____   _____
3. friendly _____   _____
4. heavy _____   _____
5. nice   _____   _____

6. noisy _____   _____
7. old _____   _____
8. safe _____   _____
9. small _____   _____
10. wet _____   _____

3 *Complete this conversation. Use the superlative of the words given.*

Ian: So where did you go for your vacation, Val?

Val: Italy.

Ian: How exciting! Did you have a good time?

Val: It was terrific! I think Italy is

_____the most exciting_____ (exciting)

country in Europe.

Ian: Well, it certainly has some of

_____ (famous)

cities in the world – Rome, Milan, and Venice.

Val: Yeah. I had _____ (good)

time in Venice. It's _____

(beautiful) city I've ever seen. Of course, it's also

one of _____ (popular)

tourist attractions. It was _____ (crowded)

city I visited this summer, and there weren't even any cars!

Ian: I've always wanted to visit Venice. What's it like in the winter?

Val: Actually, that's _____ (bad) time to visit unless

you want to avoid the summer crowds. Venice is one of

_____ (cold and foggy) places in Italy in the winter.

the Grand Canal

4 *Complete these sentences. Use the comparative or the superlative of the words given.*

Mont Blanc

Muscat, Oman

the Suez Canal

1. Mont Blanc in the French Alps is ___higher than___ (high) the Matterhorn in the Swiss Alps.

2. ___The hottest___ (hot) capital city in the world is Muscat, in Oman.

3. The Suez Canal joins the Mediterranean and Red seas. It is 190 kilometers (118 miles) long. It is _____ (long) the Panama Canal.

4. Canada and Russia are _____ (large) countries in the world.

5. Russia is _____ (large) Canada.

6. _____ (high) waterfall in the world is in Venezuela.

7. The Atacama Desert in Chile is _____ (dry) place in the world.

8. Mount Waialeale in Hawaii gets 1,170 centimeters (460 inches) of rain a year. It is _____ (wet) place on earth!

9. The continent of Antarctica is _____ (cold) any other place in the world.

10. The Himalayas are some of _____ (dangerous) mountains to climb.

11. Badwater, in California's Death Valley, is _____ (low) point in North America.

12. The Pacific Ocean is _____ (deep) the Atlantic Ocean. At one place, the Pacific Ocean is 11,033 meters (36,198 feet) deep.

5 *The coldest and the windiest!*

A Scan the article about Antarctica. In what ways is it different from other places on earth? Why do scientists work there?

ANTARCTICA is the most southern continent in the world. It's like nowhere else on earth. It's much larger than Europe and nearly twice the size of Australia. It's an icy plateau with the South Pole at its center. Antarctica is the coldest and windiest place in the world, even colder and windier than the North Pole. Although 98 percent of Antarctica is covered in ice, it is considered a desert. Along the coast, annual precipitation is only 200 millimeters (eight inches) a year. Very few plants grow there, but there is some wildlife, including whales, seals, and penguins. In the summer, the sun shines for 24 hours a day, but in the winter, it's completely dark for about three months.

When Captain James Cook sailed around the continent in the 1770s, he found no one living there. Today, a few scientists work in Antarctica, but they only spend fairly short periods of time there. Many of these scientists live and work on the Antarctic Peninsula. This area is the closest part of Antarctica to South America, the continent's nearest neighbor. Many of these scientists are studying the effects of climate change there.

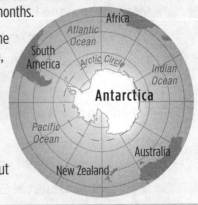

Scientists think that this cold and lonely place can teach us a lot about the earth and how to keep it safe.

B Read about Antarctica. Check (✓) True or False.

	True	False
1. Europe is bigger than Antarctica.	☐	☐
2. The North Pole is the coldest place in the world.	☐	☐
3. The coasts in Antarctica get a lot of snow.	☐	☐
4. In Antarctica, it never gets dark in the summer.	☐	☐
5. Captain Cook found a few people living in Antarctica.	☐	☐
6. The South Pole is the closest part of Antarctica to South America.	☐	☐
7. Scientists there are studying changes in climate.	☐	☐

6 Geography quiz

Use the words in the box. Write questions about the pictures.
Then circle the correct answers.

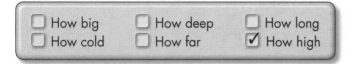

| ☐ How big | ☐ How deep | ☐ How long |
| ☐ How cold | ☐ How far | ☑ How high |

Angel Falls

1. <u>How high is Angel Falls?</u>
   a. It's 979 meters (3,212 feet) tall.
   b. It's 979 meters high.

Australia to New Zealand

2. _____
   a. It's about 2,000 kilometers (1,200 miles).
   b. It's about 2,000 square kilometers.

the Yangtze River

3. _____
   a. It's 6,300 kilometers (3,917 miles) long.
   b. It's 6,300 kilometers high.

Antarctica

4. _____
   a. It gets up to –88.3 degrees Celsius
      (–126.9 degrees Fahrenheit).
   b. It gets down to –88.3 degrees Celsius.

the Amazon Rain Forest

5. _____
   a. It's 6 million square kilometers (2.5 million square miles).
   b. It's 6 million kilometers long.

the Grand Canyon

6. _____
   a. It's about 1.6 kilometers (1 mile) big.
   b. It's about 1.6 kilometers deep.

7 Answer these questions about your country.

1. How big is the largest city?

_____

2. What's the wettest month?

_____

3. What's the driest month?

_____

4. How hot does it get in the summer?

_____

5. How cold does it get in the winter?

_____

6. How high is the highest mountain?

_____

7. What's the most beautiful town to visit?

_____

8 Write the opposites to complete the crossword puzzle.

Across

2 biggest
6 bad
7 shorter
8 worse
9 worst
10 near
11 lowest
13 driest
14 hot
15 shortest

Down

1 hotter
3 smaller
4 least crowded
   (2 words)
5 coldest
9 smallest
10 not famous
11 cold
12 best

15 I'm going to a soccer match.

1 *Match the words in columns A and B. Write the names of the activities.*
(More than one answer may be possible.)

A	B	
☑ baseball	☐ concert	1. _baseball game_
☐ beach	☐ contest	2. _____
☐ bicycle	☑ game	3. _____
☐ dance	☐ match	4. _____
☐ rock	☐ party	5. _____
☐ singing	☐ performance	6. _____
☐ tennis	☐ race	7. _____
☐ volleyball	☐ tournament	8. _____

2 *Read Anna's calendar and write about her plans. Use the present continuous.*

« July »

Sunday	Monday	Tuesday	Wednesday	Thursday	Friday	Saturday
6	**7**	**8**	**9**	**10**	**11**	**12**
afternoon – go to Jeremy's birthday party	work overtime to finish the report	7:00 P.M. – see a play with Tony	night – watch the tennis match with Kate & Sam	12:00 noon – have lunch with Candy	stay home and watch the baseball game on TV	evening – go to the dance performance with Maria

1. _On Sunday afternoon, Anna is going to Jeremy's birthday party._
2. _____
3. _____
4. _____
5. _____
6. _____
7. _____

3 Complete this conversation. Use *be going to* and the verbs given.

Marta: What _are_ you _going to do_ this weekend, Mark? (do)

Mark: I _____ to a rock concert on Saturday. (go)

Marta: That sounds interesting.

Mark: Yeah. There's a free concert in the park. And how about you, Marta?

Marta: Well, Brian and I _____ a basketball game in the afternoon. (see)

Mark: And what _____ you _____ in the evening? (do)

Marta: Brian _____ his mother in the hospital. (visit)

But I _____ not _____ anything really. (do)

Mark: Well, I _____ some friends over for a barbecue. Would you like to come? (have)

Marta: Thanks. I'd love to!

4 Choose the correct responses.

1. A: There's a singing contest on TV tonight. Do you want to watch it?

   B: _I'm sorry. I'm working late tonight._____

   • How about this evening?
   • I'm sorry. I'm working late tonight.
   • Yes, it does.

2. A: Would you like to have dinner at Rosa's tonight?

   B: _____

   • No, I'm not doing anything.
   • Sorry, I'm going away next week.
   • Great! But it's my turn to pay.

3. A: Do you want to go on a picnic tomorrow?

   B: _____

   • Yes, I'm going to.
   • Can we go to a late show?
   • Sure, I'd love to.

4. A: How about going to a movie on Saturday?

   B: _____

   • Oh, I'm sorry. I can't.
   • Nothing special.
   • No, I wouldn't.

5 *Write invitations to this week's events in Princeville.*

| | Exciting things to do this week in | **Princeville!** | All events scheduled to begin at 8:00 P.M. |

Wednesday	Thursday	Friday	Saturday
Rock concert Coldplay	**Amusement park** Lots to do for everyone!	**Musical** *Mamma Mia!*	**Museum** Exhibition of modern art

1. Are you doing anything on Wednesday evening? Do you want to see a rock concert?

   OR I'm going to see Coldplay on Wednesday. Would you like to come?

2. _____

3. _____

4. _____

6 *Write about how often you do these leisure activities. Use the expressions in the box.*

> I often . . .
> I . . . almost every weekend.
> I sometimes . . . in the summer.
> I . . . three or four times a year.
> I never . . .

1. _____
2. _____
3. _____
4. _____
5. _____
6. _____

1. go to the park

2. go to concerts

3. have parties at home

4. see plays

5. watch old movies

6. go on picnics

A Read the article. What exactly are text messages?

Text me!

Text messages are short, typed messages of up to about 150 characters. At first, the messages included letters, numbers, and spaces – they were sent by Short Message Services, or SMS. However, nowadays, text messages can include images, videos, and sound. Such messages are sent by Multimedia Message Services, or MMS. This technology allows you to send and receive text messages on your cell phone. You can also send text messages from computers to cell phones, and vice versa. Texting is fast and cheap, and it's a lot of fun!

Text messages use a kind of "text talk" language. Words in text messages are often spelled the way they sound. For example, "Talk to you later" becomes "TLK2UL8R." When you abbreviate your words in this way, you can write messages faster. And you can fit more words into a short message on a small cell phone screen.

Text messages often contain *emoticons.* You can create these icons or small pictures with your keyboard.

(^_^) equals "happy/smile"   (;_;) equals "sad"   (o.o) equals "surprise"

Sometimes, it's easier to understand them vertically, so turn your head to the left to look at these examples:

:-) equals "happy/smile"   :-(equals "sad"   :-o equals "surprise"

Most people now use this kind of electronic language in Internet chat rooms and in instant messaging. The problem is that there are thousands of text abbreviations and emoticons! Have you ever received a message but didn't know what it meant? Were you confused? The more you use this electronic way to communicate, the better you'll become at using it. B4N (Bye for now) and BOL (Best of luck)!

B Can you guess what these text abbreviations mean? Match each one with its meaning.

1. BBL	_h_	a. I see.
2. ILBL8	___	b. Where are you?
3. TTYL	___	c. Laughing out loud.
4. SUP	___	d. In my opinion.
5. ILY	___	e. I'll be late.
6. WRU?	___	f. Talk to you later.
7. IC	___	g. Thanks.
8. THNX	___	✓ h. Be back later.
9. LOL	___	i. What's up?
10. IMO	___	j. I love you.

8 Read these messages. What did the caller say?
Write the messages another way using **tell** or **ask**.

For: Ms. Tam
Message: The meeting is at 10:30. Bring the fax from New York.

1. Please tell Ms. Tam that the meeting is at 10:30.
   Could you . . .

For: Mr. Alvarez
Message: We need the report by noon. Call Ms. James as soon as possible.

2. _____

For: Miss Lowe
Message: The new laptop is ready. Pick it up this afternoon.

3. _____

9 Look at the message slips. Ask someone to give these messages.

> **Grammar note: Negative infinitives**
>
> | **Request** | **Message** |
> | --- | --- |
> | **Don't call** him today. | Please ask Jan **not to call** him today. |
> | **Don't go** home yet. | Could you tell him **not to go** home yet? |

Michael —
Don't meet me at the airport until midnight. The plane is going to be late.

1. _____

Lucy –
We're meeting at Dino's house before the concert. Don't forget the tickets.

2. _____

Christopher –
The beach party starts at noon. Don't be late!.

3. _____

10 *Choose the correct words.*

Secretary: Hello. Schmidt and Lee.

Ms. Curtis: <u>May I</u> speak to Ms. Grace Schmidt, please?
           (May I / Would you)

Secretary: I'm _____ . She's not in. _____
          (busy / sorry)   (Can I leave / Can I take)

a message?

Ms. Curtis: Yes, please. This is Ms. Curtis. _____ you
                (Would / Please)

_____ I'm staying at the Plaza Hotel?
(tell her that / ask her to)

The number is 555-9001, Room 605. _____
               (Please / Could)

you _____ ?
(ask her to call me / ask her to call her)

Secretary: OK, Ms. Curtis. I'll _____
            (give her / tell her)

the message.

Ms. Curtis: Thank you very much. Good-bye.

11 *Match the questions with the correct responses.*

☐ Yes, please. Could you tell him Roz called?	☐ Let me see if he's in.
☐ That's OK. I'll call back.	☐ My name's Graham. Graham Lock.
☐ Yes. My number is (303) 555-3241.	☑ Yes, that would be great. Thanks.

1. Would you like to come to a party?

   <u>Yes, that would be great. Thanks.</u>

2. Could I ask her to call you back?

   _____

3. Who's calling, please?

   _____

4. Can I take a message?

   _____

5. Could I speak to Paul, please?

   _____

6. I'm sorry. She's busy at the moment.

   _____

16 A change for the better!

1 Choose the correct responses.

1. A: Say, you really look different.

   B: _Well, my hair is a little longer now._

   - I moved into a new house.
   - I'm more outgoing than before.
   - Well, my hair is a little longer now.

2. A: I haven't seen you for ages.

   B: _____

   - I know. How have you been?
   - Well, I got a bank loan.
   - My new job is more stressful.

3. A: You know, I have three kids now.

   B: _____

   - Well, I've grown a mustache.
   - That's terrific!
   - Say, you've really changed your hair.

4. A: How are you?

   B: _____

   - I do more aerobics these days.
   - Well, actually, I turned 18.
   - I'm doing really well.

2 Complete the sentences. Use information in the box and the present perfect.

☐ move to a new apartment	☐ start going to the gym	☐ stop eating in restaurants

1. Judy _____ .

   Her old one was too small.

2. Kim and Anna _____ .

   Now they cook dinner at home every evening. It's much cheaper.

3. Alex _____ .

   He looks healthier, and he has more energy.

3 *Describe how these people have changed. Use the present or the past tense.*

Shawn

Elena

1. Shawn grew a lot.

2. _____

Mr. and Mrs. Jones

Eddie

3. _____

4. _____

4 *Rewrite these sentences. Find another way to say each sentence using the words given.*

1. Alice quit eating rich food.

   Alice eats healthier food now. _____ (healthier)

2. James lost a lot of weight.

   _____ (heavier)

3. Mary goes to a new school now.

   _____ (change)

4. Tess got divorced last year.

   _____ (married)

5. I've grown out my hair.

   _____ (longer)

6. We quit working out at the gym.

   _____ (go)

A Read the passages on the left in Part B. Complete these sentences.

1. _____ had an interesting job two years ago.

2. _____ had a money problem two years ago.

3. _____ was a student two years ago.

B Now read the passages on the right. Match the people's lives two years ago with their lives now.

Aki

Luis and his wife

Rosie

Two years ago	Now
1. **Aki** Two years ago, I was a student, and I thought life was really good. I got up late. I spent the day talking to friends, and then I studied all night. I wore jeans and sweatshirts and had long hair and a mustache. I felt free. _____	a. Now my life has completely changed. I got married six months ago! My wife and I often have friends over for dinner. We're taking classes several nights a week. It's great! We're even talking about starting a family soon.
2. **Luis** I moved to a new town two years ago. My job was interesting, but I was single and I didn't have any friends. People at work were friendly but not very outgoing. We never did anything after work. _____	b. Now I work as a computer programmer for an international company. I've moved to Seoul and have started to learn Korean. Korean food is great, and I've gained several kilos. I feel much happier and healthier.
3. **Rosie** My life seemed to come to an end two years ago. I lost my job. Then I lost weight, and looked terrible. Money became a problem. I was very sad. I needed some good luck. _____	c. Now I actually look forward to getting up early in the morning and going to work. Of course, I dress up now, and my hair is shorter. But I don't really mind. At least my evenings are free!

C Underline at least two changes in each person's life.

6 Complete the sentences. Use words in the box.

☐ broke   ☑ graduation   ☐ responsibilities
☐ career   ☐ loan   ☐ successful

1. After ___graduation___ , Nancy and Kirk plan to look for jobs.

2. What _____ do you think you're most interested in pursuing?

3. I go to school, and I have a family and a part-time job. I have a lot of _____ .

4. Lucy wants to pay off her student _____ before she buys a car.

5. Marie lost her job. Now she's _____ , and she can't pay her rent.

6. I'd like to be _____ in my first job. Then I can get a better job and a raise.

7 Complete this conversation. Use the words given.

Melissa: ___What do you plan to do___ (plan, do) this summer, Leo?

Leo: I _____ (want, get) a summer job.

I _____ (like, save) money for a vacation.

Melissa: Really? Where _____ (like, go)?

Leo: I _____ (love, travel) to Latin America. What about you, Melissa?

Melissa: Well, I _____ (not go, get) a job right away.

First, I _____ (want, go) to Spain and Portugal.

Leo: Sounds great, but how _____ (go, pay) for it?

Melissa: I _____ (hope, borrow) some money from my brother. I have a good excuse. I _____ (plan, take) courses in Spanish and Portuguese.

Leo: Oh, I'm tired of studying!

Melissa: So am I. But I also _____ (hope, take) people on tours to Latin America. Why don't you come on my first tour?

Leo: Count me in!

8 *Imagine you have these problems. Write three sentences about changing each situation. Use words in the box.*

1. I'm not interested in my job these days. I spend three hours driving to and from work every day, and I don't make enough money! I can't find a new job, though, because of my poor computer skills.

> I hope to . . .   I want to . . .   I plan to . . .

_____

_____

_____

2. I've become less careful about my health lately. I've stopped jogging because I'm bored with it. I've started eating more fast food because I'm too tired to cook after work. And I can't sleep at night.

> I'm going to . . .   I'd like to . . .   I'd love to . . .

_____

_____

_____

3. I just moved to a new town, and I don't know anyone. I never do anything after work. People at work don't really talk to me. I haven't had a date in about four months. And I never seem to do anything fun in the evenings.

> I'm going to . . .   I want to . . .   I plan to . . .

_____

_____

_____

9 **Choose the correct words to complete each sentence. Use the correct form of the word and add any words if necessary.**

1. I hope to buy a house soon. I need _____to get_____
   (open / start / get)
   a bank loan.

2. Heather's salary is much _____ before.
   (low / short / high)
   She had to take a pay cut.

3. After graduation, Jack plans _____ for an
   (play / work / move)
   international company.

4. This job is _____ my last job.
   (outgoing / stressful / expensive)

5. Mel hopes _____ to a small town.
   (move / live / change)

6. William and Donna got _____ last summer.
   (engage / marry)
   The wedding will be in April.

10 **Advise people how to make changes in their lives. Use expressions like the ones in the box.**

> You should . . .   You shouldn't . . .   Why don't you . . .

1. I've gained a lot of weight this year.

   _____

2. My hair is longer, but it doesn't look good.

   _____

3. I've gotten tired of wearing the same old clothes.

   _____

4. I want to start a successful business.

   _____

5. I'm often bored on weekends.

   _____

6. I don't seem to have any goals.

   _____

7. I've finished this textbook, but I still want to improve my English!

   _____